THE
Acker & Blacker Present...

THRILLING
ADVENTURE
HOUR

Phil Hester
Mauricio Wallace

Frank & Sadie Doyle in...

A SPIRITED ROMANCE

BOOM!
STUDIOS

**A Comic Collection
Produced in Spectacular
WORKJUICE COLOR
for a Superior Reading
Experience**

WARNING:
This volume contains two-fisted action,
full-hearted romance and spine-tingling terror.
Sometimes concurrently.
**PLEASE READ
RESPONSIBLY.**

DESIGNER
SCOTT NEWMAN

ORIGINAL SERIES EDITOR
NATE COSBY

COLLECTION ASSOCIATE EDITOR
MATTHEW LEVINE

COLLECTION EDITOR
CAMERON CHITTOCK

Ross Richie CEO & Founder
Matt Gagnon Editor-in-Chief
Filip Sablik President of Publishing & Marketing
Stephen Christy President of Development
Lance Kreiter VP of Licensing & Merchandising
Phil Barbaro VP of Finance
Arune Singh VP of Marketing
Bryce Carlson Managing Editor
Scott Newman Production Design Manager
Kate Henning Operations Manager
Spencer Simpson Sales Manager
Sierra Hahn Senior Editor
Dafna Pleban Editor, Talent Development
Shannon Watters Editor
Eric Harburn Editor
Whitney Leopard Editor
Cameron Chittock Editor
Chris Rosa Associate Editor
Matthew Levine Associate Editor
Sophie Philips-Roberts Assistant Editor

Gavin Gronenthal Assistant Editor
Michael Moccio Assistant Editor
Amanda LaFranco Executive Assistant
Katalina Holland Editorial Administrative Assistant
Jillian Crab Design Coordinator
Michelle Ankley Design Coordinator
Kara Leopard Production Designer
Marie Krupina Production Designer
Grace Park Production Design Assistant
Chelsea Roberts Production Design Assistant
Elizabeth Loughridge Accounting Coordinator
Stephanie Hocutt Social Media Coordinator
José Meza Event Coordinator
Holly Aitchison Operations Coordinator
Megan Christopher Operations Assistant
Rodrigo Hernandez Mailroom Assistant
Morgan Perry Direct Market Representative
Cat O'Grady Marketing Assistant
Cornelia Tzana Publicity Assistant
Liz Almendarez Accounting Administrative Assistant

THE THRILLING ADVENTURE HOUR: A SPIRITED ROMANCE, October 2018. Published by BOOM! Studios, a
division of Boom Entertainment, Inc. The Thrilling Adventure Hour is ™ & © 2018 Workjuice Corp. Originally
published in single magazine form as THE THRILLING ADVENTURE HOUR PRESENTS: BEYOND BELIEF No. 0-4. ™
& © 2014-2016 Workjuice Corp. All rights reserved. BOOM! Studios™ and the BOOM! Studios logo are trademarks
of Boom Entertainment, Inc., registered in various countries and categories. All characters, events, and
institutions depicted herein are fictional. Any similarity between any of the names, characters, persons, events,
and/or institutions in this publication to actual names, characters, and persons, whether living or dead, events,
and/or institutions is unintended and purely coincidental. BOOM! Studios does not read or accept unsolicited
submissions of ideas, stories, or artwork.

BOOM! Studios, 5670 Wilshire Boulevard, Suite 400, Los Angeles, CA 90036-5679. Printed in China. First Printing.

ISBN: 978-1-68415-231-5, eISBN: 978-1-64144-093-6

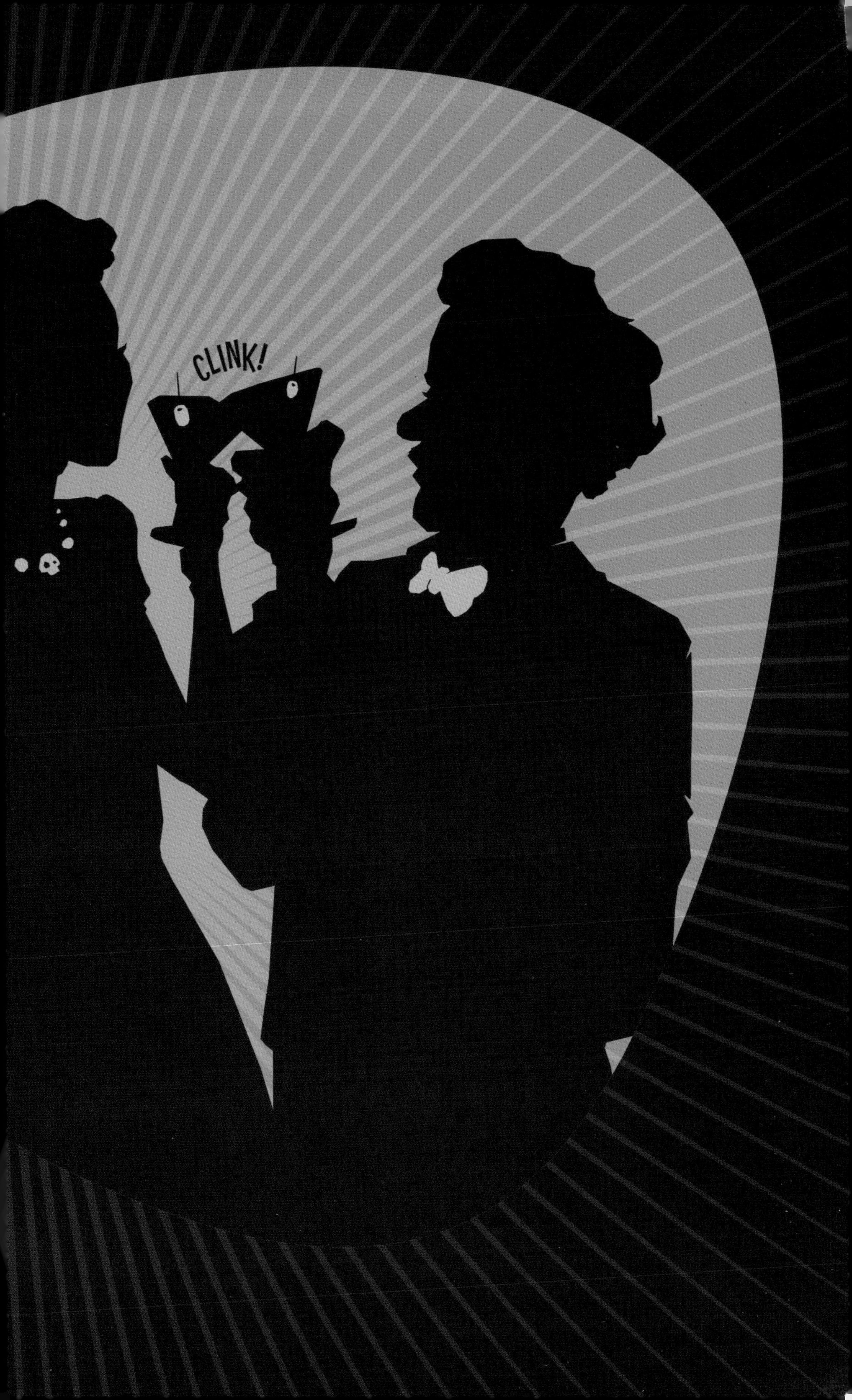
CLINK!

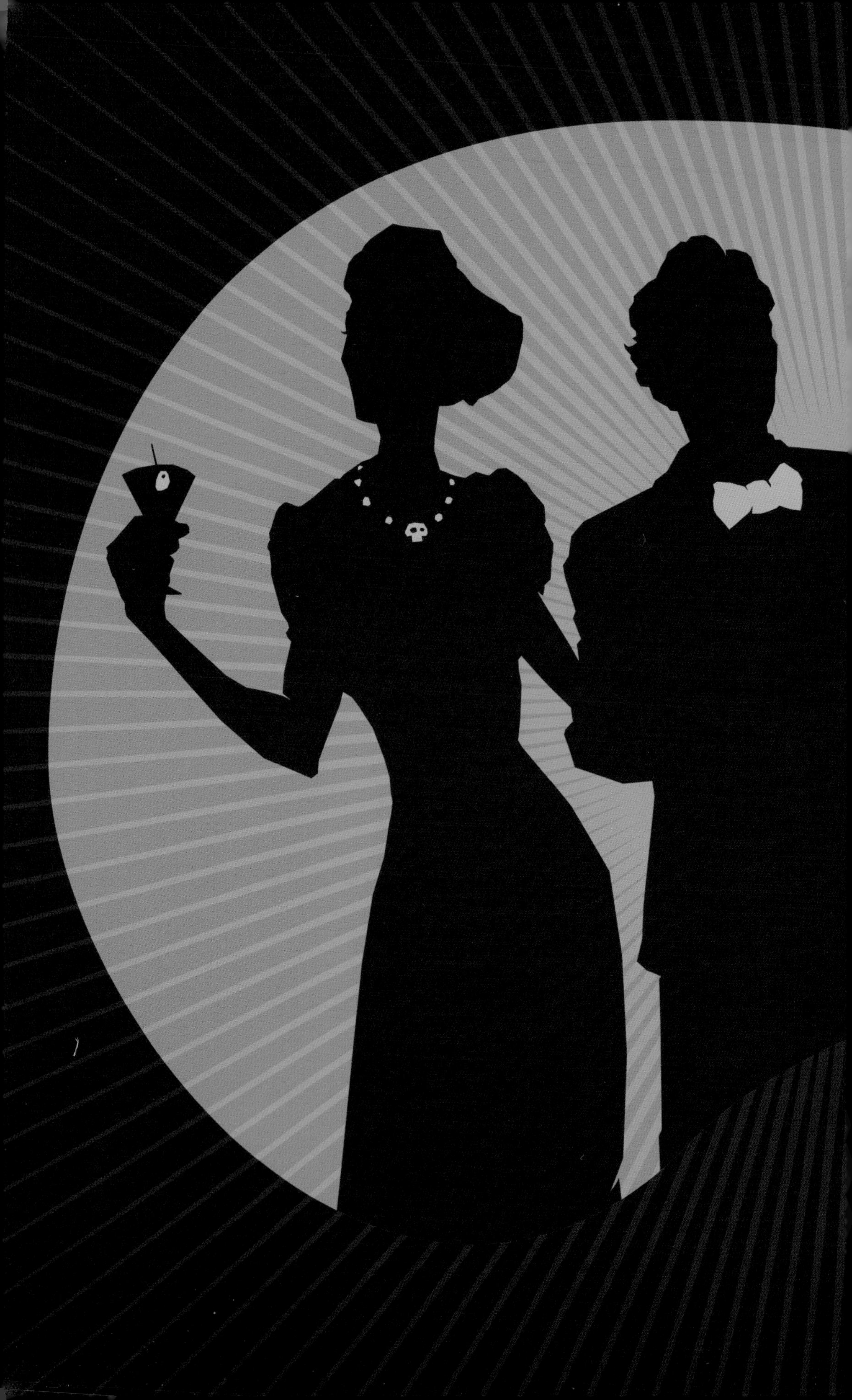

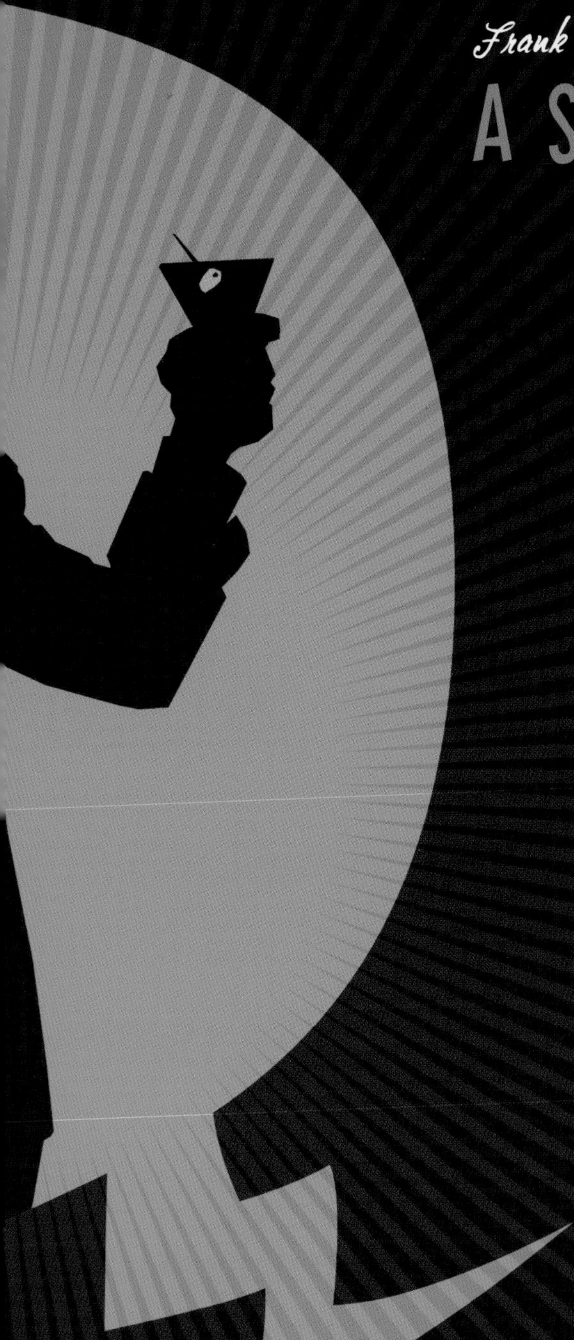

Frank & Sadie Doyle in...

A SPIRITED ROMANCE

WRITTEN BY
BEN ACKER & BEN BLACKER

PENCILED BY
PHIL HESTER

INKED BY
ERIC GAPSTUR
MARK STEGBAUER
ANDE J. PARKS

COLORED BY
MAURICIO WALLACE
JOHN RAUCH

LETTERED BY
MARSHALL DILLON

COVER BY
SCOTT NEWMAN

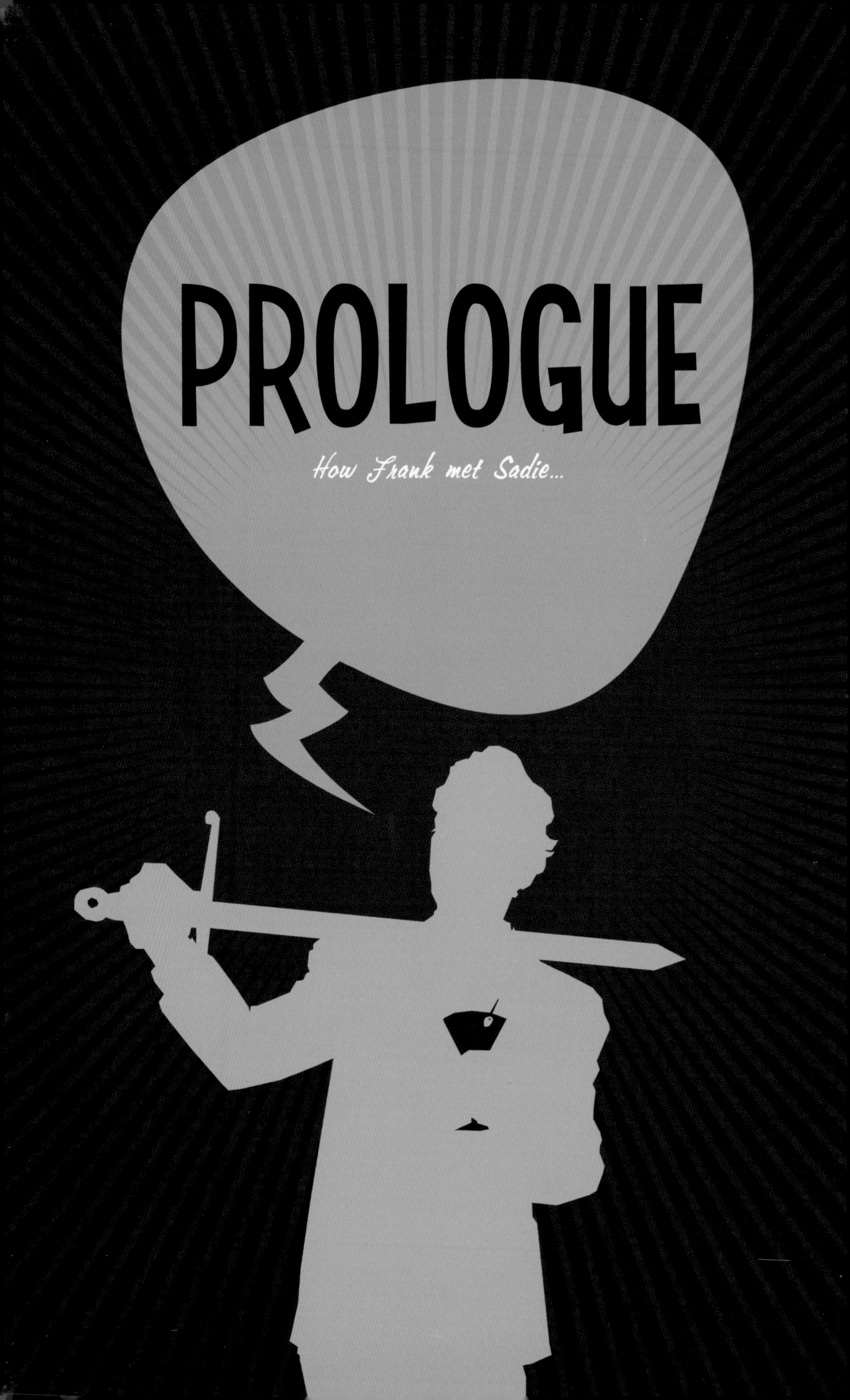
PROLOGUE
How Frank met Sadie...

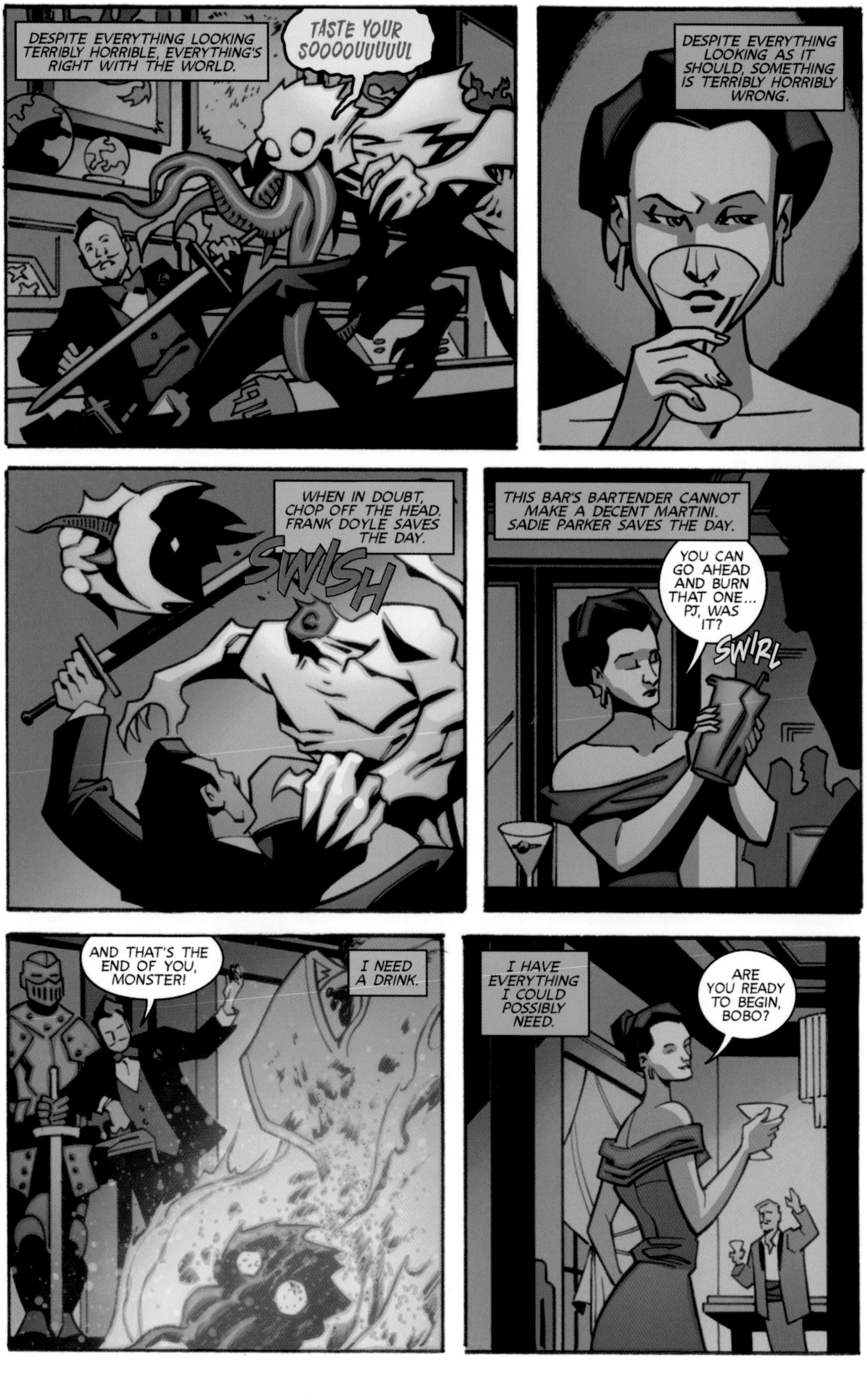
DESPITE EVERYTHING LOOKING TERRIBLY HORRIBLE, EVERYTHING'S RIGHT WITH THE WORLD.
TASTE YOUR SOOOOUUUUUL
DESPITE EVERYTHING LOOKING AS IT SHOULD, SOMETHING IS TERRIBLY HORRIBLY WRONG.
WHEN IN DOUBT, CHOP OFF THE HEAD. FRANK DOYLE SAVES THE DAY.
SWISH
THIS BAR'S BARTENDER CANNOT MAKE A DECENT MARTINI. SADIE PARKER SAVES THE DAY.
YOU CAN GO AHEAD AND BURN THAT ONE... PJ, WAS IT?
SWIRL
AND THAT'S THE END OF YOU, MONSTER!
I NEED A DRINK.
I HAVE EVERYTHING I COULD POSSIBLY NEED.
ARE YOU READY TO BEGIN, BOBO?

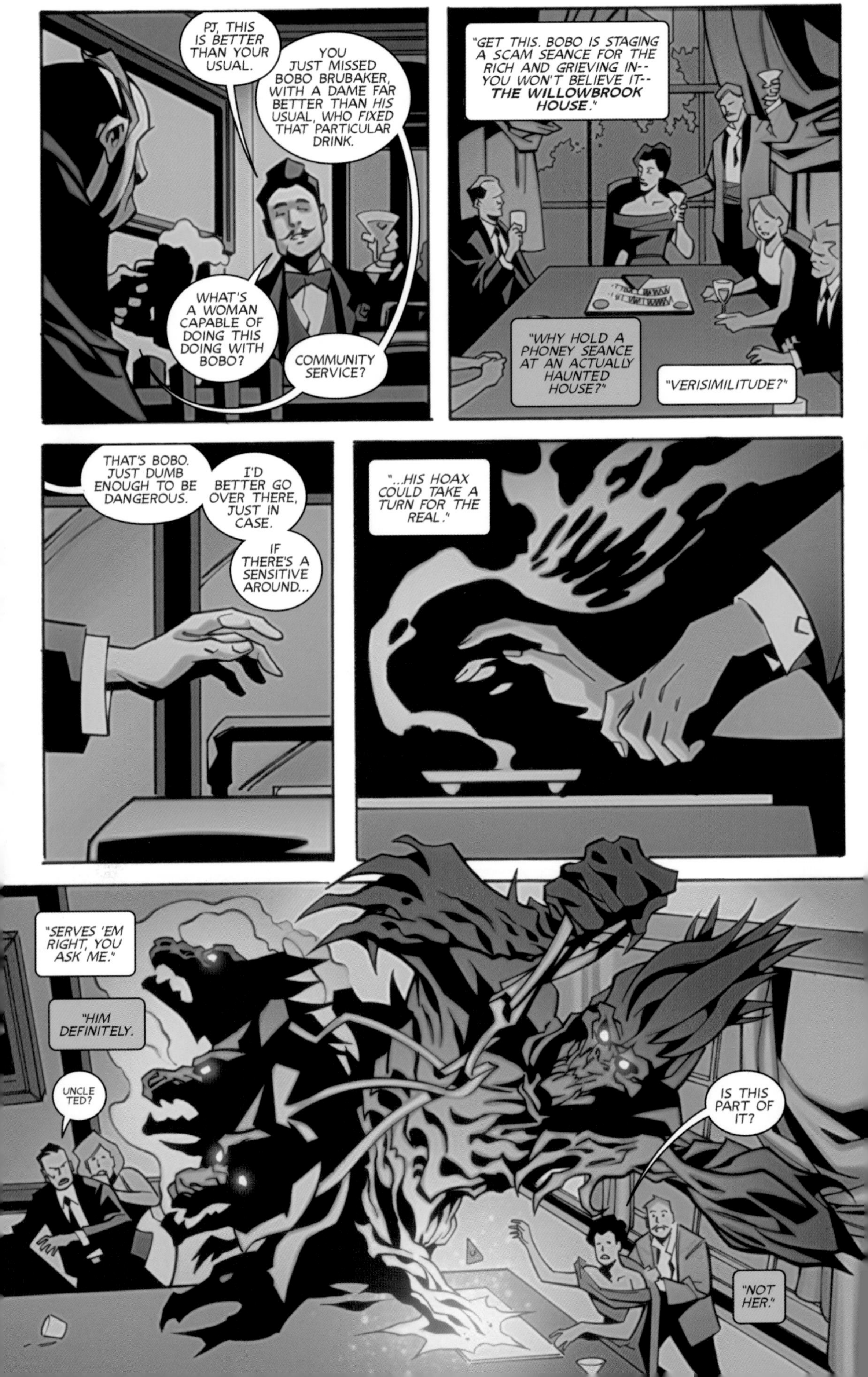
PJ, THIS IS BETTER THAN YOUR USUAL.
YOU JUST MISSED BOBO BRUBAKER, WITH A DAME FAR BETTER THAN HIS USUAL, WHO FIXED THAT PARTICULAR DRINK.
WHAT'S A WOMAN CAPABLE OF DOING THIS DOING WITH BOBO?
COMMUNITY SERVICE?
"GET THIS. BOBO IS STAGING A SCAM SEANCE FOR THE RICH AND GRIEVING IN-- YOU WON'T BELIEVE IT-- THE WILLOWBROOK HOUSE."
"WHY HOLD A PHONEY SEANCE AT AN ACTUALLY HAUNTED HOUSE?"
"VERISIMILITUDE?"
THAT'S BOBO. JUST DUMB ENOUGH TO BE DANGEROUS.
I'D BETTER GO OVER THERE, JUST IN CASE.
IF THERE'S A SENSITIVE AROUND...
"...HIS HOAX COULD TAKE A TURN FOR THE REAL."
"SERVES 'EM RIGHT, YOU ASK ME."
"HIM DEFINITELY.
UNCLE TED?
IS THIS PART OF IT?
"NOT HER."

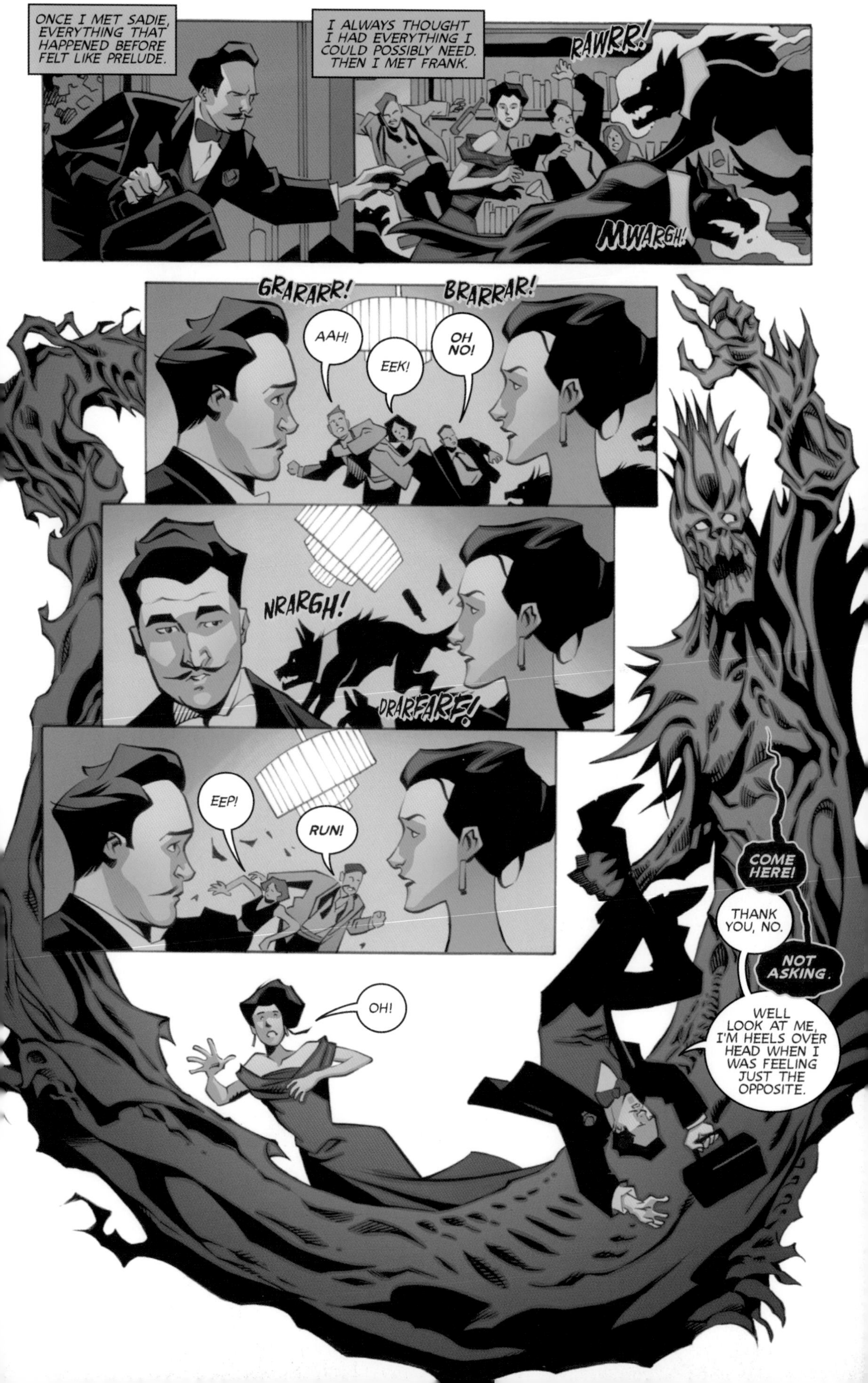
ONCE I MET SADIE, EVERYTHING THAT HAPPENED BEFORE FELT LIKE PRELUDE.
I ALWAYS THOUGHT I HAD EVERYTHING I COULD POSSIBLY NEED. THEN I MET FRANK.
RAWRR!
MWARGH!
GRARARR!
BRARRAR!
AAH!
EEK!
OH NO!
NRARGH!
DRARFARF!
EEP!
RUN!
COME HERE!
THANK YOU, NO.
NOT ASKING.
OH!
WELL LOOK AT ME, I'M HEELS OVER HEAD WHEN I WAS FEELING JUST THE OPPOSITE.

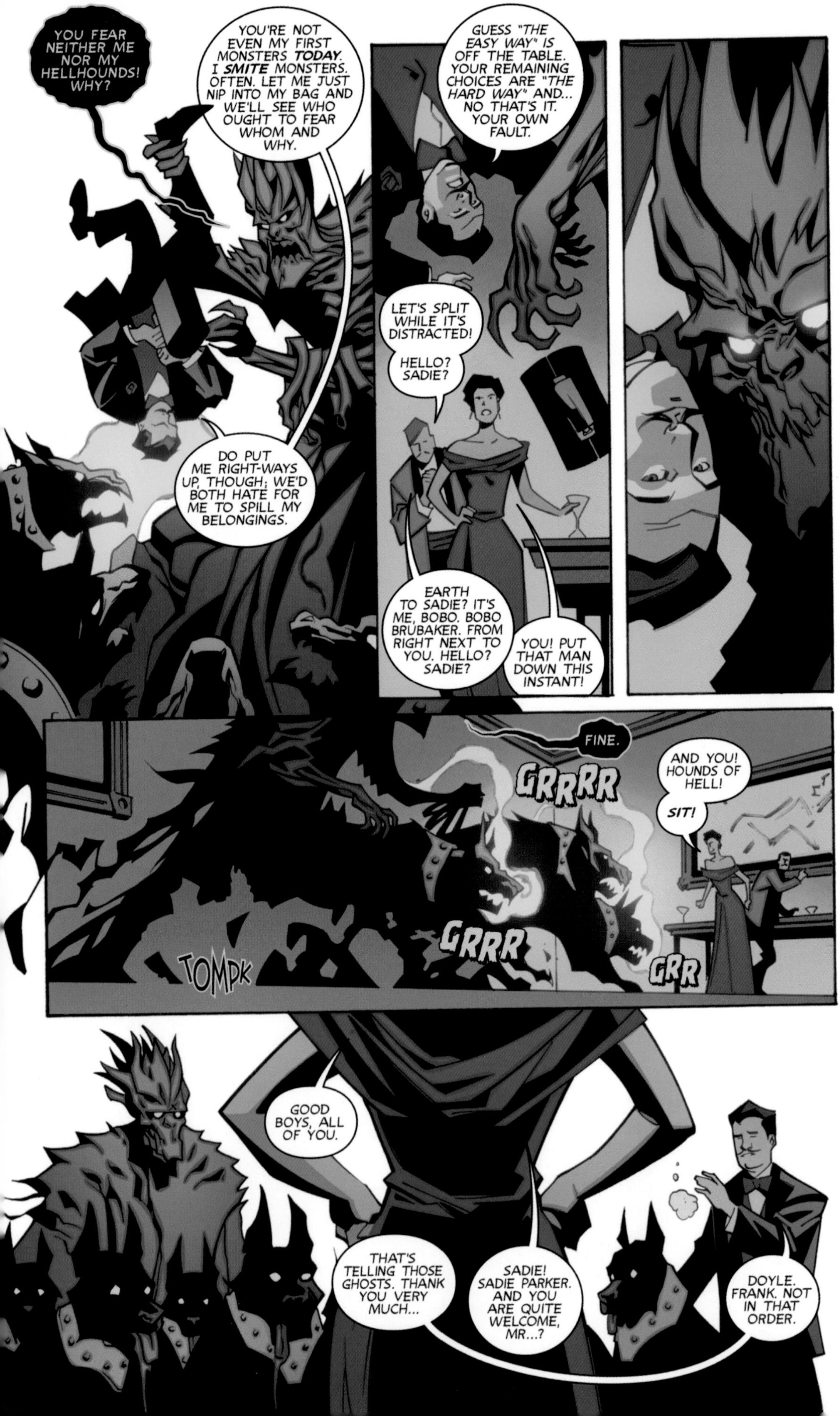
YOU FEAR NEITHER ME NOR MY HELLHOUNDS! WHY?
YOU'RE NOT EVEN MY FIRST MONSTERS TODAY. I SMITE MONSTERS. OFTEN. LET ME JUST NIP INTO MY BAG AND WE'LL SEE WHO OUGHT TO FEAR WHOM AND WHY.
DO PUT ME RIGHT-WAYS UP, THOUGH; WE'D BOTH HATE FOR ME TO SPILL MY BELONGINGS.
GUESS "THE EASY WAY" IS OFF THE TABLE. YOUR REMAINING CHOICES ARE "THE HARD WAY" AND... NO THAT'S IT. YOUR OWN FAULT.
LET'S SPLIT WHILE IT'S DISTRACTED!
HELLO? SADIE?
EARTH TO SADIE? IT'S ME, BOBO. BOBO BRUBAKER. FROM RIGHT NEXT TO YOU. HELLO? SADIE?
YOU! PUT THAT MAN DOWN THIS INSTANT!
FINE.
GRRRR
AND YOU! HOUNDS OF HELL!
SIT!
TOMPK
GRRR
GRR
GOOD BOYS, ALL OF YOU.
THAT'S TELLING THOSE GHOSTS. THANK YOU VERY MUCH...
SADIE! SADIE PARKER. AND YOU ARE QUITE WELCOME, MR...?
DOYLE. FRANK. NOT IN THAT ORDER.

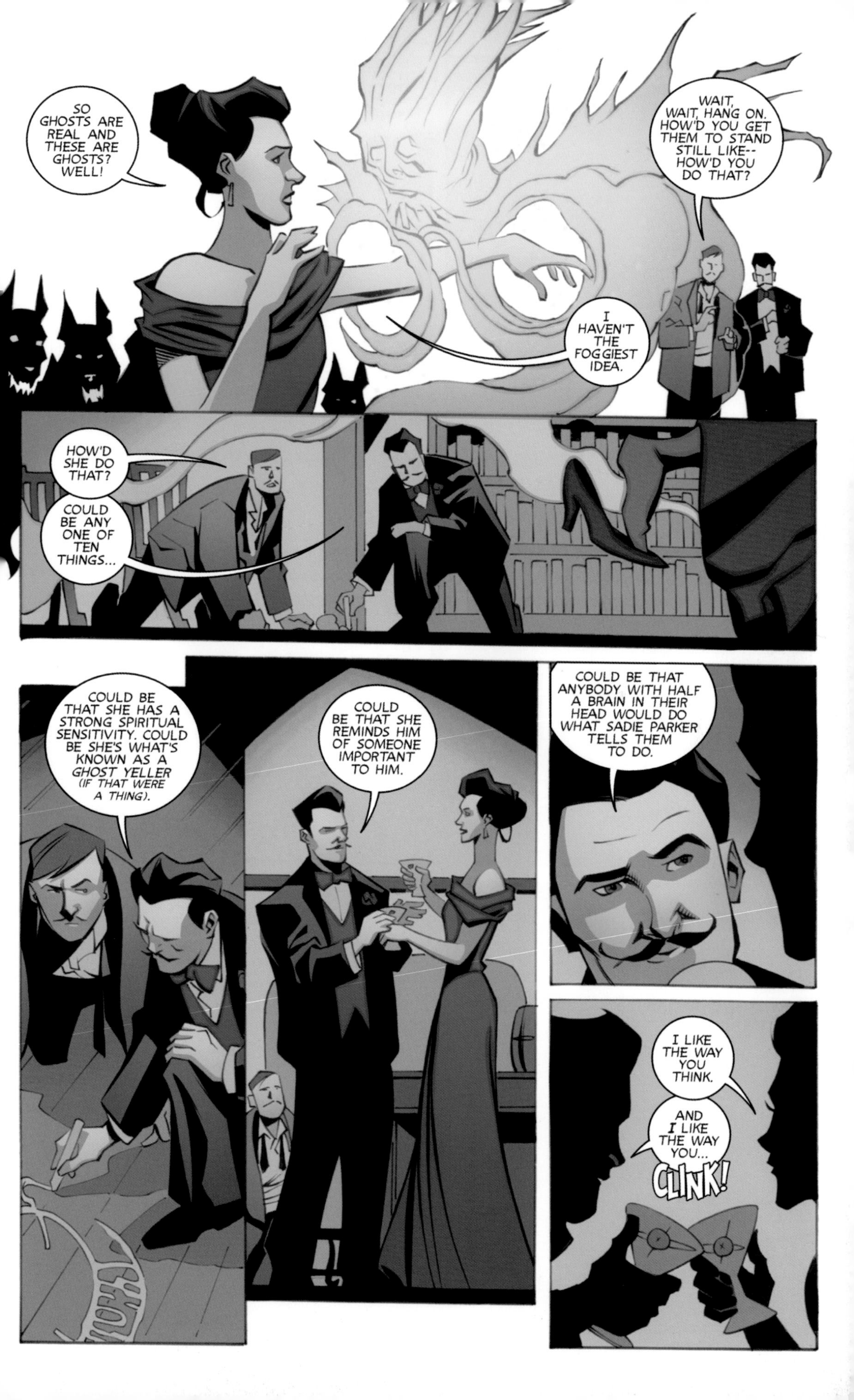
SO GHOSTS ARE REAL AND THESE ARE GHOSTS? WELL!
WAIT, WAIT, HANG ON. HOW'D YOU GET THEM TO STAND STILL LIKE-- HOW'D YOU DO THAT?
I HAVEN'T THE FOGGIEST IDEA.
HOW'D SHE DO THAT?
COULD BE ANY ONE OF TEN THINGS...
COULD BE THAT SHE HAS A STRONG SPIRITUAL SENSITIVITY. COULD BE SHE'S WHAT'S KNOWN AS A *GHOST YELLER* (IF THAT WERE A THING).
COULD BE THAT SHE REMINDS HIM OF SOMEONE IMPORTANT TO HIM.
COULD BE THAT ANYBODY WITH HALF A BRAIN IN THEIR HEAD WOULD DO WHAT SADIE PARKER TELLS THEM TO DO.
I LIKE THE WAY YOU THINK.
AND **I** LIKE THE WAY YOU...
CLINK!

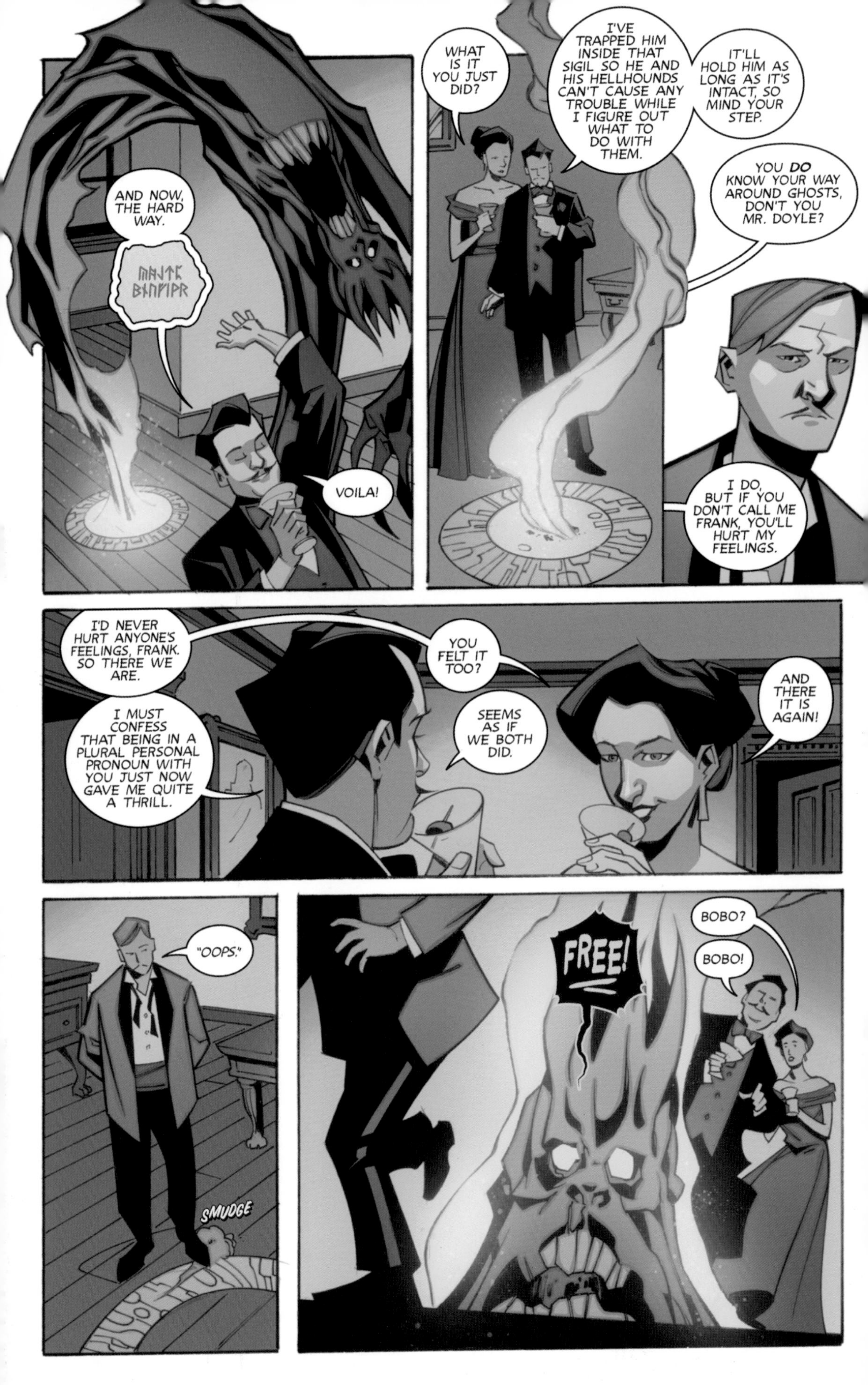
AND NOW, THE HARD WAY.
VOILA!
WHAT IS IT YOU JUST DID?
I'VE TRAPPED HIM INSIDE THAT SIGIL SO HE AND HIS HELLHOUNDS CAN'T CAUSE ANY TROUBLE WHILE I FIGURE OUT WHAT TO DO WITH THEM.
IT'LL HOLD HIM AS LONG AS IT'S INTACT, SO MIND YOUR STEP.
YOU DO KNOW YOUR WAY AROUND GHOSTS, DON'T YOU MR. DOYLE?
I DO, BUT IF YOU DON'T CALL ME FRANK, YOU'LL HURT MY FEELINGS.
I'D NEVER HURT ANYONE'S FEELINGS, FRANK. SO THERE WE ARE.
YOU FELT IT TOO?
I MUST CONFESS THAT BEING IN A PLURAL PERSONAL PRONOUN WITH YOU JUST NOW GAVE ME QUITE A THRILL.
SEEMS AS IF WE BOTH DID.
AND THERE IT IS AGAIN!
"OOPS."
SMUDGE
FREE!
BOBO?
BOBO!

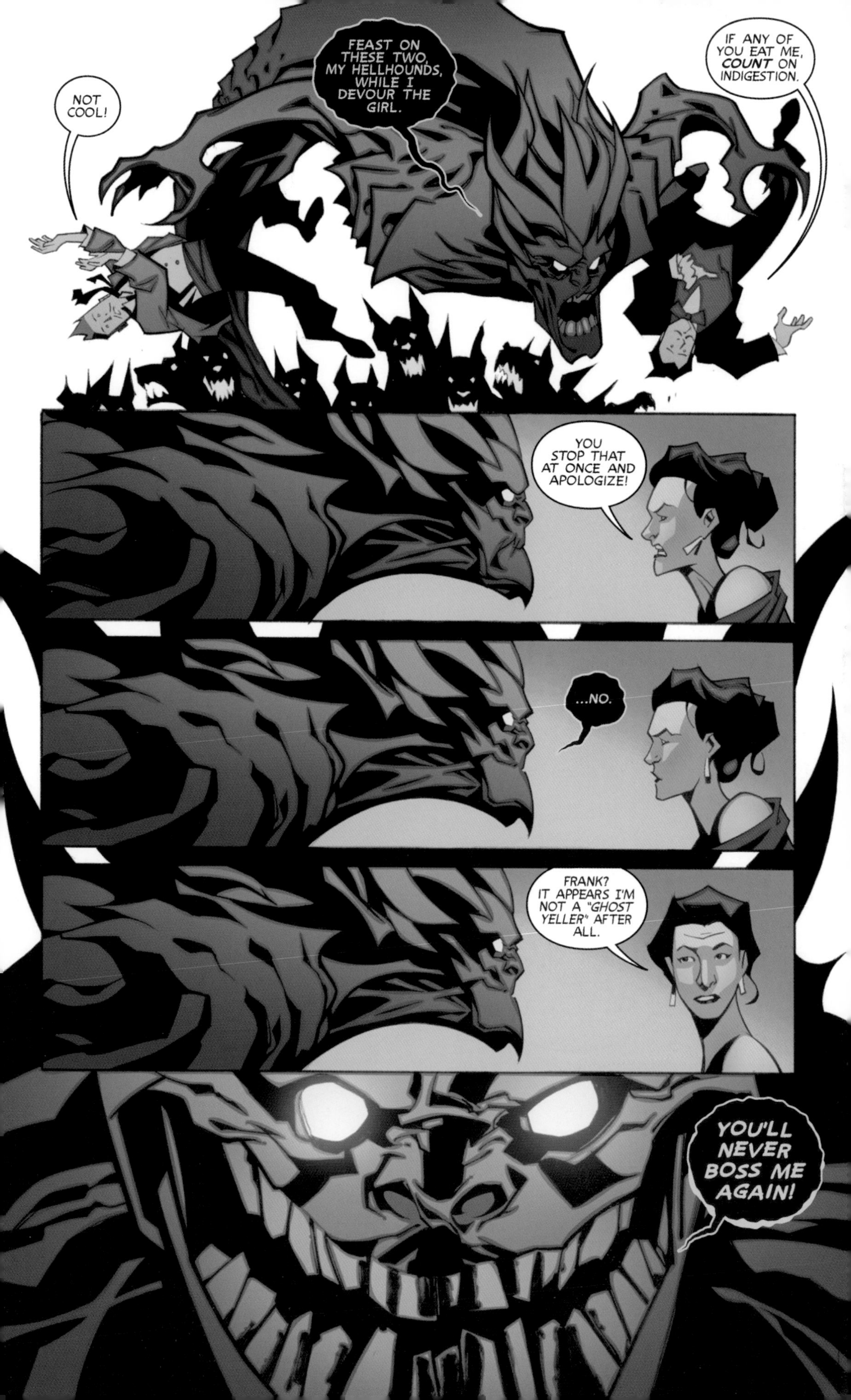
NOT COOL!
FEAST ON THESE TWO, MY HELLHOUNDS, WHILE I DEVOUR THE GIRL.
IF ANY OF YOU EAT ME, COUNT ON INDIGESTION.
YOU STOP THAT AT ONCE AND APOLOGIZE!
...NO.
FRANK? IT APPEARS I'M NOT A "GHOST YELLER" AFTER ALL.
YOU'LL NEVER BOSS ME AGAIN!

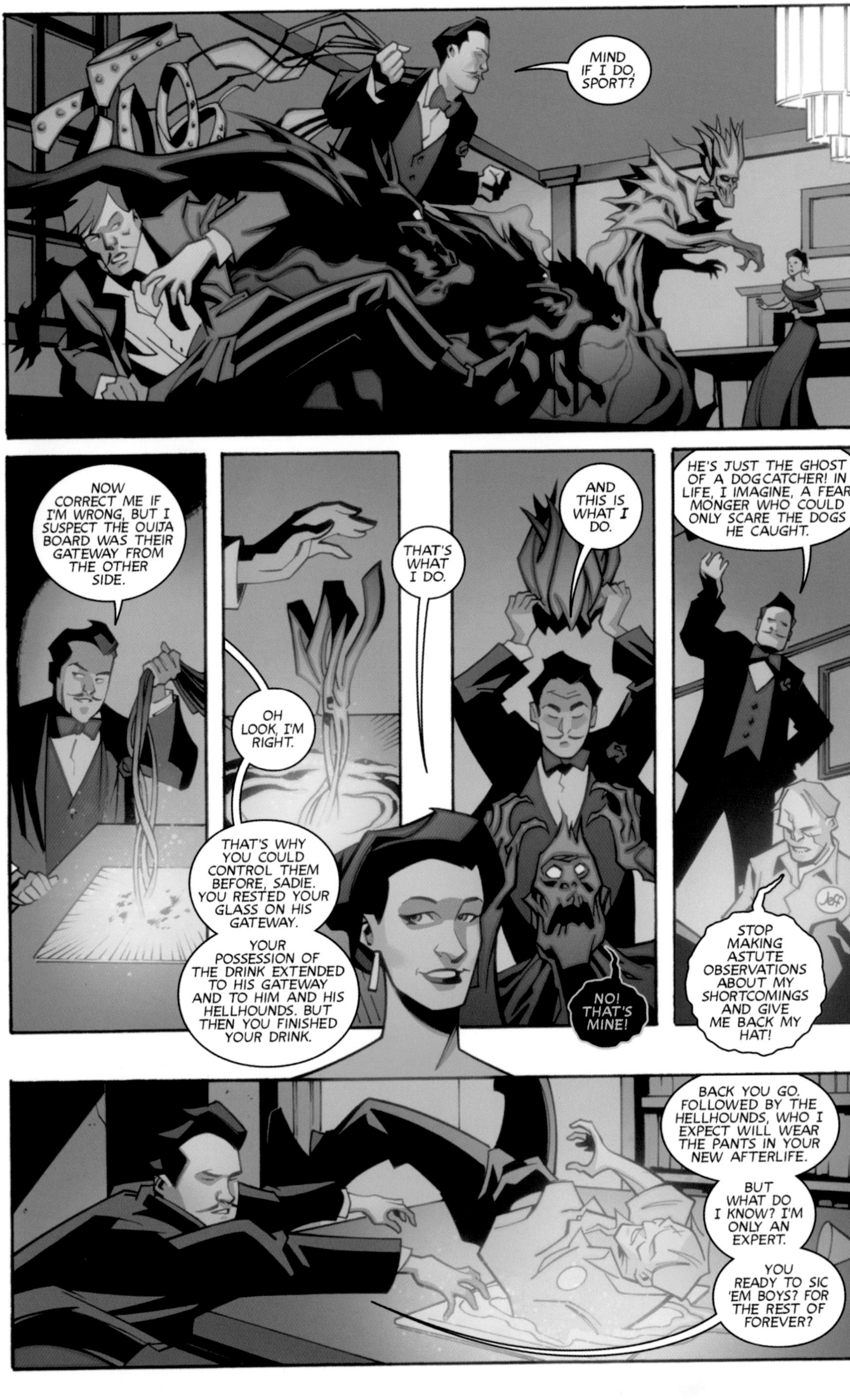
MIND IF I DO, SPORT?
NOW CORRECT ME IF I'M WRONG, BUT I SUSPECT THE OUIJA BOARD WAS THEIR GATEWAY FROM THE OTHER SIDE.
OH LOOK, I'M RIGHT.
THAT'S WHY YOU COULD CONTROL THEM BEFORE, SADIE. YOU RESTED YOUR GLASS ON HIS GATEWAY.
YOUR POSSESSION OF THE DRINK EXTENDED TO HIS GATEWAY AND TO HIM AND HIS HELLHOUNDS. BUT THEN YOU FINISHED YOUR DRINK.
THAT'S WHAT I DO.
AND THIS IS WHAT I DO.
NO! THAT'S MINE!
HE'S JUST THE GHOST OF A DOGCATCHER! IN LIFE, I IMAGINE, A FEAR MONGER WHO COULD ONLY SCARE THE DOGS HE CAUGHT.
JEFF
STOP MAKING ASTUTE OBSERVATIONS ABOUT MY SHORTCOMINGS AND GIVE ME BACK MY HAT!
BACK YOU GO. FOLLOWED BY THE HELLHOUNDS, WHO I EXPECT WILL WEAR THE PANTS IN YOUR NEW AFTERLIFE.
BUT WHAT DO I KNOW? I'M ONLY AN EXPERT.
YOU READY TO SIC 'EM BOYS? FOR THE REST OF FOREVER?

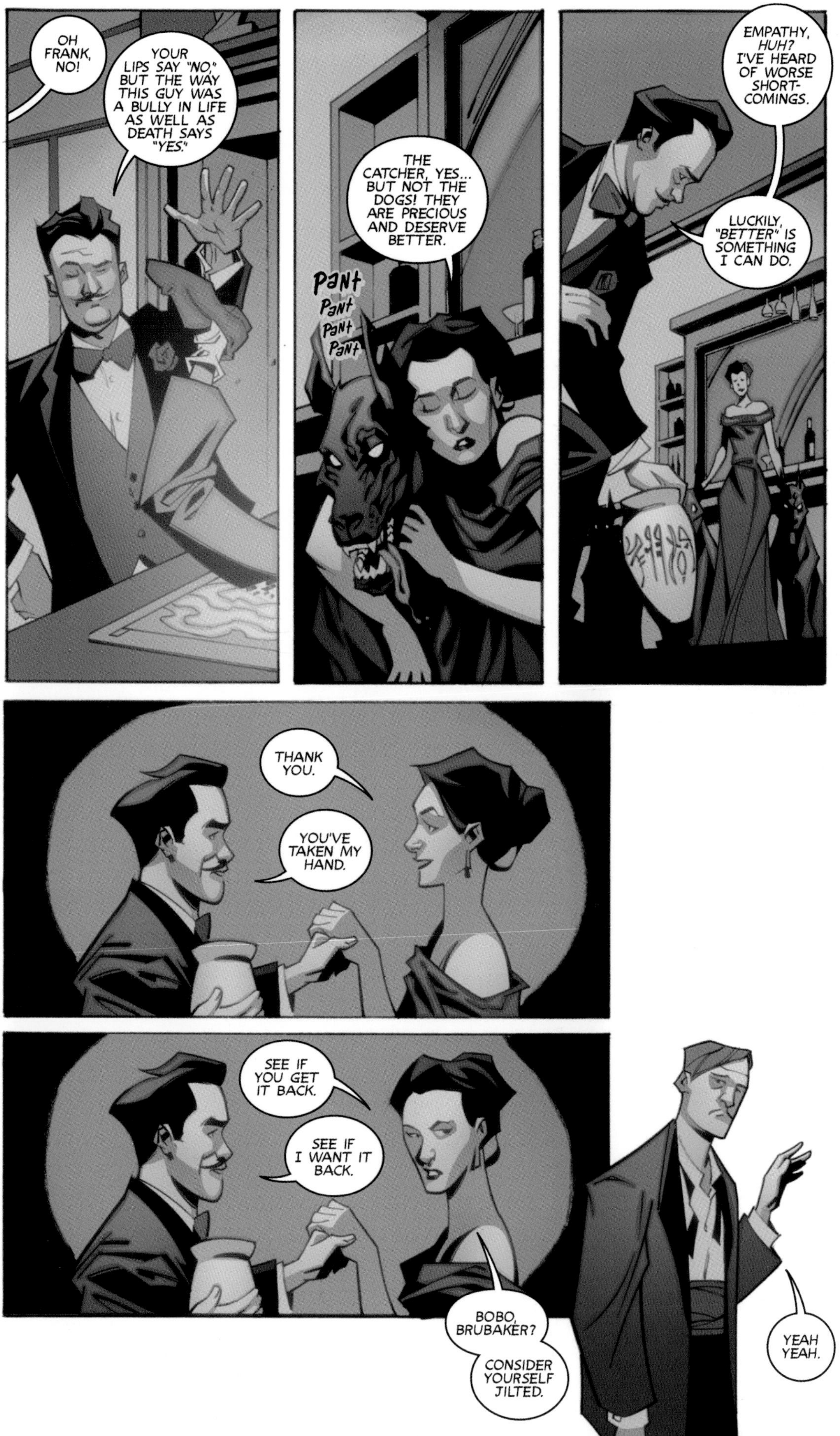
OH FRANK, NO!
YOUR LIPS SAY "NO," BUT THE WAY THIS GUY WAS A BULLY IN LIFE AS WELL AS DEATH SAYS "YES."
THE CATCHER, YES... BUT NOT THE DOGS! THEY ARE PRECIOUS AND DESERVE BETTER.
PANT PANT PANT PANT
EMPATHY, HUH? I'VE HEARD OF WORSE SHORT-COMINGS.
LUCKILY, "BETTER" IS SOMETHING I CAN DO.
THANK YOU.
YOU'VE TAKEN MY HAND.
SEE IF YOU GET IT BACK.
SEE IF I WANT IT BACK.
BOBO, BRUBAKER?
CONSIDER YOURSELF JILTED.
YEAH YEAH.

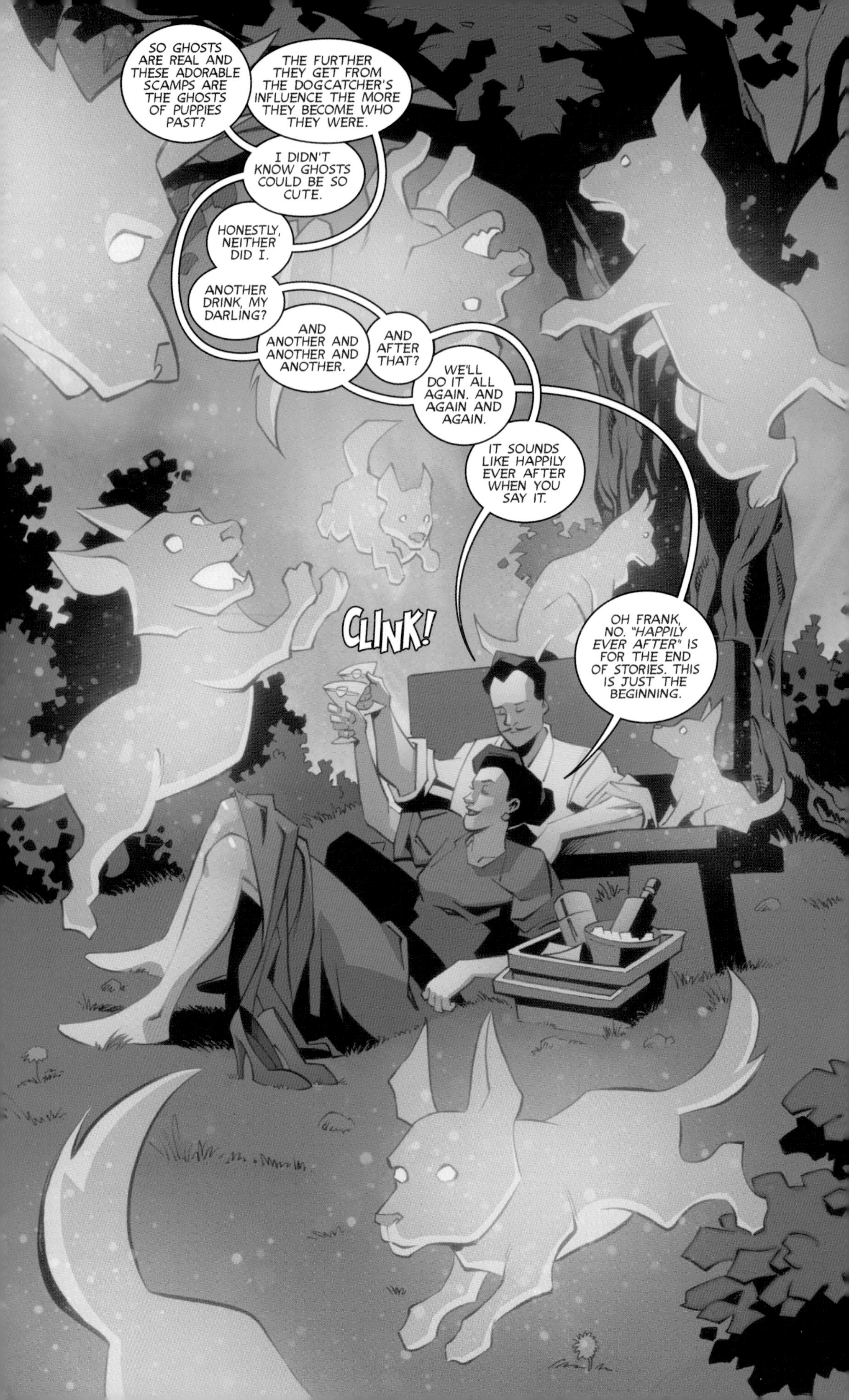
SO GHOSTS ARE REAL AND THESE ADORABLE SCAMPS ARE THE GHOSTS OF PUPPIES PAST?
THE FURTHER THEY GET FROM THE DOGCATCHER'S INFLUENCE THE MORE THEY BECOME WHO THEY WERE.
I DIDN'T KNOW GHOSTS COULD BE SO CUTE.
HONESTLY, NEITHER DID I.
ANOTHER DRINK, MY DARLING?
AND ANOTHER AND ANOTHER AND ANOTHER.
AND AFTER THAT?
WE'LL DO IT ALL AGAIN. AND AGAIN AND AGAIN.
IT SOUNDS LIKE HAPPILY EVER AFTER WHEN YOU SAY IT.
CLINK!
OH FRANK, NO. "HAPPILY EVER AFTER" IS FOR THE END OF STORIES. THIS IS JUST THE BEGINNING.

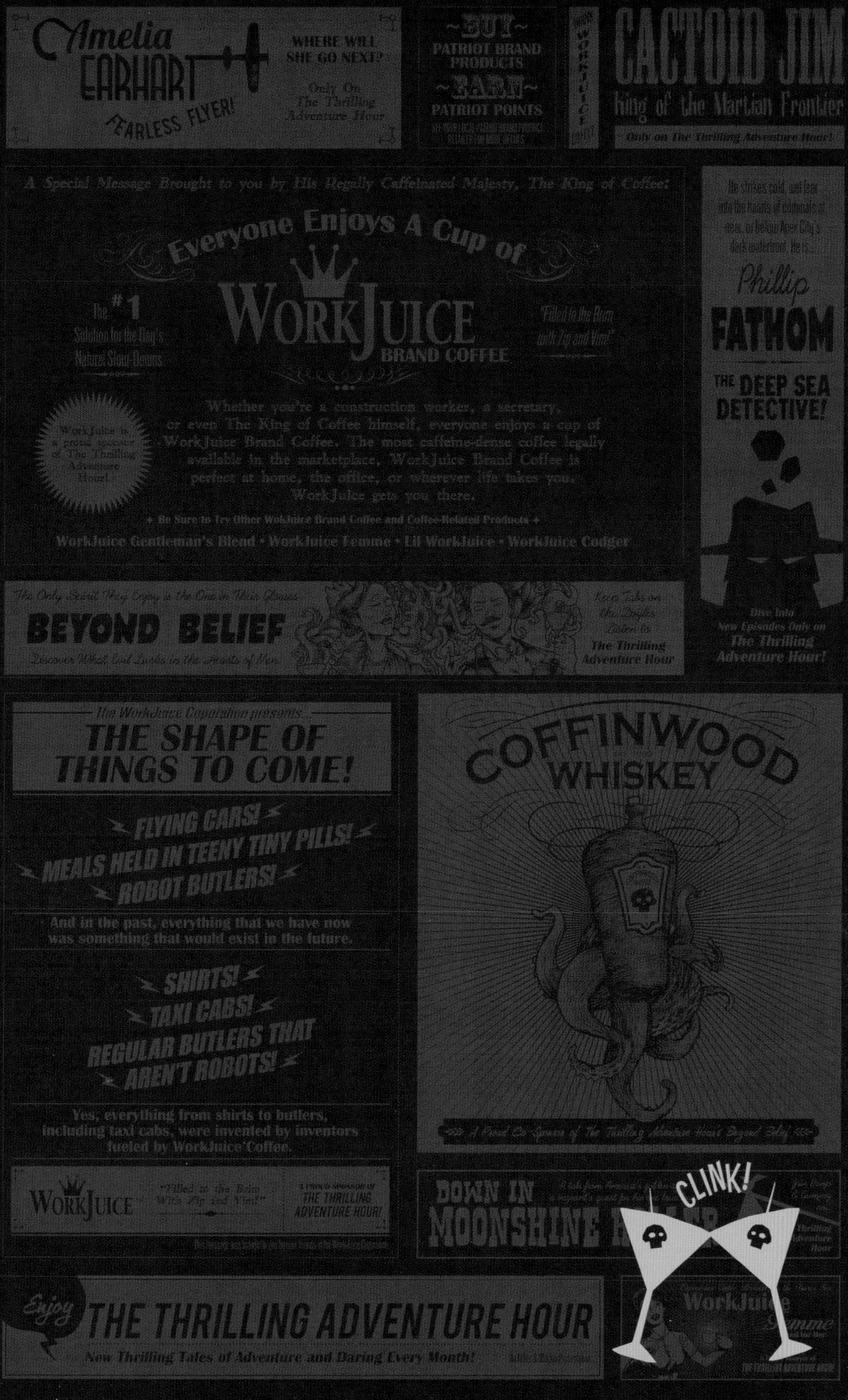

Amelia
EARHART
FEARLESS FLYER!
WHERE WILL SHE GO NEXT?
Only On The Thrilling Adventure Hour
~BUY~
PATRIOT BRAND PRODUCTS
~EARN~
PATRIOT POINTS
WORKJUICE
CACTOID JIM
King of the Martian Frontier
Only on The Thrilling Adventure Hour!
A Special Message Brought to you by His Regally Caffeinated Majesty, The King of Coffee:
Everyone Enjoys A Cup of
WORKJUICE
BRAND COFFEE
The #1 Solution for the Day's Natural Slow-Downs
"Filled to the Brim with Zip and Vim!"
WorkJuice is a proud sponsor of The Thrilling Adventure Hour!
Whether you're a construction worker, a secretary, or even The King of Coffee himself, everyone enjoys a cup of WorkJuice Brand Coffee. The most caffeine-dense coffee legally available in the marketplace. WorkJuice Brand Coffee is perfect at home, the office, or wherever life takes you. WorkJuice gets you there.
+ Be Sure to Try Other WorkJuice Brand Coffee and Coffee-Related Products +
WorkJuice Gentleman's Blend • WorkJuice Femme • Lil WorkJuice • WorkJuice Codger
He strikes cold, wet fear into the hearts of criminals at, near, or below Apex City's dark waterfront. He is...
Phillip
FATHOM
THE DEEP SEA DETECTIVE!
Dive Into New Episodes Only on The Thrilling Adventure Hour!
The Only Spirit They Enjoy is the One in Their Glasses
BEYOND BELIEF
Discover What Evil Lurks in the Hearts of Men
Keep Tabs on the Doyles Listen to The Thrilling Adventure Hour
The WorkJuice Corporation presents...
THE SHAPE OF THINGS TO COME!
FLYING CARS!
MEALS HELD IN TEENY TINY PILLS!
ROBOT BUTLERS!
And in the past, everything that we have now was something that would exist in the future.
SHIRTS!
TAXI CABS!
REGULAR BUTLERS THAT AREN'T ROBOTS!
Yes, everything from shirts to butlers, including taxi cabs, were invented by inventors fueled by WorkJuice Coffee.
WORKJUICE
"Filled to the Brim With Zip and Vim!"
A PROUD SPONSOR OF THE THRILLING ADVENTURE HOUR!
COFFINWOOD WHISKEY
A Proud Co-Sponsor of The Thrilling Adventure Hour Beyond Belief
DOWN IN MOONSHINE
CLINK!
The Thrilling Adventure Hour
WorkJuice
Femme
Enjoy
THE THRILLING ADVENTURE HOUR
New Thrilling Tales of Adventure and Daring Every Month!

Chapter ONE

A Haunted Housewarming...

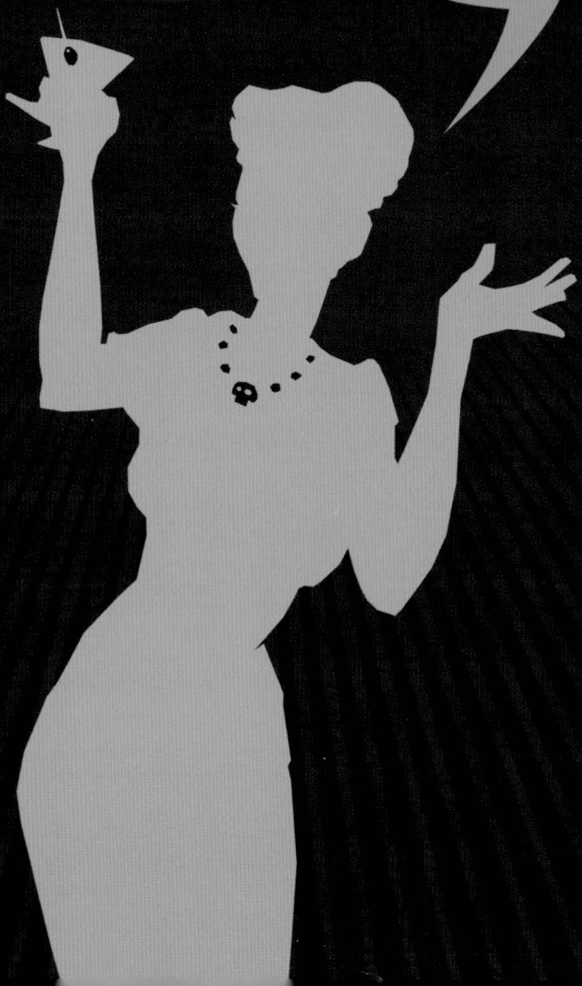

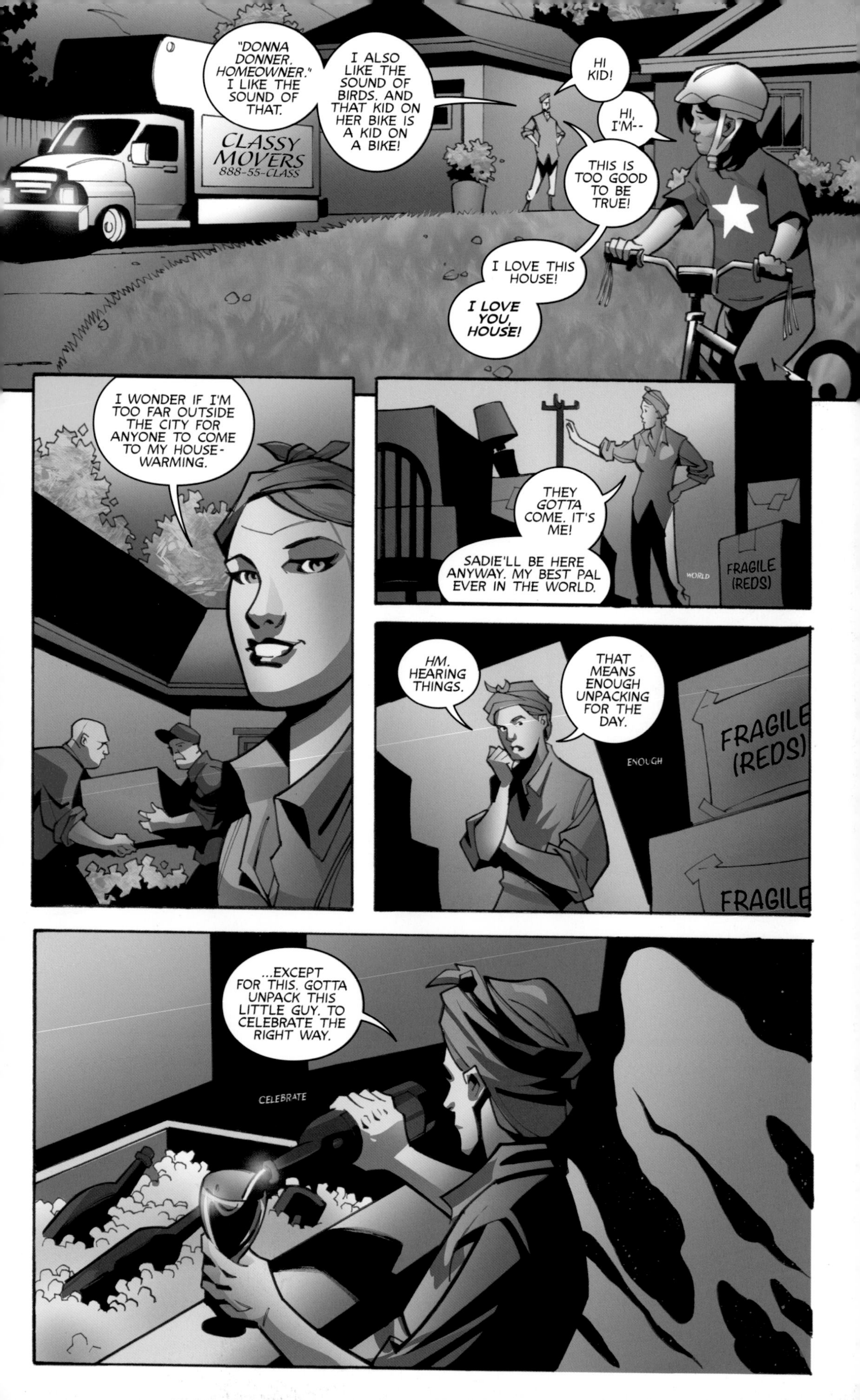
"DONNA DONNER. HOMEOWNER." I LIKE THE SOUND OF THAT.
CLASSY MOVERS
888-55-CLASS
I ALSO LIKE THE SOUND OF BIRDS. AND THAT KID ON HER BIKE IS A KID ON A BIKE!
HI KID!
HI, I'M--
THIS IS TOO GOOD TO BE TRUE!
I LOVE THIS HOUSE!
I LOVE YOU, HOUSE!
I WONDER IF I'M TOO FAR OUTSIDE THE CITY FOR ANYONE TO COME TO MY HOUSE-WARMING.
THEY *GOTTA* COME. IT'S ME!
SADIE'LL BE HERE ANYWAY. MY BEST PAL EVER IN THE WORLD.
WORLD
FRAGILE (REDS)
HM. HEARING THINGS.
THAT MEANS ENOUGH UNPACKING FOR THE DAY.
ENOUGH
FRAGILE (REDS)
FRAGILE
...EXCEPT FOR THIS. GOTTA UNPACK THIS LITTLE GUY. TO CELEBRATE THE RIGHT WAY.
CELEBRATE

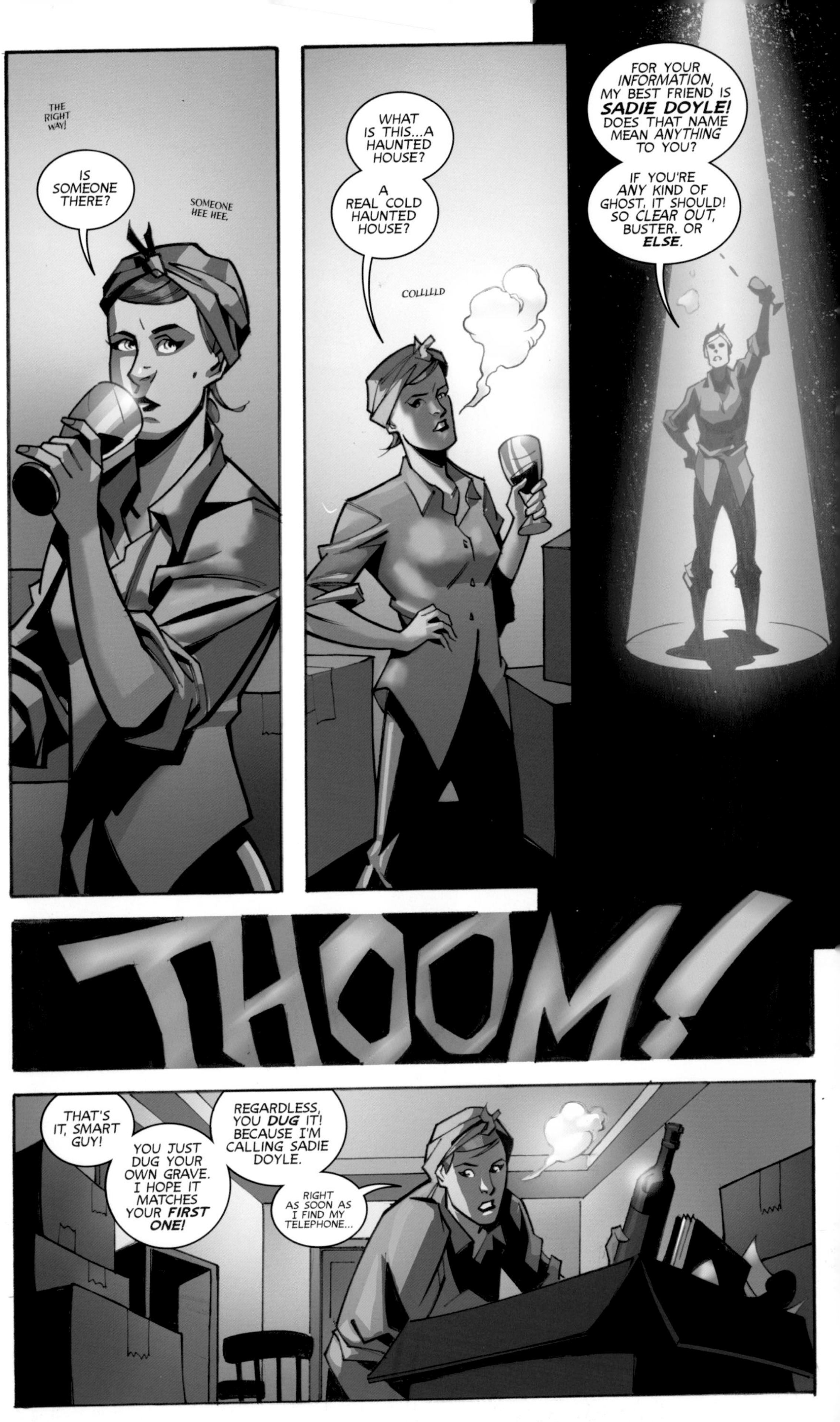
THE RIGHT WAY!
IS SOMEONE THERE?
SOMEONE HEE HEE.
WHAT IS THIS...A HAUNTED HOUSE?
A REAL COLD HAUNTED HOUSE?
COLLLLD
FOR YOUR *INFORMATION*, MY BEST FRIEND IS ***SADIE DOYLE!*** DOES THAT NAME MEAN *ANYTHING* TO YOU?
IF YOU'RE *ANY* KIND OF GHOST, IT SHOULD! SO *CLEAR OUT*, BUSTER. OR ***ELSE***.
THOOM!
THAT'S IT, SMART GUY!
YOU JUST DUG YOUR OWN GRAVE. I HOPE IT MATCHES YOUR ***FIRST ONE!***
REGARDLESS, YOU ***DUG*** IT! BECAUSE I'M CALLING SADIE DOYLE.
RIGHT AS SOON AS I FIND MY TELEPHONE...

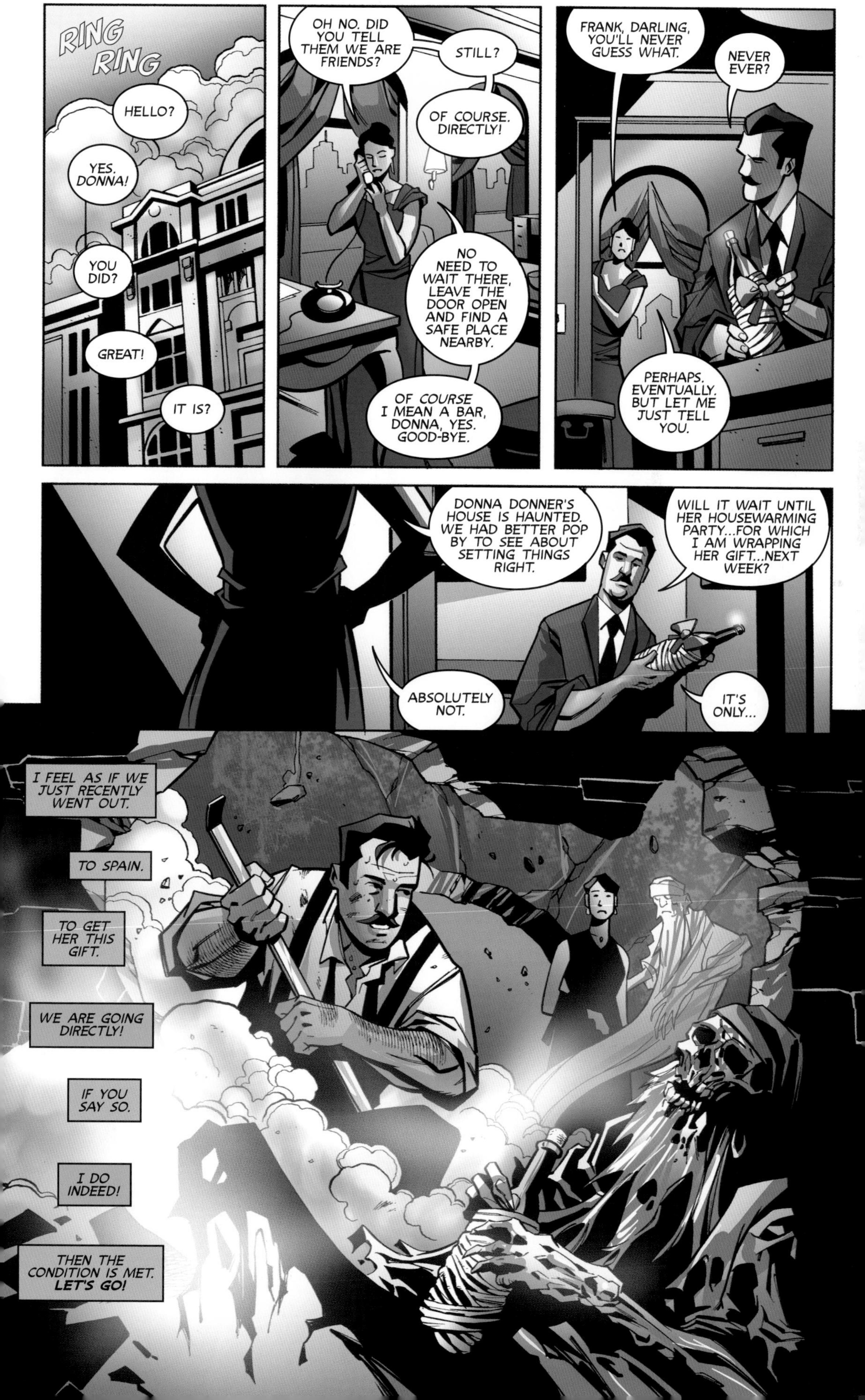
RING RING
HELLO?
YES. DONNA!
YOU DID?
GREAT!
IT IS?
OH NO. DID YOU TELL THEM WE ARE FRIENDS?
STILL?
OF COURSE. DIRECTLY!
NO NEED TO WAIT THERE, LEAVE THE DOOR OPEN AND FIND A SAFE PLACE NEARBY.
OF COURSE I MEAN A BAR, DONNA, YES. GOOD-BYE.
FRANK, DARLING, YOU'LL NEVER GUESS WHAT.
NEVER EVER?
PERHAPS. EVENTUALLY. BUT LET ME JUST TELL YOU.
DONNA DONNER'S HOUSE IS HAUNTED. WE HAD BETTER POP BY TO SEE ABOUT SETTING THINGS RIGHT.
WILL IT WAIT UNTIL HER HOUSEWARMING PARTY...FOR WHICH I AM WRAPPING HER GIFT...NEXT WEEK?
ABSOLUTELY NOT.
IT'S ONLY...
I FEEL AS IF WE JUST RECENTLY WENT OUT.
TO SPAIN.
TO GET HER THIS GIFT.
WE ARE GOING DIRECTLY!
IF YOU SAY SO.
I DO INDEED!
THEN THE CONDITION IS MET. LET'S GO!

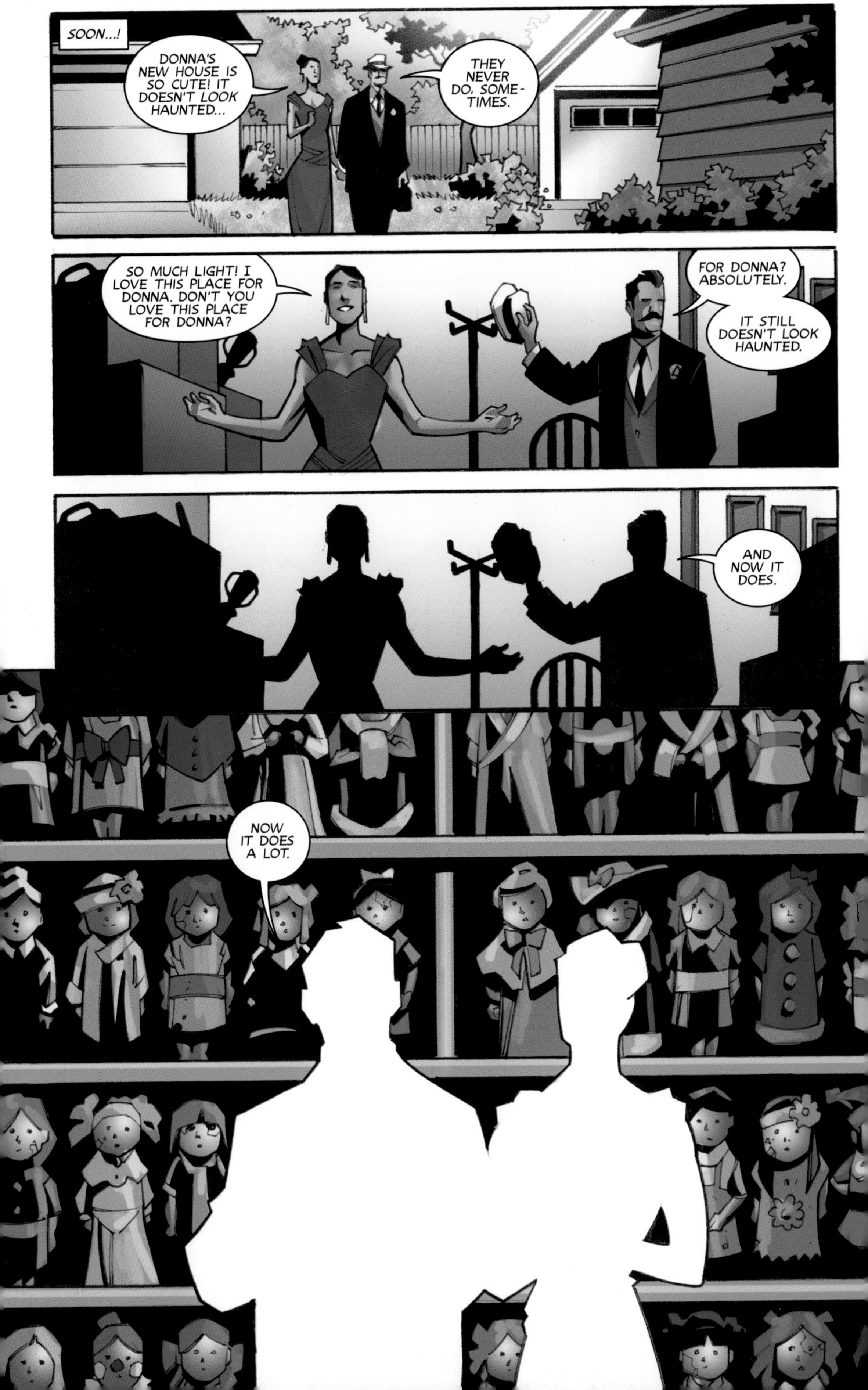
SOON...!
DONNA'S NEW HOUSE IS SO CUTE! IT DOESN'T LOOK HAUNTED...
THEY NEVER DO, SOME-TIMES.
SO MUCH LIGHT! I LOVE THIS PLACE FOR DONNA. DON'T YOU LOVE THIS PLACE FOR DONNA?
FOR DONNA? ABSOLUTELY.
IT STILL DOESN'T LOOK HAUNTED.
AND NOW IT DOES.
NOW IT DOES A LOT.

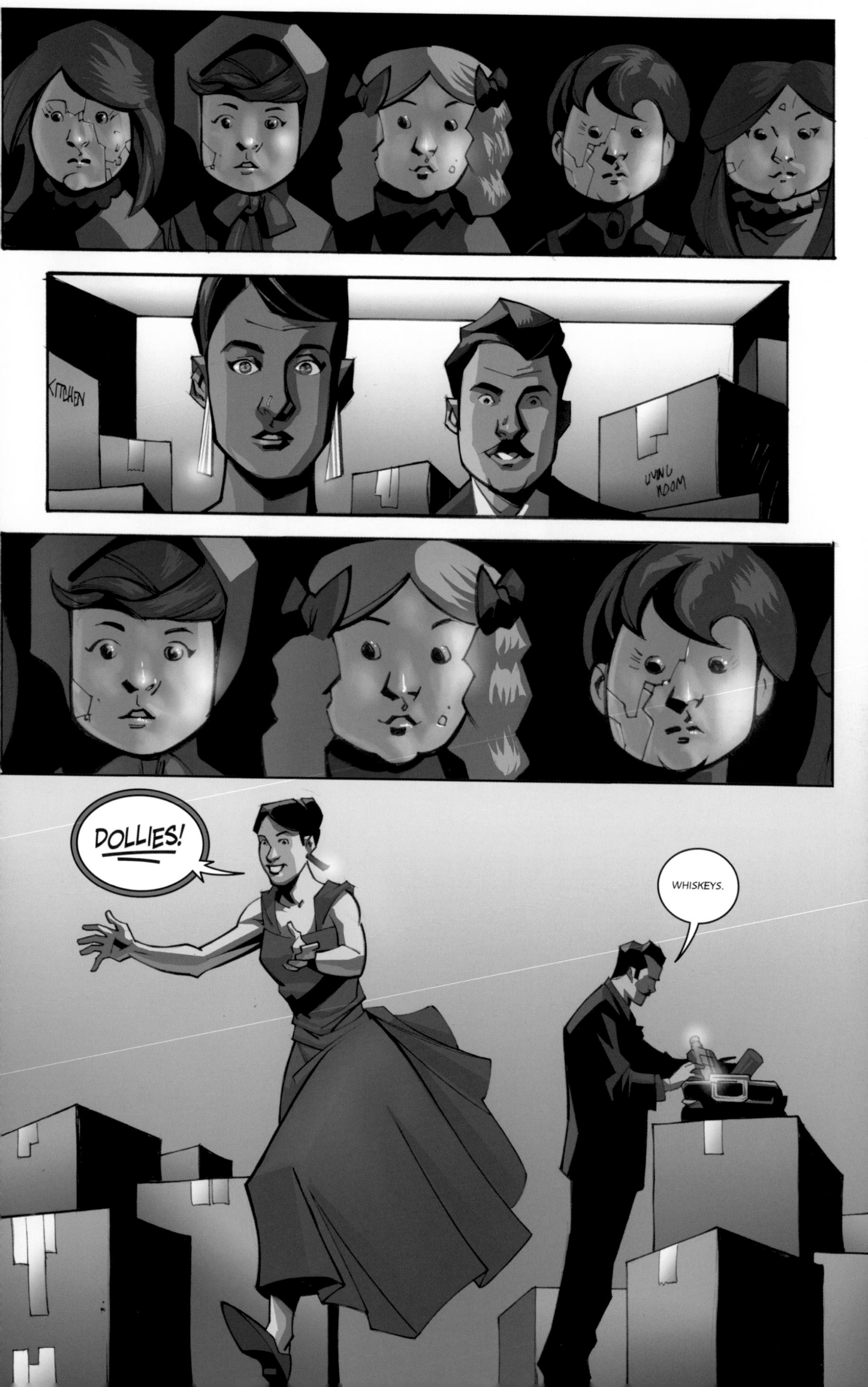
KITCHEN
LIVING ROOM
DOLLIES!
WHISKEYS.

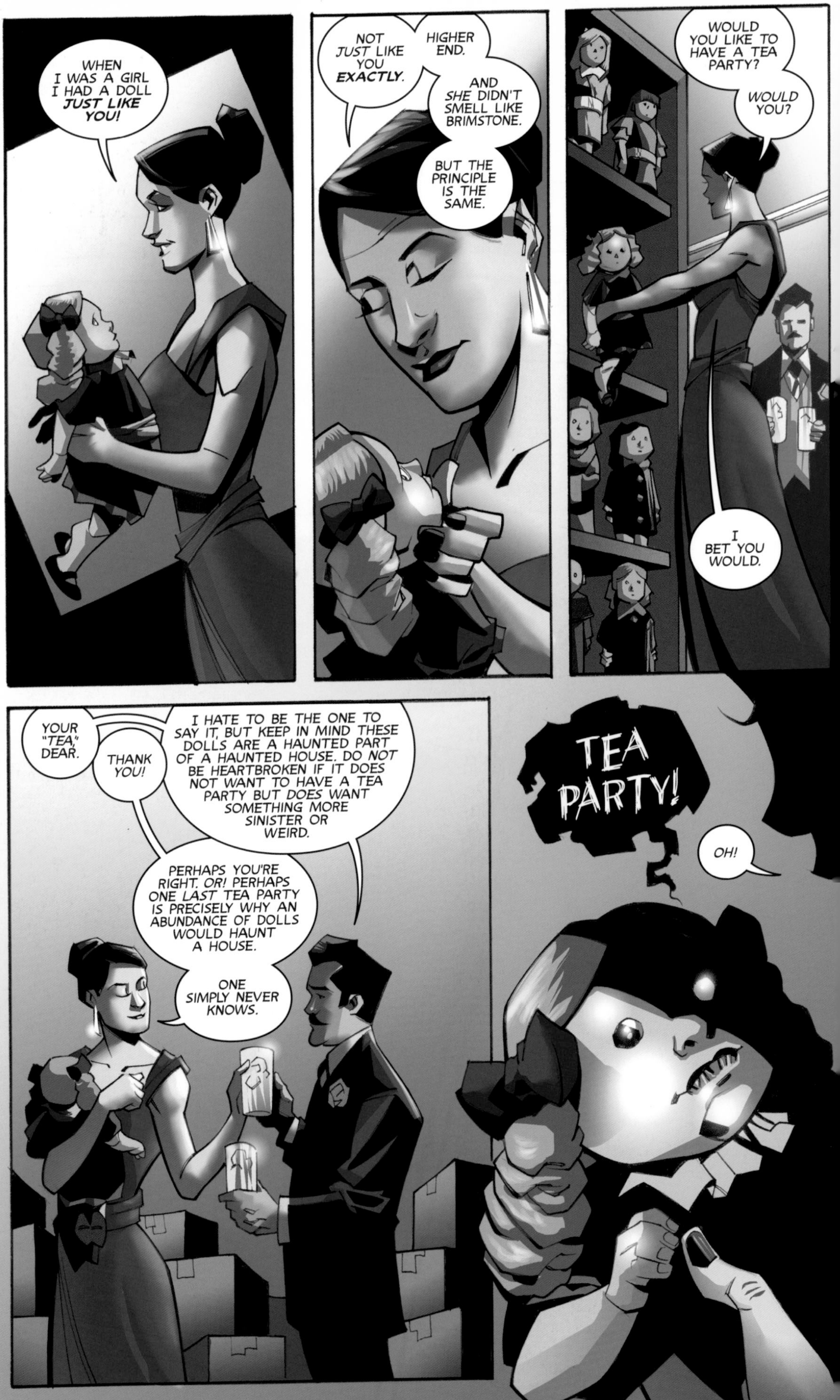
WHEN I WAS A GIRL I HAD A DOLL **JUST LIKE YOU!**
NOT *JUST* LIKE YOU **EXACTLY**.
HIGHER END.
AND *SHE* DIDN'T SMELL LIKE BRIMSTONE.
BUT THE PRINCIPLE IS THE SAME.
WOULD YOU LIKE TO HAVE A TEA PARTY?
WOULD YOU?
I BET YOU WOULD.
YOUR "*TEA*," DEAR.
THANK *YOU!*
I HATE TO BE THE ONE TO SAY IT, BUT KEEP IN MIND THESE DOLLS ARE A HAUNTED PART OF A HAUNTED HOUSE. DO *NOT* BE HEARTBROKEN IF IT DOES NOT WANT TO HAVE A TEA PARTY BUT *DOES* WANT SOMETHING MORE SINISTER OR WEIRD.
PERHAPS YOU'RE RIGHT. *OR!* PERHAPS ONE *LAST* TEA PARTY IS PRECISELY WHY AN ABUNDANCE OF DOLLS WOULD HAUNT A HOUSE.
ONE SIMPLY NEVER KNOWS.
TEA PARTY!
OH!

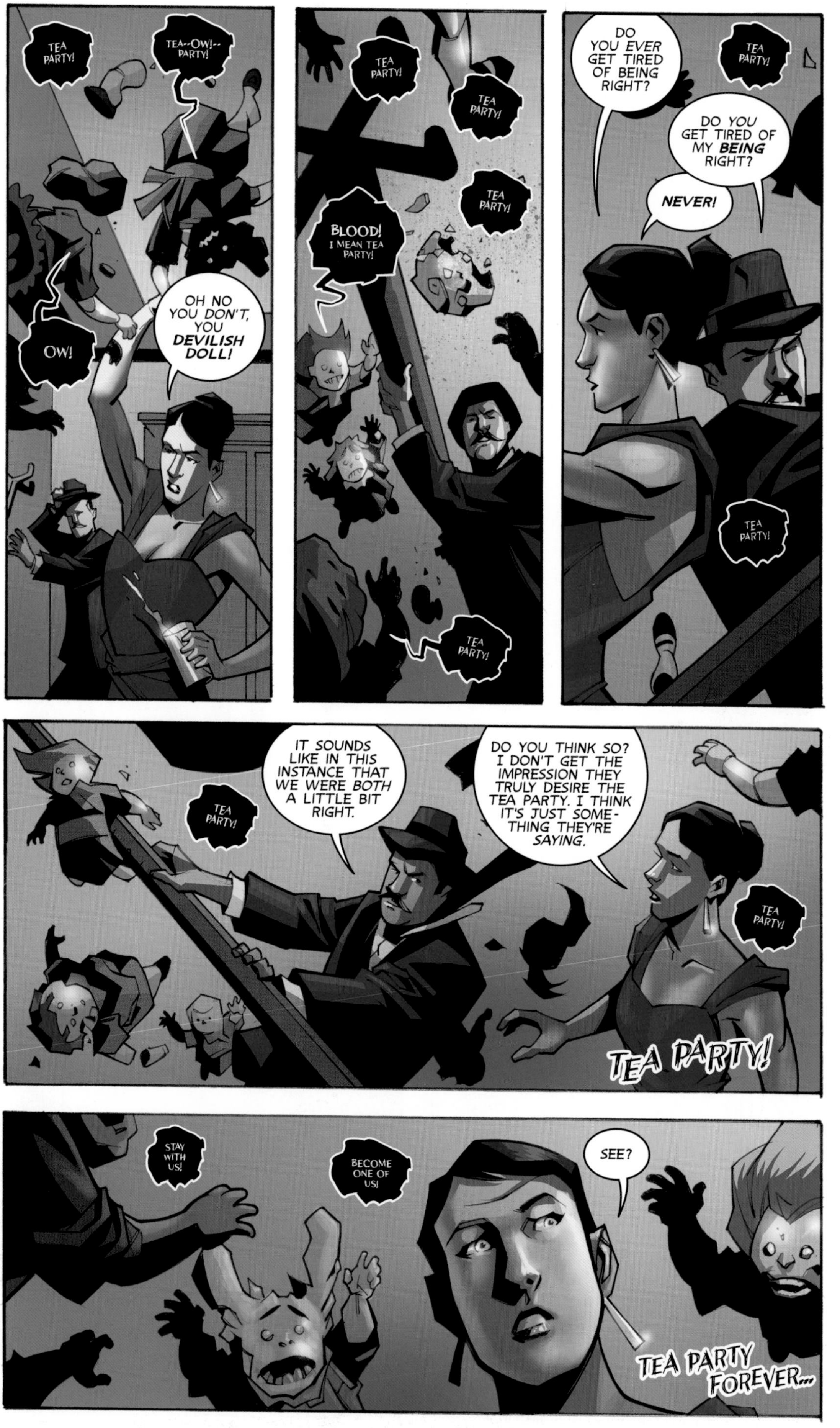
TEA PARTY!
TEA--OW!--PARTY!
OW!
OH NO YOU DON'T, YOU DEVILISH DOLL!
TEA PARTY!
TEA PARTY!
TEA PARTY!
BLOOD! I MEAN TEA PARTY!
TEA PARTY!
DO YOU EVER GET TIRED OF BEING RIGHT?
TEA PARTY!
DO YOU GET TIRED OF MY BEING RIGHT?
NEVER!
TEA PARTY!
TEA PARTY!
IT SOUNDS LIKE IN THIS INSTANCE THAT WE WERE BOTH A LITTLE BIT RIGHT.
DO YOU THINK SO? I DON'T GET THE IMPRESSION THEY TRULY DESIRE THE TEA PARTY. I THINK IT'S JUST SOME-THING THEY'RE SAYING.
TEA PARTY!
TEA PARTY!
STAY WITH US!
BECOME ONE OF US!
SEE?
TEA PARTY FOREVER...

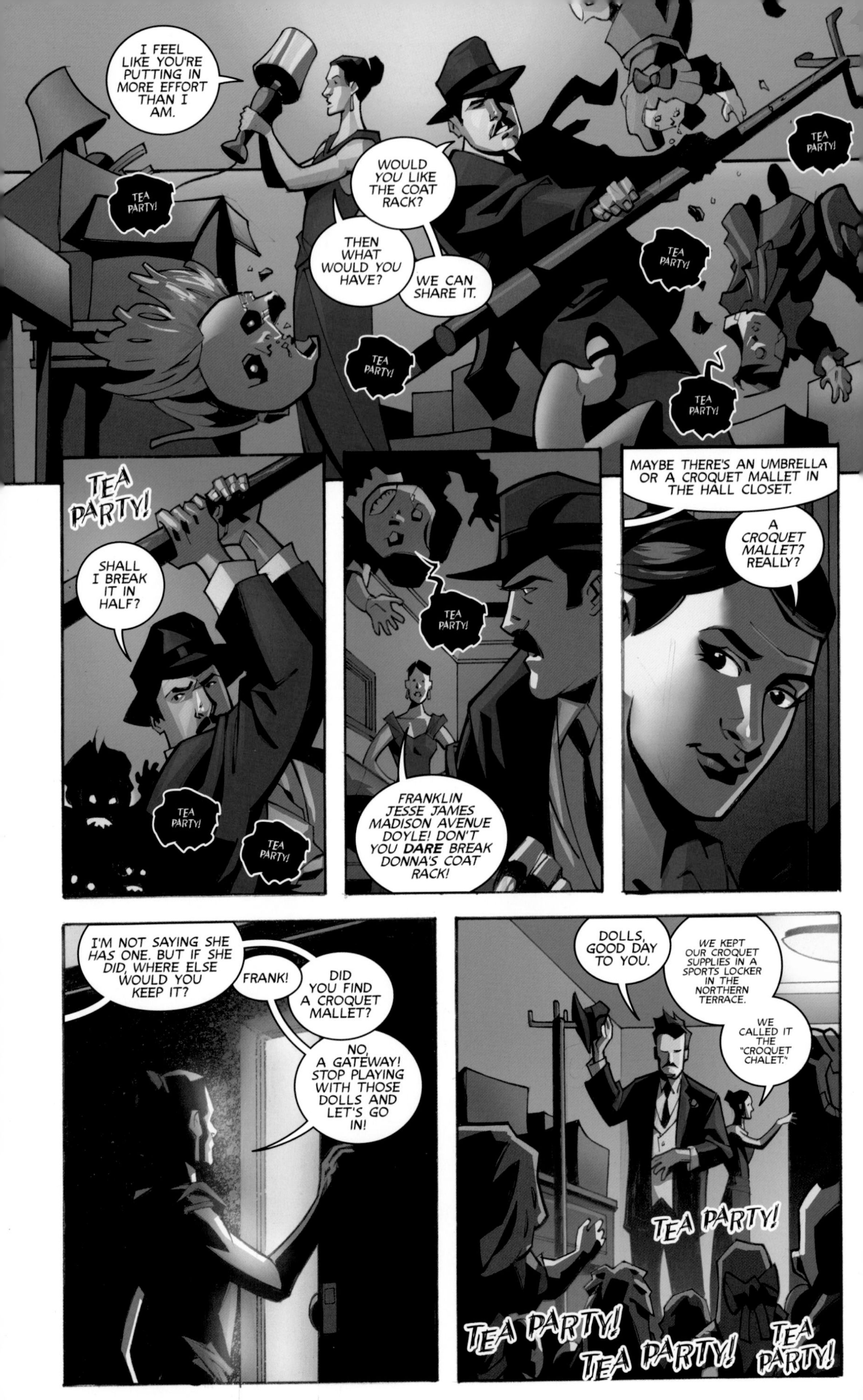
I FEEL LIKE YOU'RE PUTTING IN MORE EFFORT THAN I AM.
WOULD YOU LIKE THE COAT RACK?
THEN WHAT WOULD YOU HAVE?
WE CAN SHARE IT.
TEA PARTY!
TEA PARTY!
TEA PARTY!
TEA PARTY!
TEA PARTY!
TEA PARTY!
SHALL I BREAK IT IN HALF?
TEA PARTY!
TEA PARTY!
TEA PARTY!
FRANKLIN JESSE JAMES MADISON AVENUE DOYLE! DON'T YOU DARE BREAK DONNA'S COAT RACK!
MAYBE THERE'S AN UMBRELLA OR A CROQUET MALLET IN THE HALL CLOSET.
A CROQUET MALLET? REALLY?
I'M NOT SAYING SHE HAS ONE. BUT IF SHE DID, WHERE ELSE WOULD YOU KEEP IT?
FRANK!
DID YOU FIND A CROQUET MALLET?
NO, A GATEWAY! STOP PLAYING WITH THOSE DOLLS AND LET'S GO IN!
DOLLS, GOOD DAY TO YOU.
WE KEPT OUR CROQUET SUPPLIES IN A SPORTS LOCKER IN THE NORTHERN TERRACE.
WE CALLED IT THE "CROQUET CHALET."
TEA PARTY!
TEA PARTY!
TEA PARTY!
TEA PARTY!

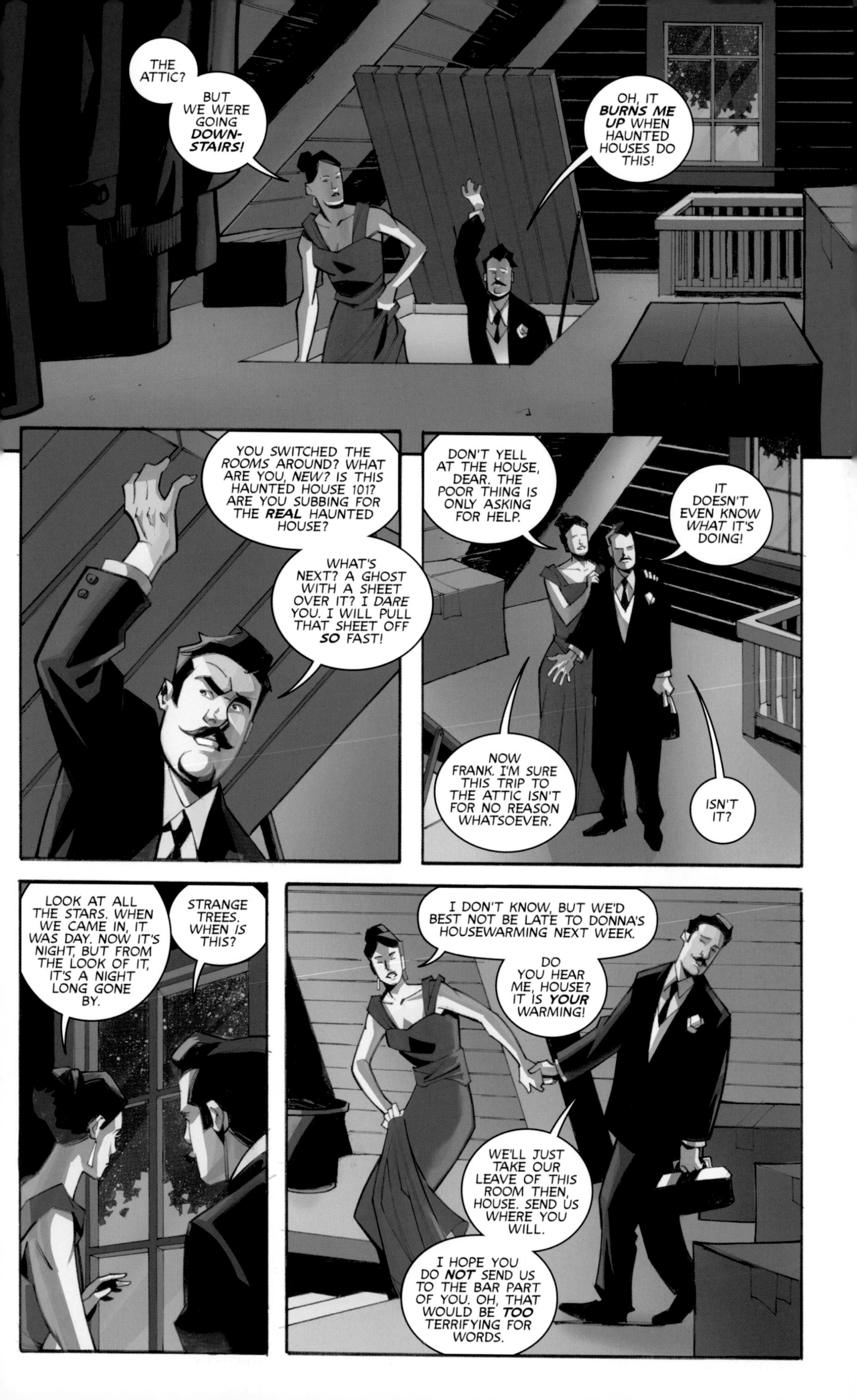
THE ATTIC?
BUT WE WERE GOING DOWN-STAIRS!
OH, IT BURNS ME UP WHEN HAUNTED HOUSES DO THIS!
YOU SWITCHED THE ROOMS AROUND? WHAT ARE YOU, NEW? IS THIS HAUNTED HOUSE 101? ARE YOU SUBBING FOR THE REAL HAUNTED HOUSE?
WHAT'S NEXT? A GHOST WITH A SHEET OVER IT? I DARE YOU. I WILL PULL THAT SHEET OFF SO FAST!
DON'T YELL AT THE HOUSE, DEAR. THE POOR THING IS ONLY ASKING FOR HELP.
IT DOESN'T EVEN KNOW WHAT IT'S DOING!
NOW FRANK. I'M SURE THIS TRIP TO THE ATTIC ISN'T FOR NO REASON WHATSOEVER.
ISN'T IT?
LOOK AT ALL THE STARS. WHEN WE CAME IN, IT WAS DAY. NOW IT'S NIGHT, BUT FROM THE LOOK OF IT, IT'S A NIGHT LONG GONE BY.
STRANGE TREES. WHEN IS THIS?
I DON'T KNOW, BUT WE'D BEST NOT BE LATE TO DONNA'S HOUSEWARMING NEXT WEEK.
DO YOU HEAR ME, HOUSE? IT IS YOUR WARMING!
WE'LL JUST TAKE OUR LEAVE OF THIS ROOM THEN, HOUSE. SEND US WHERE YOU WILL.
I HOPE YOU DO NOT SEND US TO THE BAR PART OF YOU. OH, THAT WOULD BE TOO TERRIFYING FOR WORDS.

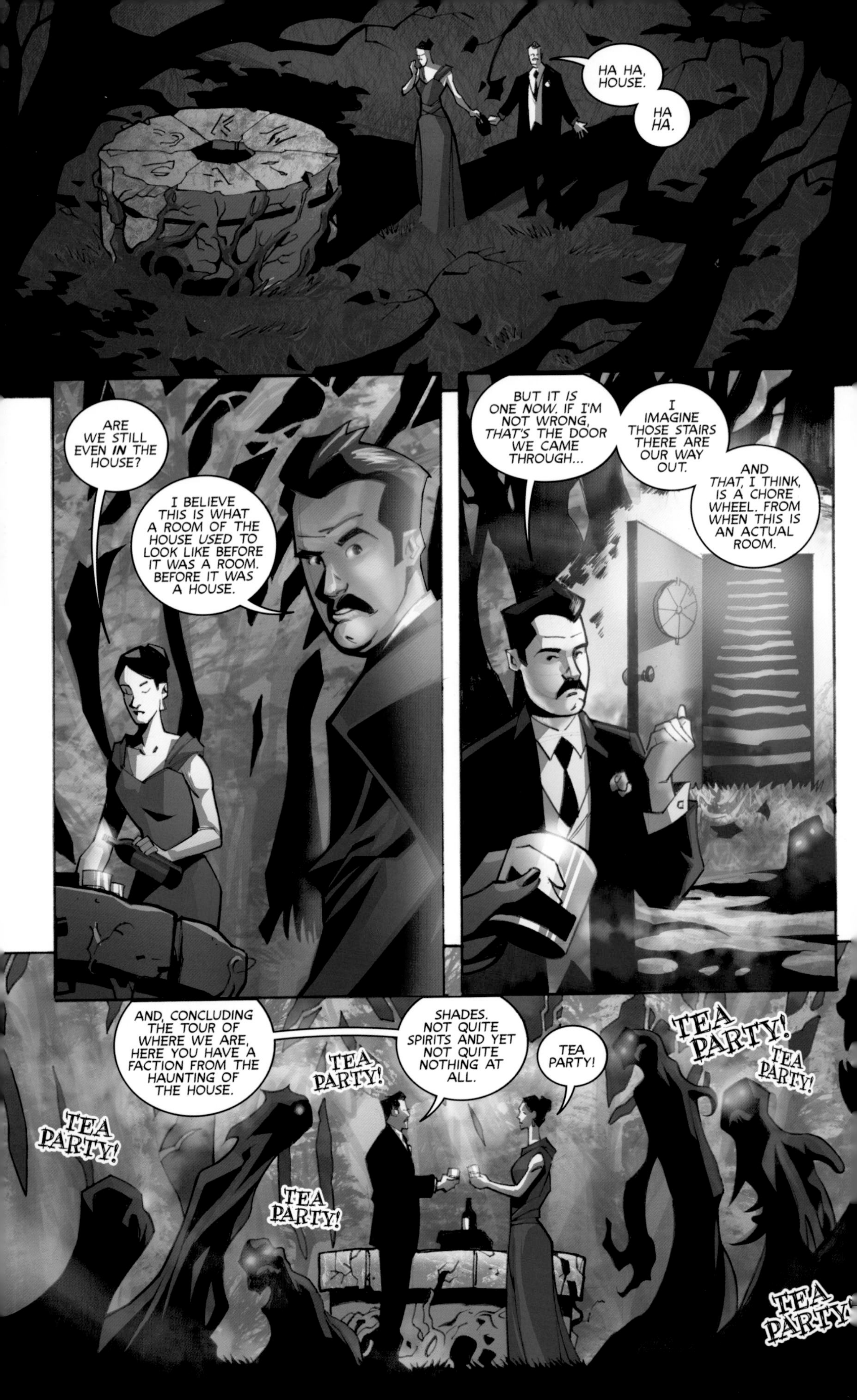
HA HA, HOUSE.
HA HA.
ARE WE STILL EVEN IN THE HOUSE?
I BELIEVE THIS IS WHAT A ROOM OF THE HOUSE USED TO LOOK LIKE BEFORE IT WAS A ROOM. BEFORE IT WAS A HOUSE.
BUT IT IS ONE NOW. IF I'M NOT WRONG, THAT'S THE DOOR WE CAME THROUGH...
I IMAGINE THOSE STAIRS THERE ARE OUR WAY OUT.
AND THAT, I THINK, IS A CHORE WHEEL. FROM WHEN THIS IS AN ACTUAL ROOM.
AND, CONCLUDING THE TOUR OF WHERE WE ARE, HERE YOU HAVE A FACTION FROM THE HAUNTING OF THE HOUSE.
SHADES. NOT QUITE SPIRITS AND YET NOT QUITE NOTHING AT ALL.
TEA PARTY!
TEA PARTY!
TEA PARTY!
TEA PARTY!
TEA PARTY!
TEA PARTY!
TEA PARTY!

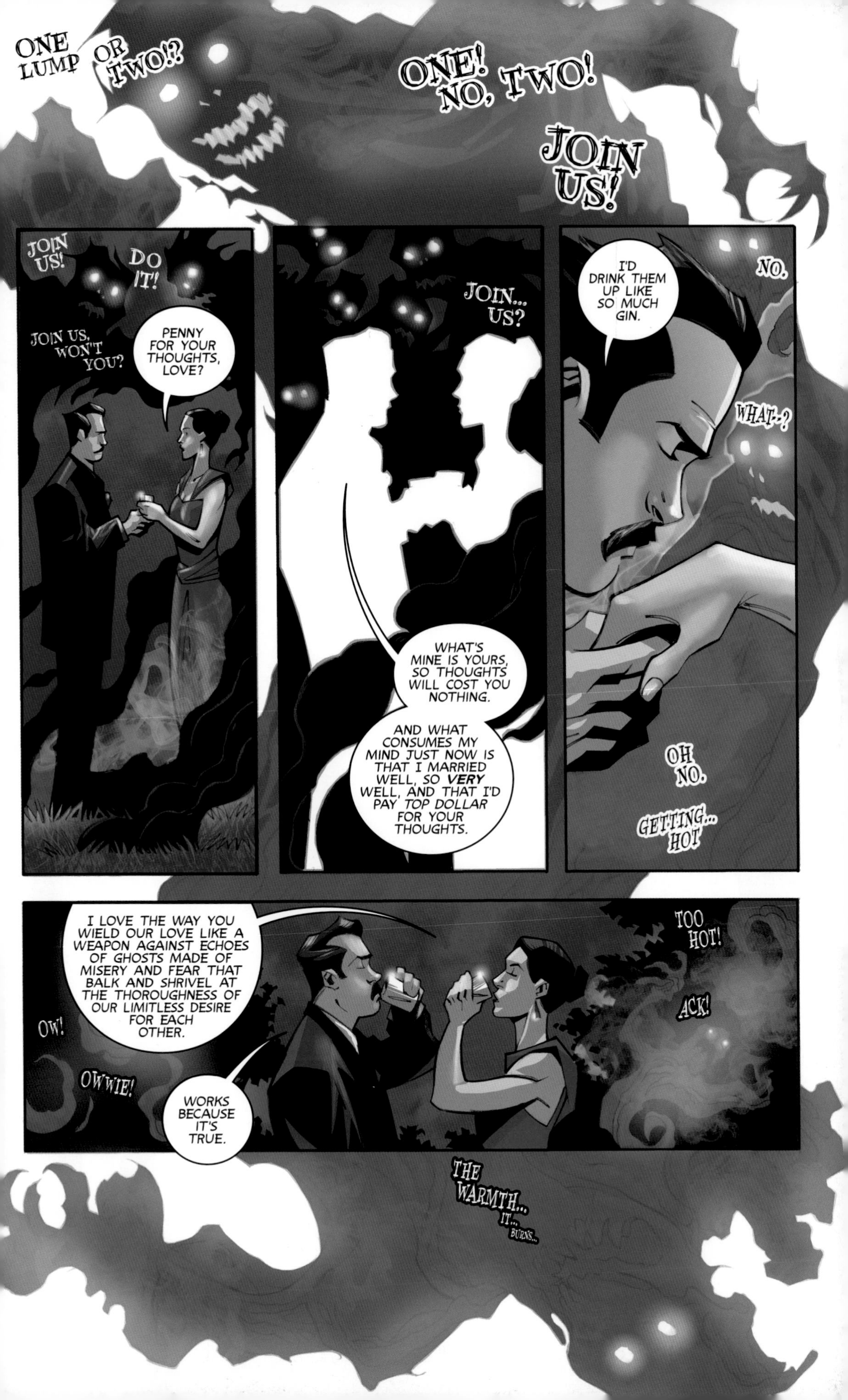
ONE LUMP OR TWO!?
ONE! NO, TWO!
JOIN US!
JOIN US!
DO IT!
JOIN US, WON'T YOU?
PENNY FOR YOUR THOUGHTS, LOVE?
JOIN... US?
WHAT'S MINE IS YOURS, SO THOUGHTS WILL COST YOU NOTHING.
AND WHAT CONSUMES MY MIND JUST NOW IS THAT I MARRIED WELL, SO VERY WELL, AND THAT I'D PAY TOP DOLLAR FOR YOUR THOUGHTS.
I'D DRINK THEM UP LIKE SO MUCH GIN.
NO.
WHAT-?
OH NO.
GETTING... HOT
I LOVE THE WAY YOU WIELD OUR LOVE LIKE A WEAPON AGAINST ECHOES OF GHOSTS MADE OF MISERY AND FEAR THAT BALK AND SHRIVEL AT THE THOROUGHNESS OF OUR LIMITLESS DESIRE FOR EACH OTHER.
WORKS BECAUSE IT'S TRUE.
OW!
OWWIE!
TOO HOT!
ACK!
THE WARMTH... IT... BURNS...

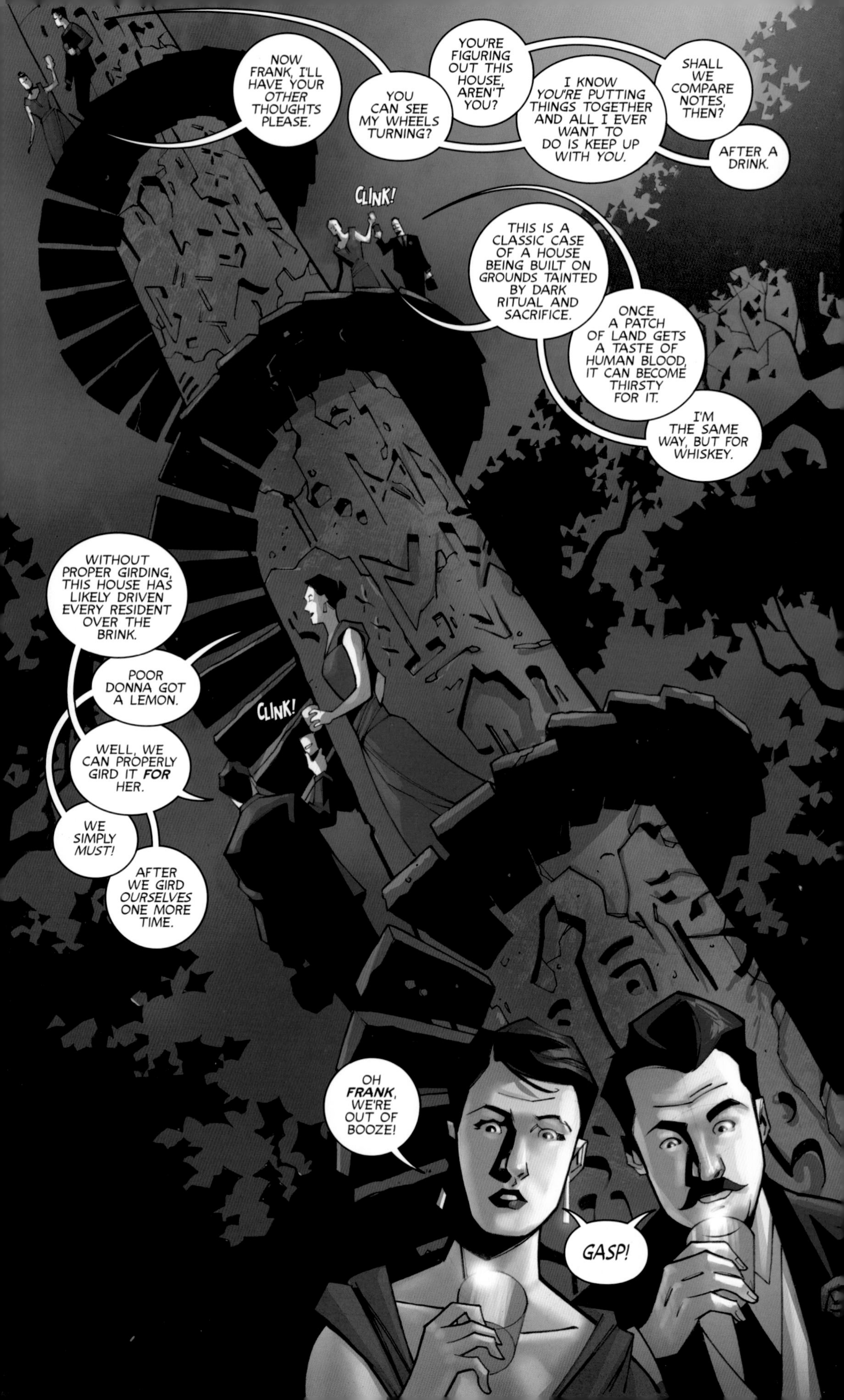
NOW FRANK, I'LL HAVE YOUR OTHER THOUGHTS PLEASE.
YOU CAN SEE MY WHEELS TURNING?
YOU'RE FIGURING OUT THIS HOUSE, AREN'T YOU?
I KNOW YOU'RE PUTTING THINGS TOGETHER AND ALL I EVER WANT TO DO IS KEEP UP WITH YOU.
SHALL WE COMPARE NOTES, THEN?
AFTER A DRINK.
CLINK!
THIS IS A CLASSIC CASE OF A HOUSE BEING BUILT ON GROUNDS TAINTED BY DARK RITUAL AND SACRIFICE.
ONCE A PATCH OF LAND GETS A TASTE OF HUMAN BLOOD, IT CAN BECOME THIRSTY FOR IT.
I'M THE SAME WAY, BUT FOR WHISKEY.
WITHOUT PROPER GIRDING, THIS HOUSE HAS LIKELY DRIVEN EVERY RESIDENT OVER THE BRINK.
POOR DONNA GOT A LEMON.
CLINK!
WELL, WE CAN PROPERLY GIRD IT FOR HER.
WE SIMPLY MUST!
AFTER WE GIRD OURSELVES ONE MORE TIME.
OH FRANK, WE'RE OUT OF BOOZE!
GASP!

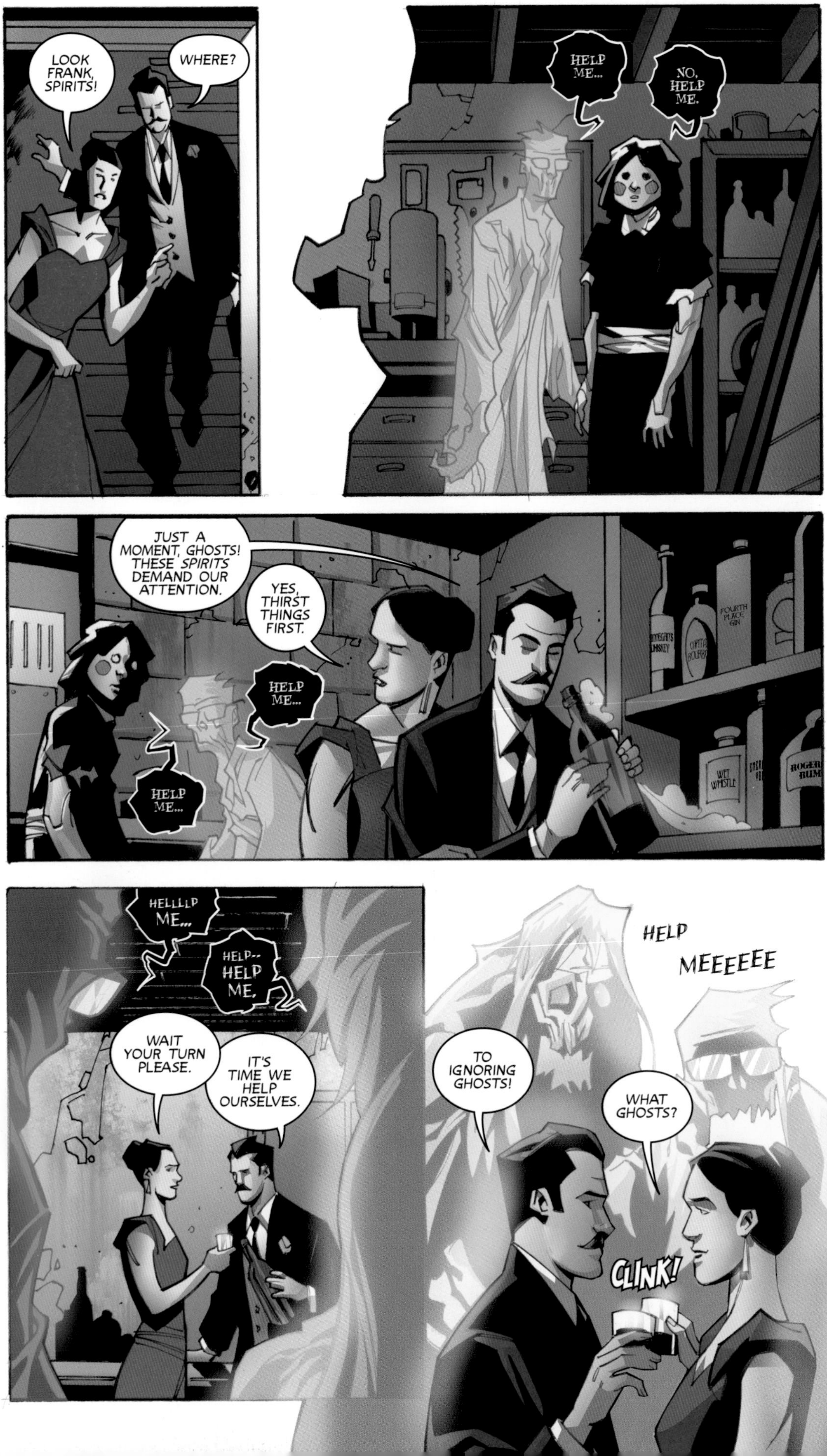

LOOK FRANK, SPIRITS!
WHERE?
HELP ME...
NO, HELP ME.
JUST A MOMENT, GHOSTS! THESE SPIRITS DEMAND OUR ATTENTION.
YES, THIRST THINGS FIRST.
HELP ME...
HELP ME...
FOURTH PLACE GIN
WET WHISTLE
HELLLLP ME...
HELP-- HELP ME,
WAIT YOUR TURN PLEASE.
IT'S TIME WE HELP OURSELVES.
HELP MEEEEEE
TO IGNORING GHOSTS!
WHAT GHOSTS?
CLINK!

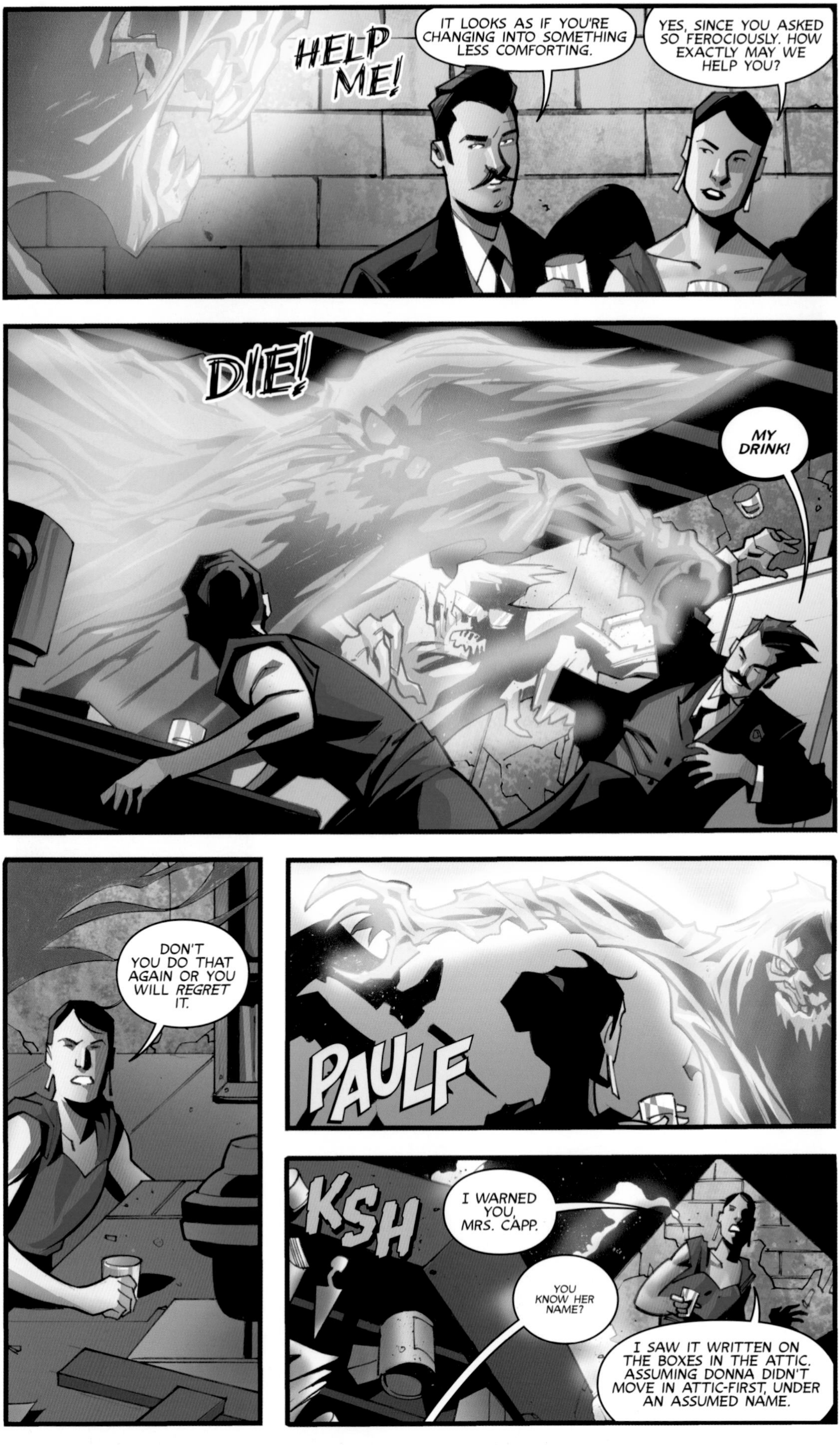
HELP ME!
IT LOOKS AS IF YOU'RE CHANGING INTO SOMETHING LESS COMFORTING.
YES, SINCE YOU ASKED SO FEROCIOUSLY. HOW EXACTLY MAY WE HELP YOU?
DIE!
MY DRINK!
DON'T YOU DO THAT AGAIN OR YOU WILL *REGRET* IT.
PAULF
KSH
I WARNED YOU, MRS. CAPP.
YOU KNOW HER NAME?
I SAW IT WRITTEN ON THE BOXES IN THE ATTIC. ASSUMING DONNA DIDN'T MOVE IN ATTIC-FIRST, UNDER AN ASSUMED NAME.

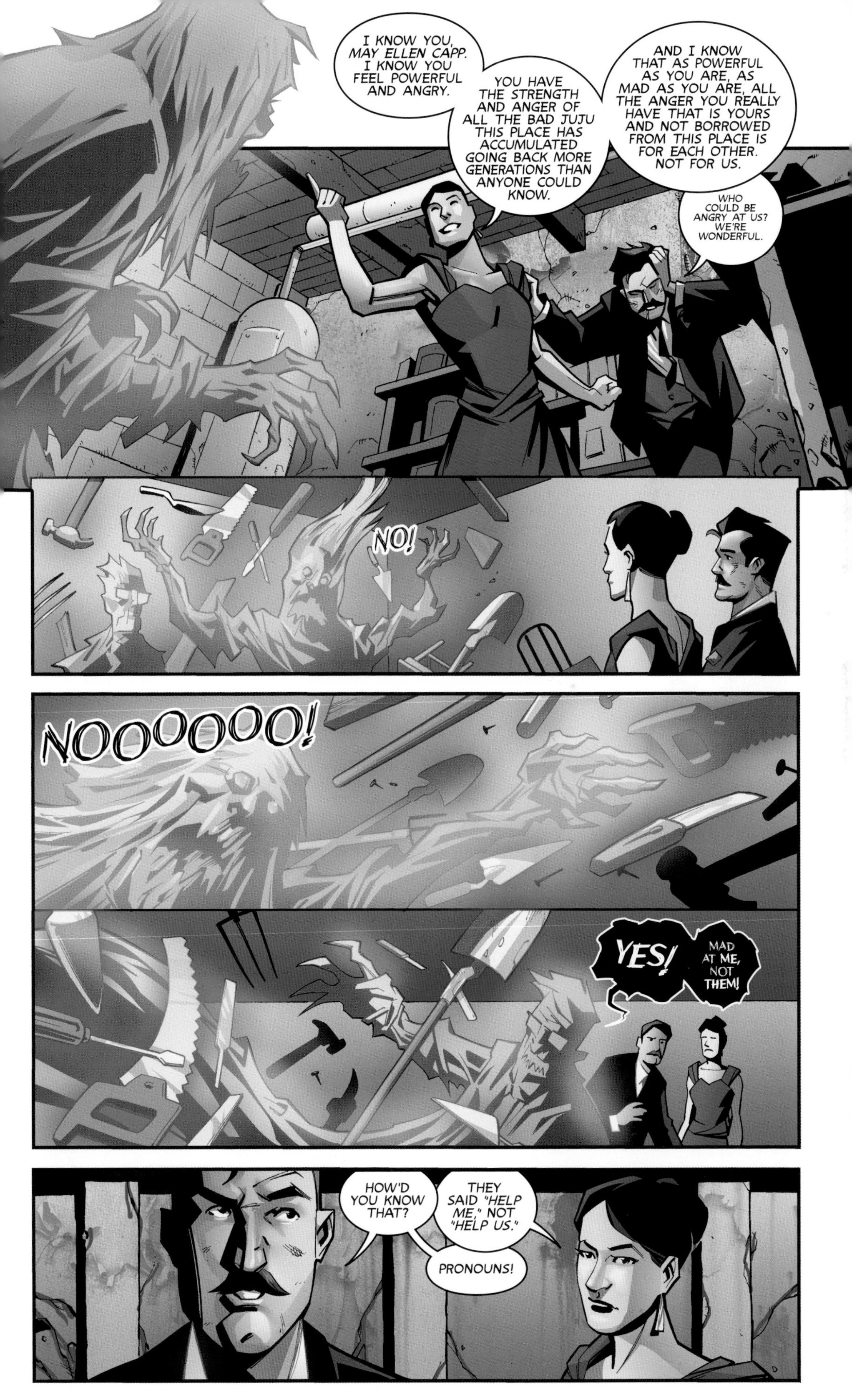

I KNOW YOU, MAY ELLEN CAPP. I KNOW YOU FEEL POWERFUL AND ANGRY.
YOU HAVE THE STRENGTH AND ANGER OF ALL THE BAD JUJU THIS PLACE HAS ACCUMULATED GOING BACK MORE GENERATIONS THAN ANYONE COULD KNOW.
AND I KNOW THAT AS POWERFUL AS YOU ARE, AS MAD AS YOU ARE, ALL THE ANGER YOU REALLY HAVE THAT IS YOURS AND NOT BORROWED FROM THIS PLACE IS FOR EACH OTHER. NOT FOR US.
WHO COULD BE ANGRY AT US? WE'RE WONDERFUL.
NO!
NOOOOOO!
YES!
MAD AT ME, NOT THEM!
HOW'D YOU KNOW THAT?
THEY SAID "HELP ME," NOT "HELP US."
PRONOUNS!

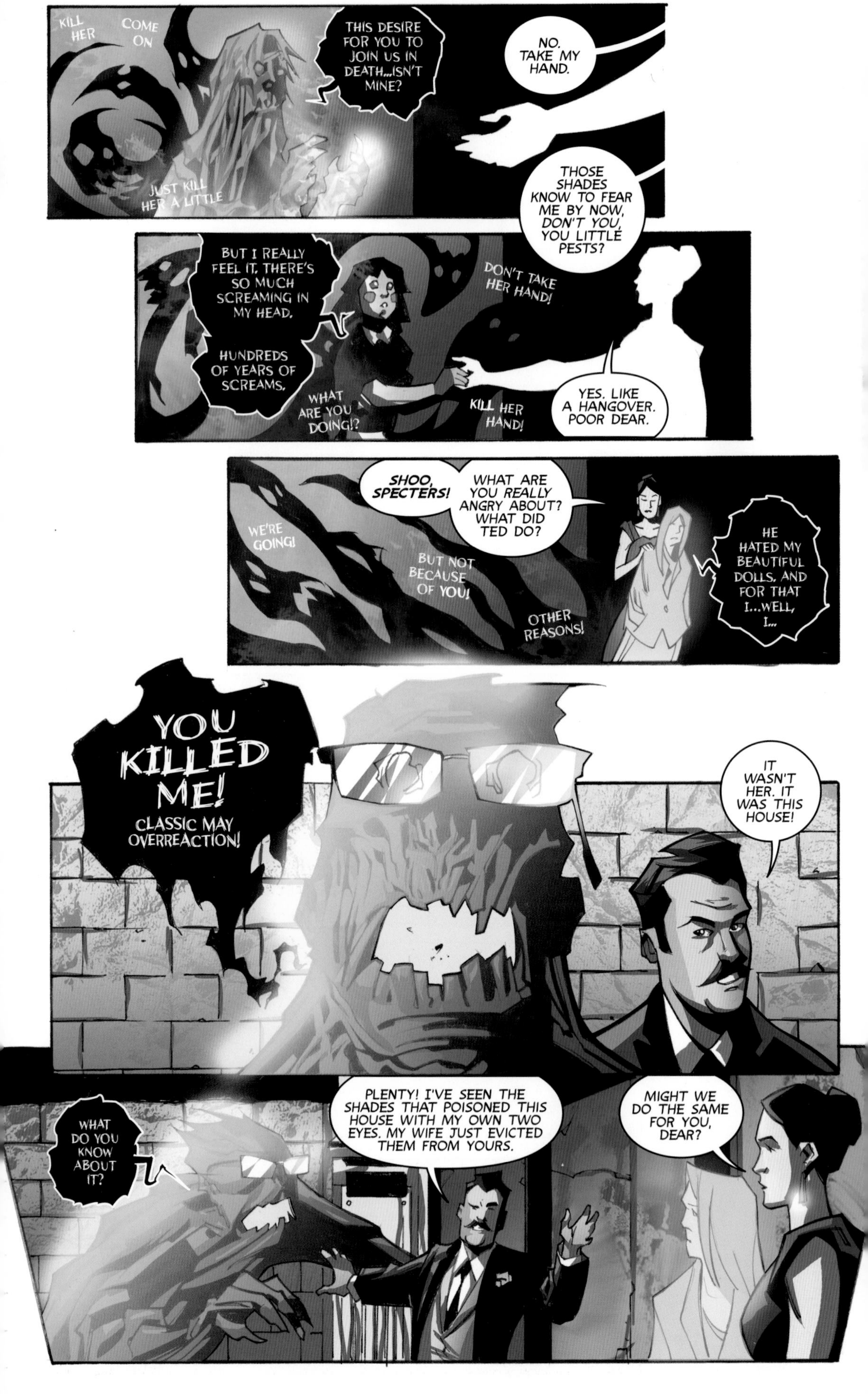
KILL HER
COME ON
THIS DESIRE FOR YOU TO JOIN US IN DEATH...ISN'T MINE?
JUST KILL HER A LITTLE
NO. TAKE MY HAND.
THOSE SHADES KNOW TO FEAR ME BY NOW, *DON'T YOU*, YOU LITTLE PESTS?
BUT I REALLY FEEL IT. THERE'S SO MUCH SCREAMING IN MY HEAD.
HUNDREDS OF YEARS OF SCREAMS.
DON'T TAKE HER HAND!
WHAT ARE YOU DOING!?
KILL HER HAND!
YES. LIKE A HANGOVER. POOR DEAR.
SHOO, SPECTERS!
WHAT ARE YOU *REALLY* ANGRY ABOUT? WHAT DID TED DO?
WE'RE GOING!
BUT NOT BECAUSE OF YOU!
OTHER REASONS!
HE HATED MY BEAUTIFUL DOLLS. AND FOR THAT I...WELL, I...
YOU KILLED ME!
CLASSIC MAY OVERREACTION!
IT WASN'T HER. IT WAS THIS HOUSE!
WHAT DO YOU KNOW ABOUT IT?
PLENTY! I'VE SEEN THE SHADES THAT POISONED THIS HOUSE WITH MY OWN TWO EYES. MY WIFE JUST EVICTED THEM FROM YOURS.
MIGHT WE DO THE SAME FOR YOU, DEAR?

NO! SO ANGRY!

I NEED YOU LISTEN TO ME, TED.

YOU HAVE *EVERY RIGHT* TO BE ANGRY AT MAY FOR KILLING YOU, BUT *ONLY* FOR KILLING YOU.

YOU HAVE *EVERY RIGHT* TO BE *STEAMING* MAD AT MAY FOR KILLING YOU.

HECK, IF SADIE KILLED ME I'D PROBABLY BE VERY UPSET.

FOCUS ON *THAT THREAD* OF YOUR ANGER TAPESTRY. HOLD ON TO THAT STRAND BUT LET ALL THE OTHERS...I DON'T KNOW, RAVEL AWAY?

I'M BAD AT TAPESTRY METAPHORS.

I AM MAD AT HER FOR THAT AND MANY OTHER THINGS! NONE OF WHICH SHE DID!

BUT OTHER WIVES DID TO OTHER HUSBANDS! HERE! IN GENERATIONS PAST!

AND YET...

AND YET...

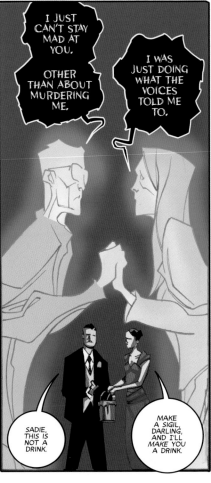

I JUST CAN'T STAY MAD AT YOU.

OTHER THAN ABOUT MURDERING ME.

I WAS JUST DOING WHAT THE VOICES TOLD ME TO.

SADIE, THIS IS NOT A DRINK.

MAKE A SIGIL, DARLING, AND I'LL MAKE YOU A DRINK.

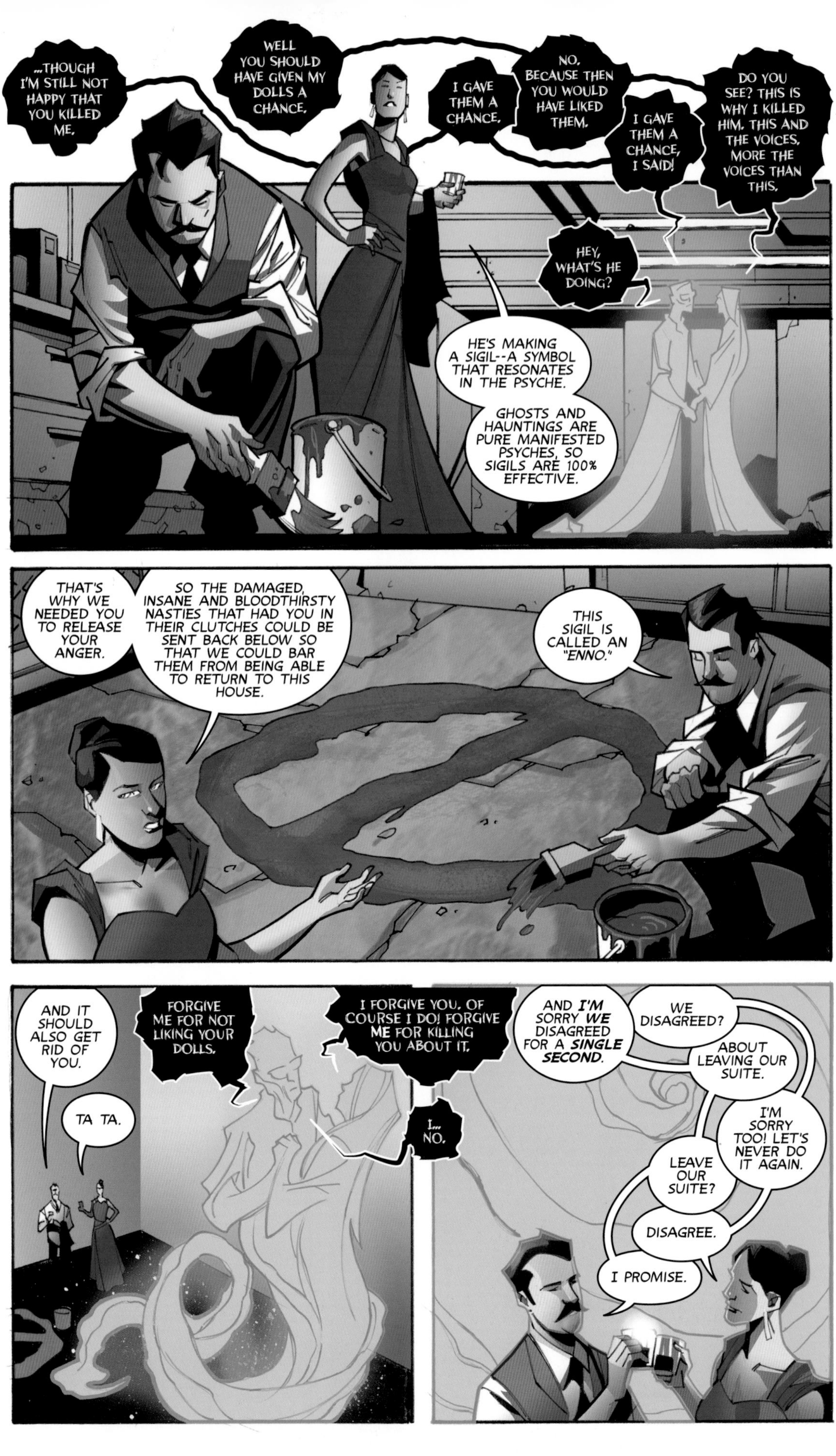
...THOUGH I'M STILL NOT HAPPY THAT YOU KILLED ME.
WELL YOU SHOULD HAVE GIVEN MY DOLLS A CHANCE.
I GAVE THEM A CHANCE.
NO, BECAUSE THEN YOU WOULD HAVE LIKED THEM.
I GAVE THEM A CHANCE, I SAID!
DO YOU SEE? THIS IS WHY I KILLED HIM. THIS AND THE VOICES. MORE THE VOICES THAN THIS.
HEY, WHAT'S HE DOING?
HE'S MAKING A SIGIL--A SYMBOL THAT RESONATES IN THE PSYCHE.
GHOSTS AND HAUNTINGS ARE PURE MANIFESTED PSYCHES, SO SIGILS ARE 100% EFFECTIVE.
THAT'S WHY WE NEEDED YOU TO RELEASE YOUR ANGER.
SO THE DAMAGED, INSANE AND BLOODTHIRSTY NASTIES THAT HAD YOU IN THEIR CLUTCHES COULD BE SENT BACK BELOW SO THAT WE COULD BAR THEM FROM BEING ABLE TO RETURN TO THIS HOUSE.
THIS SIGIL IS CALLED AN "*ENNO*."
AND IT SHOULD ALSO GET RID OF YOU.
TA TA.
FORGIVE ME FOR NOT LIKING YOUR DOLLS.
I FORGIVE YOU. OF COURSE I DO! FORGIVE **ME** FOR KILLING YOU ABOUT IT.
I... NO.
AND ***I'M*** SORRY ***WE*** DISAGREED FOR A ***SINGLE SECOND***.
WE DISAGREED?
ABOUT LEAVING OUR SUITE.
I'M SORRY TOO! LET'S NEVER DO IT AGAIN.
LEAVE OUR SUITE?
DISAGREE.
I PROMISE.

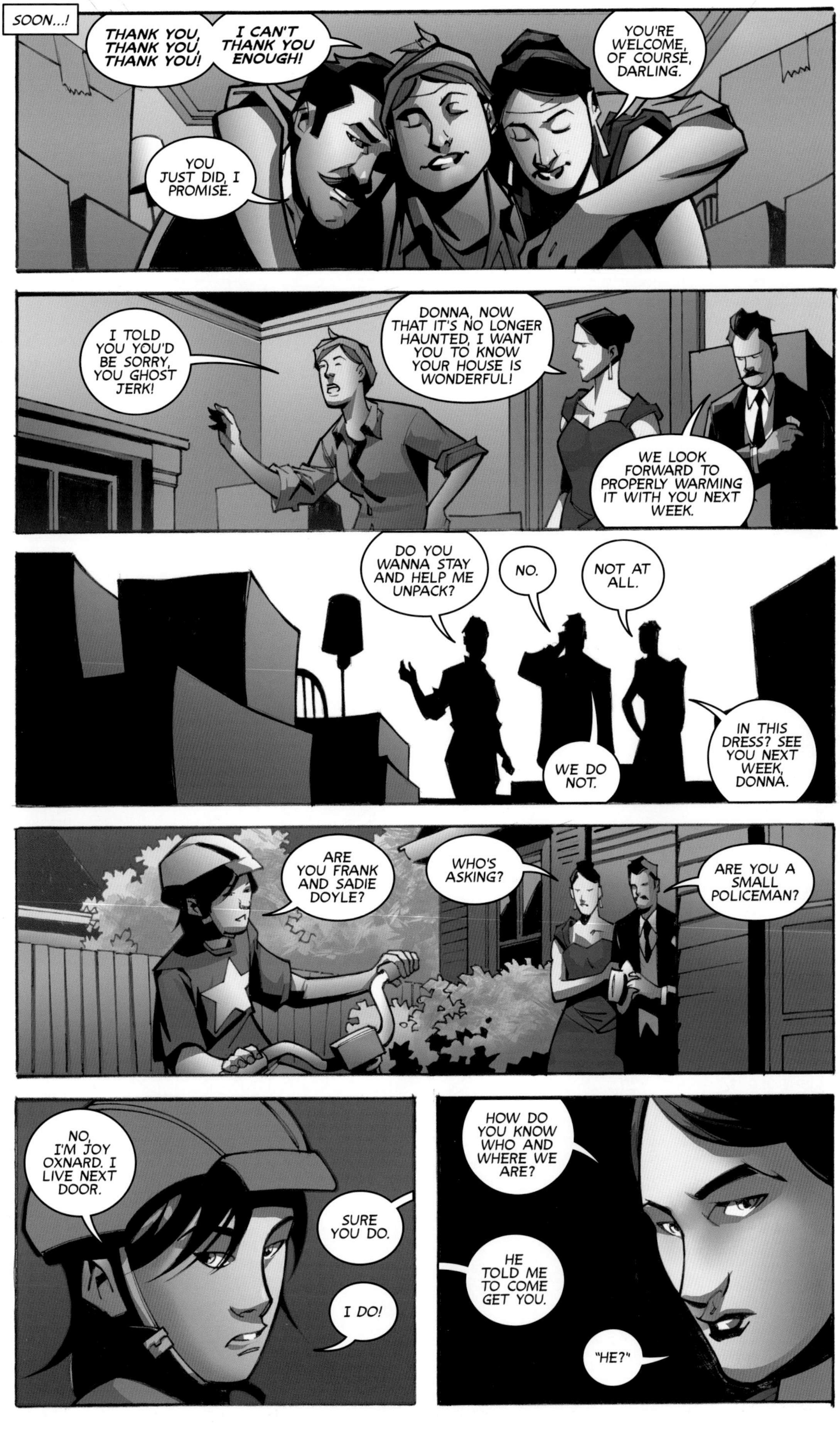
SOON...!
THANK YOU, THANK YOU, THANK YOU!
I CAN'T THANK YOU ENOUGH!
YOU'RE WELCOME, OF COURSE, DARLING.
YOU JUST DID, I PROMISE.
I TOLD YOU YOU'D BE SORRY, YOU GHOST JERK!
DONNA, NOW THAT IT'S NO LONGER HAUNTED, I WANT YOU TO KNOW YOUR HOUSE IS WONDERFUL!
WE LOOK FORWARD TO PROPERLY WARMING IT WITH YOU NEXT WEEK.
DO YOU WANNA STAY AND HELP ME UNPACK?
NO.
NOT AT ALL.
WE DO NOT.
IN THIS DRESS? SEE YOU NEXT WEEK, DONNA.
ARE YOU FRANK AND SADIE DOYLE?
WHO'S ASKING?
ARE YOU A SMALL POLICEMAN?
NO, I'M JOY OXNARD. I LIVE NEXT DOOR.
SURE YOU DO.
I DO!
HOW DO YOU KNOW WHO AND WHERE WE ARE?
HE TOLD ME TO COME GET YOU.
"HE?"

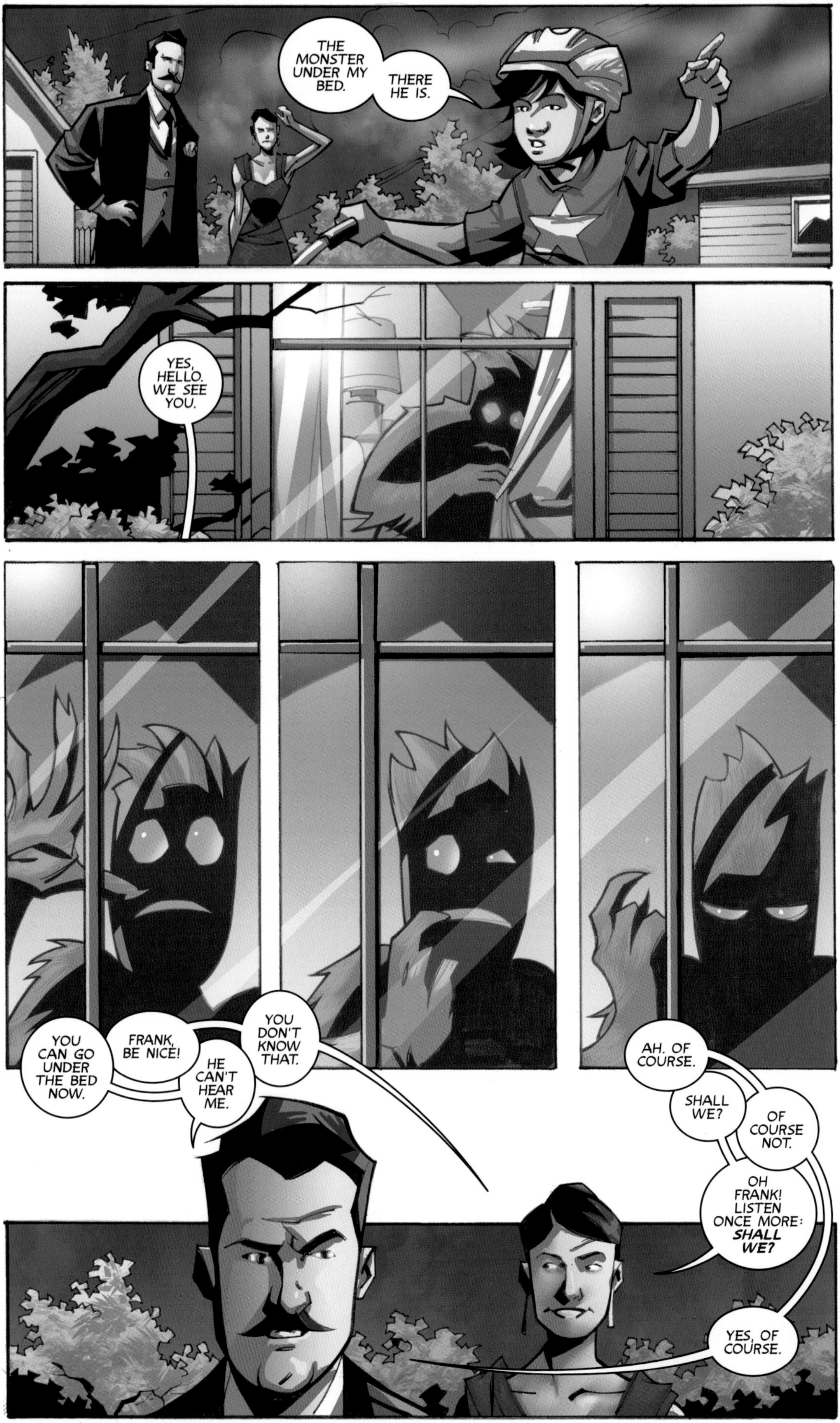
THE MONSTER UNDER MY BED.
THERE HE IS.
YES, HELLO. WE SEE YOU.
YOU CAN GO UNDER THE BED NOW.
FRANK, BE NICE!
HE CAN'T HEAR ME.
YOU DON'T KNOW THAT.
AH. OF COURSE.
SHALL WE?
OF COURSE NOT.
OH FRANK! LISTEN ONCE MORE: ***SHALL WE?***
YES, OF COURSE.

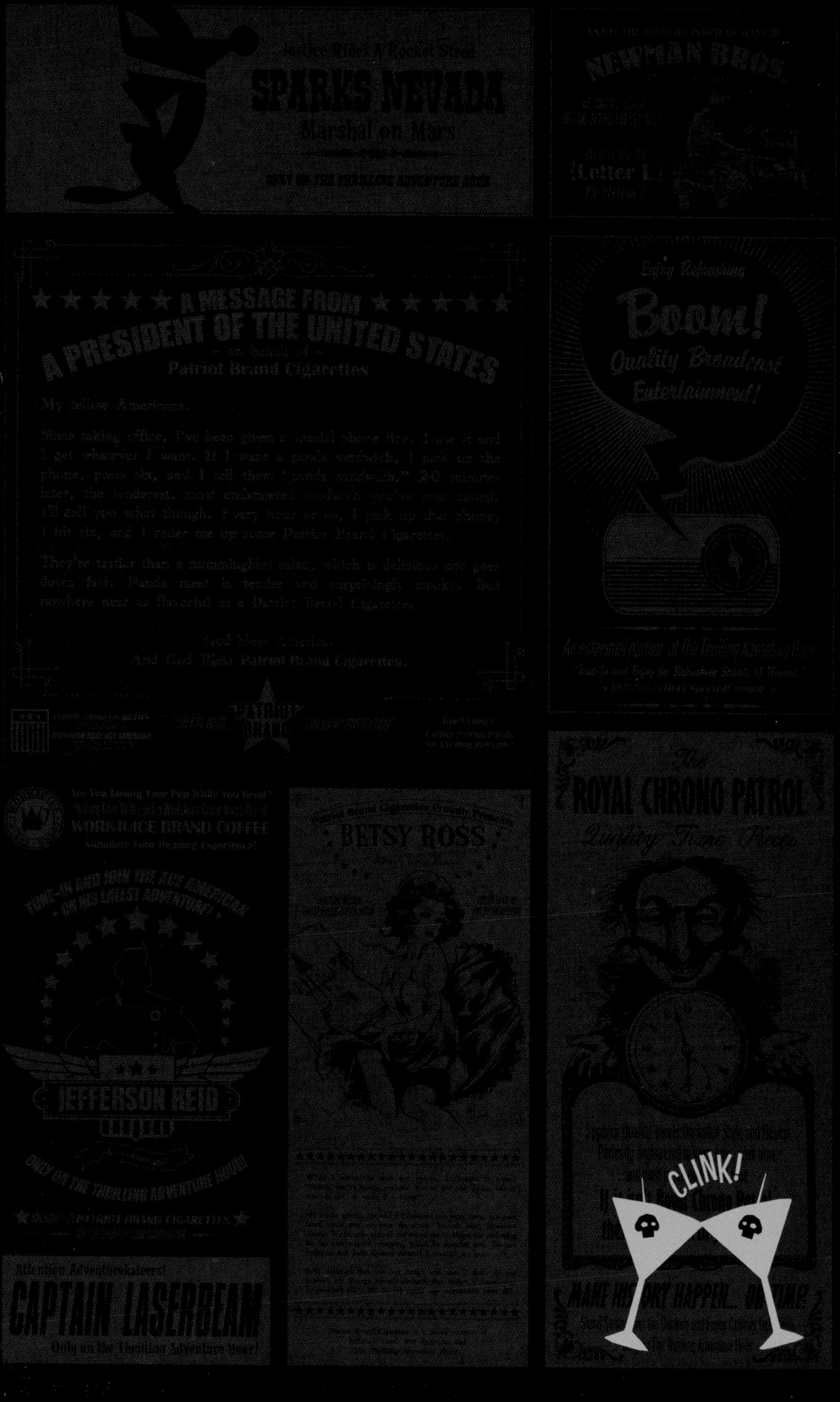

Justice Rides A Rocket Steed
SPARKS NEVADA
Marshal on Mars
ONLY ON THE THRILLING ADVENTURE HOUR
NEWMAN BROS.
Letter L
★★★★★ A MESSAGE FROM ★★★★★
A PRESIDENT OF THE UNITED STATES
– on behalf of –
Patriot Brand Cigarettes
My fellow Americans,
Since taking office, I've been given a special phone line. I use it and I get whatever I want. If I want a panda sandwich, I pick up the phone, press six, and I tell them "panda sandwich." 20 minutes later, the tenderest, most endangered sandwich you've ever tasted. I'll tell you what though. Every hour or so, I pick up that phone, I hit six, and I order me up some Patriot Brand Cigarettes.
They're tastier than a hummingbird salad, which is delicious and goes down fast. Panda meat is tender and surprisingly smoky. But nowhere near as flavorful as a Patriot Brand Cigarette.
God Bless America.
And God Bless Patriot Brand Cigarettes.
PATRIOT BRAND
Don't Forget
Collect Patriot Points
for Exciting Rewards!
Enjoy Refreshing
Boom!
Quality Broadcast
Entertainment!
An esteemed sponsor of The Thrilling Adventure Hour
Are You Losing Your Pep While You Read?
WORKJUICE BRAND COFFEE
Stimulate Your Reading Experience!
TUNE-IN AND JOIN THE AIR AMERICAN ON HIS LATEST ADVENTURE!
JEFFERSON REID
ONLY ON THE THRILLING ADVENTURE HOUR
PATRIOT BRAND CIGARETTES
Attention Adventurekateers!
CAPTAIN LASERBEAM
Only on the Thrilling Adventure Hour!
Patriot Brand Cigarettes Proudly Presents
BETSY ROSS
The
ROYAL CHRONO PATROL
Quality Time Pieces
CLINK!
MAKE HISTORY HAPPEN... ON TIME

Chapter

TWO

Of Martinis and Monsters...

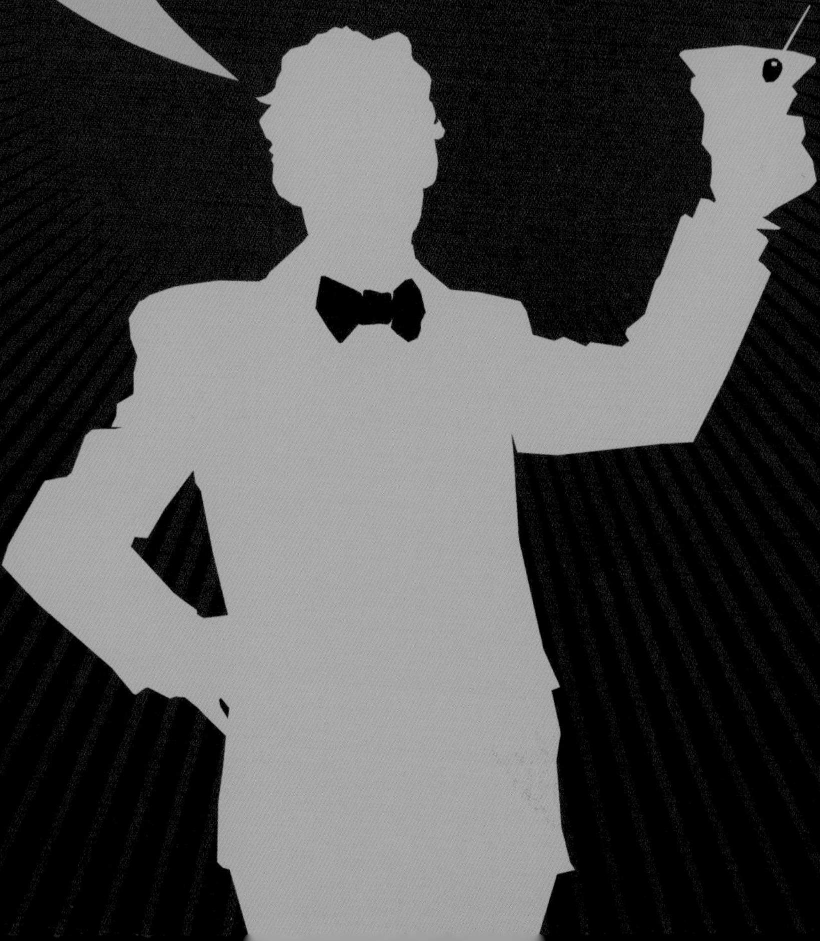

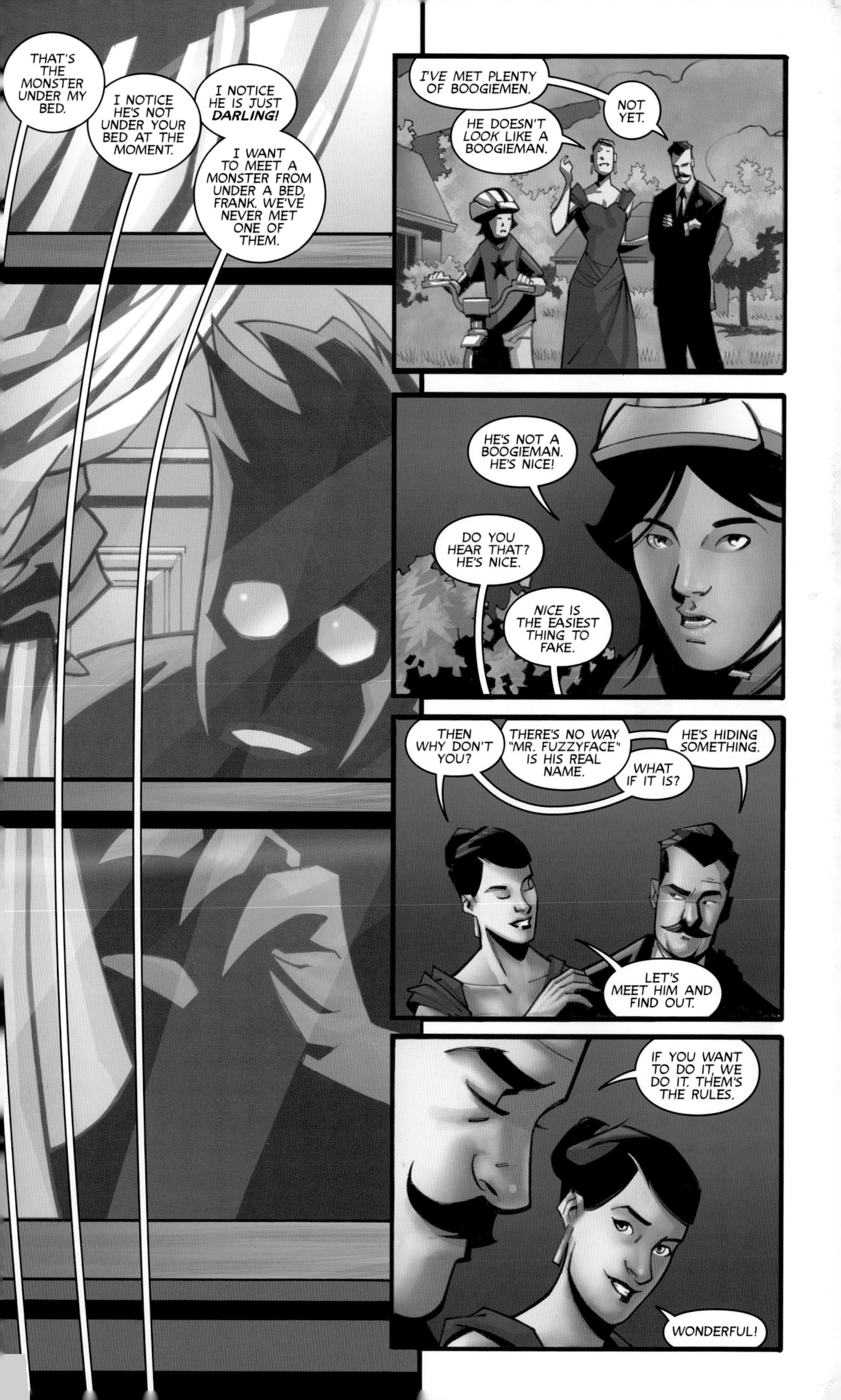
THAT'S THE MONSTER UNDER MY BED.
I NOTICE HE'S NOT UNDER YOUR BED AT THE MOMENT.
I NOTICE HE IS JUST DARLING!
I WANT TO MEET A MONSTER FROM UNDER A BED, FRANK. WE'VE NEVER MET ONE OF THEM.
I'VE MET PLENTY OF BOOGIEMEN.
NOT YET.
HE DOESN'T LOOK LIKE A BOOGIEMAN.
HE'S NOT A BOOGIEMAN. HE'S NICE!
DO YOU HEAR THAT? HE'S NICE.
NICE IS THE EASIEST THING TO FAKE.
THEN WHY DON'T YOU?
THERE'S NO WAY "MR. FUZZYFACE" IS HIS REAL NAME.
HE'S HIDING SOMETHING.
WHAT IF IT IS?
LET'S MEET HIM AND FIND OUT.
IF YOU WANT TO DO IT, WE DO IT. THEM'S THE RULES.
WONDERFUL!

THANK YOU FOR YOUR HOSPITALITY. YOU'RE QUITE A LITTLE GENTLEMAN, AREN'T YOU... MR. FUZZYFACE, WAS IT?

I'D TELL YOU TO CALL ME BY MY FIRST NAME IF I HAD ONE.

I HAVE ONE. IT'S SADIE!

I KNOW.

AND THAT'S FRANK.

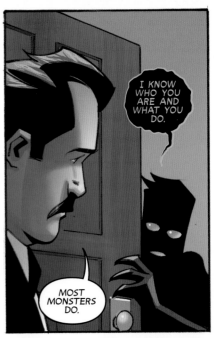

I KNOW WHO YOU ARE AND WHAT YOU DO.

MOST MONSTERS DO.

WHERE ARE YOUR PARENTS, LITTLE GIRL? DID A MONSTER EAT THEM?

NO. THEY'RE ATTENDING A *FUNCTION*. THEY'RE *ALWAYS* ATTENDING FUNCTIONS.

I'M NEVER INVITED.

ME NEITHER. IT'S ROUGH, KIDDO.

YOUR PARENTS AREN'T ALL BAD--THIS IS QUITE A LIQUOR CABINET. MAY I?

IT'S LOCKED.

I HAVE A SKELETON KEY.

AS FOR *FUNCTIONS?* THEY COULDN'T BE MORE BORING. TRUST ME. I'VE BEEN TO PLENTY. YOU'RE NOT MISSING ANYTHING.

YES, QUITE.

EVEN AT THEIR MOST FUN...

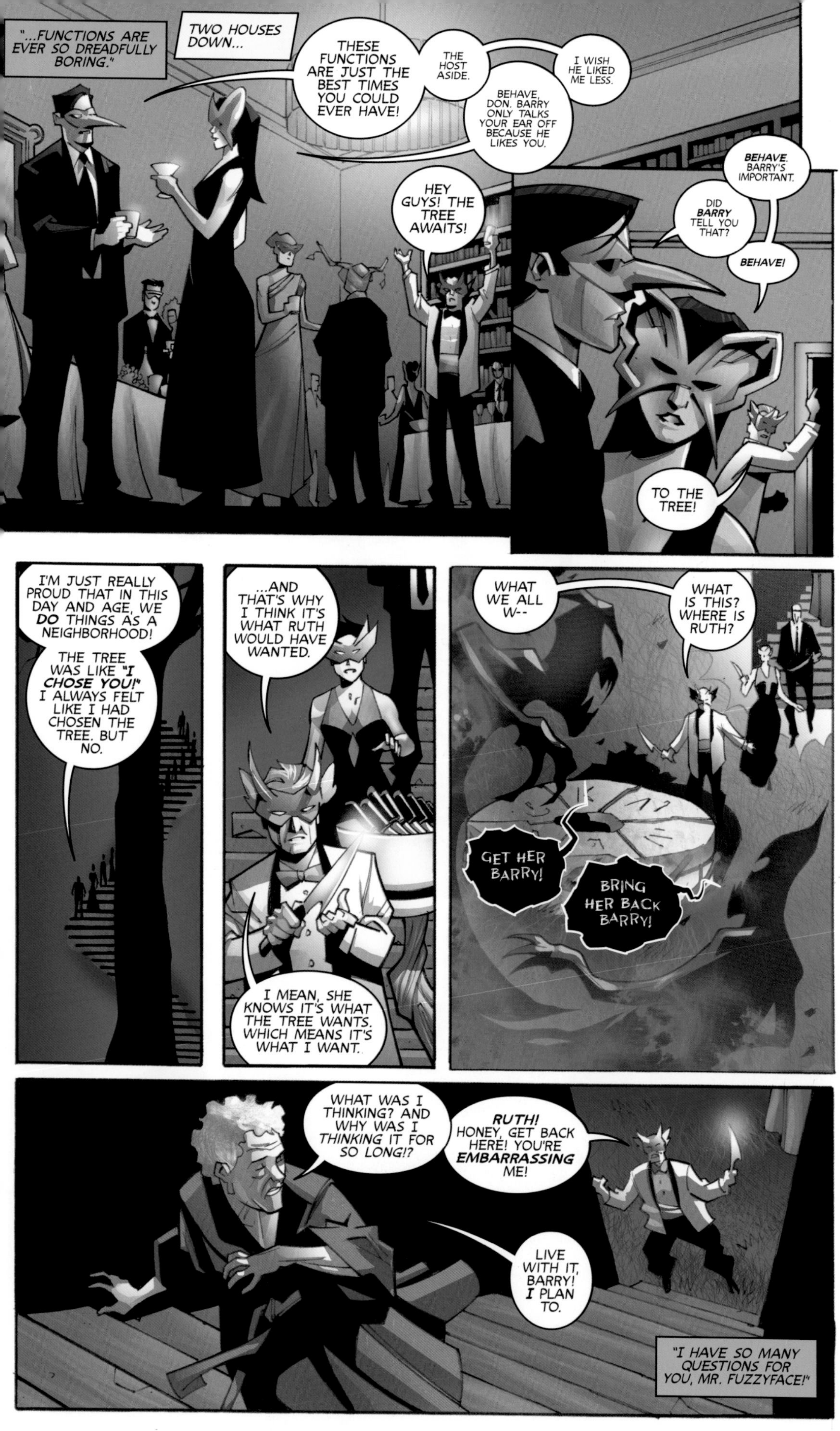
"...FUNCTIONS ARE EVER SO DREADFULLY BORING."
TWO HOUSES DOWN...
THESE FUNCTIONS ARE JUST THE BEST TIMES YOU COULD EVER HAVE!
THE HOST ASIDE.
I WISH HE LIKED ME LESS.
BEHAVE, DON. BARRY ONLY TALKS YOUR EAR OFF BECAUSE HE LIKES YOU.
HEY GUYS! THE TREE AWAITS!
BEHAVE. BARRY'S IMPORTANT.
DID BARRY TELL YOU THAT?
BEHAVE!
TO THE TREE!
I'M JUST REALLY PROUD THAT IN THIS DAY AND AGE, WE DO THINGS AS A NEIGHBORHOOD!
THE TREE WAS LIKE "I CHOSE YOU!" I ALWAYS FELT LIKE I HAD CHOSEN THE TREE. BUT NO.
...AND THAT'S WHY I THINK IT'S WHAT RUTH WOULD HAVE WANTED.
I MEAN, SHE KNOWS IT'S WHAT THE TREE WANTS. WHICH MEANS IT'S WHAT I WANT.
WHAT WE ALL W--
WHAT IS THIS? WHERE IS RUTH?
GET HER BARRY!
BRING HER BACK BARRY!
WHAT WAS I THINKING? AND WHY WAS I THINKING IT FOR SO LONG!?
RUTH! HONEY, GET BACK HERE! YOU'RE EMBARRASSING ME!
LIVE WITH IT, BARRY! I PLAN TO.
"I HAVE SO MANY QUESTIONS FOR YOU, MR. FUZZYFACE!"

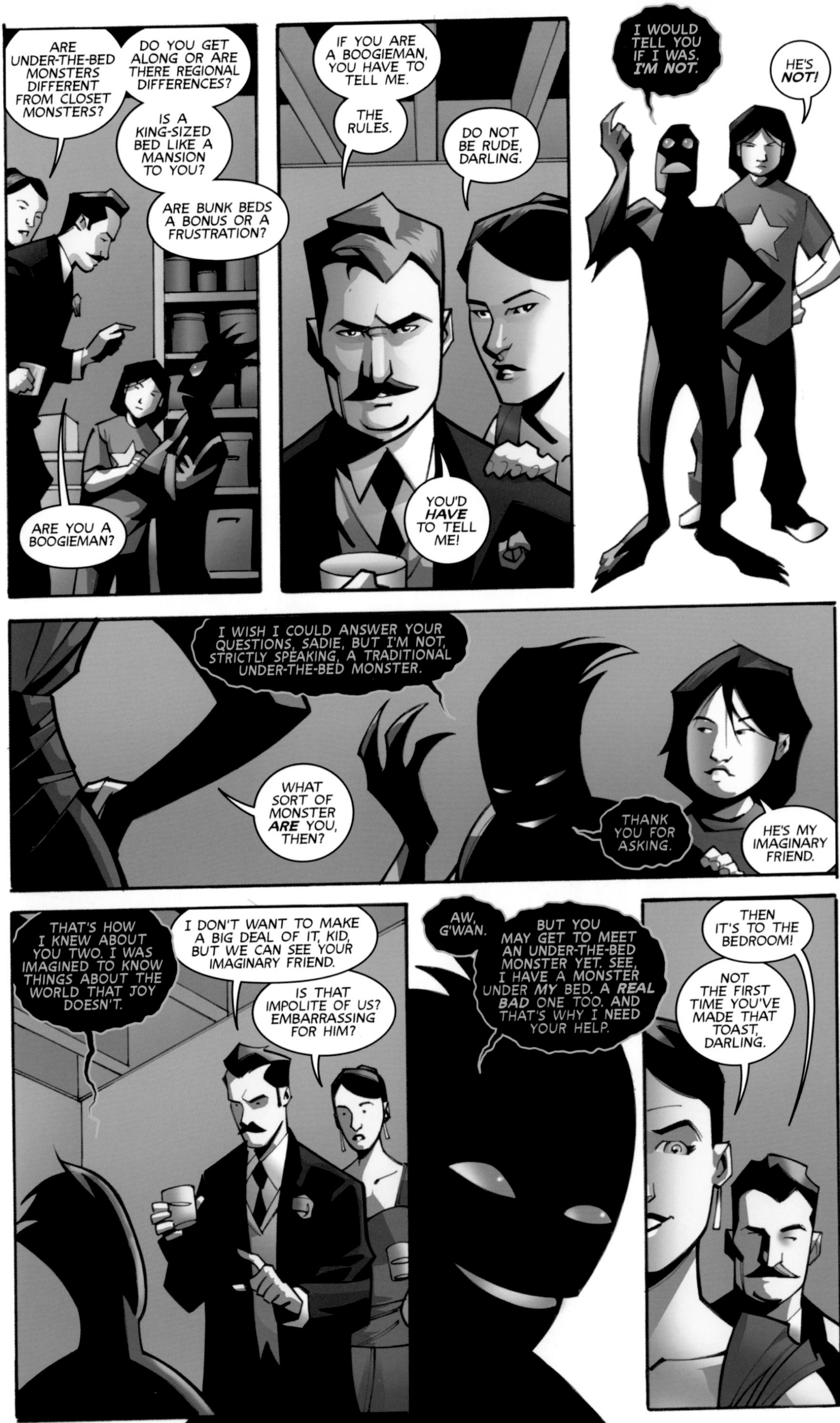
ARE UNDER-THE-BED MONSTERS DIFFERENT FROM CLOSET MONSTERS?
DO YOU GET ALONG OR ARE THERE REGIONAL DIFFERENCES?
IS A KING-SIZED BED LIKE A MANSION TO YOU?
ARE BUNK BEDS A BONUS OR A FRUSTRATION?
ARE YOU A BOOGIEMAN?
IF YOU ARE A BOOGIEMAN, YOU HAVE TO TELL ME.
THE RULES.
DO NOT BE RUDE, DARLING.
YOU'D *HAVE* TO TELL ME!
I WOULD TELL YOU IF I WAS. *I'M NOT.*
HE'S *NOT!*
I WISH I COULD ANSWER YOUR QUESTIONS, SADIE, BUT I'M NOT, STRICTLY SPEAKING, A TRADITIONAL UNDER-THE-BED MONSTER.
WHAT SORT OF MONSTER *ARE* YOU, THEN?
THANK YOU FOR ASKING.
HE'S MY IMAGINARY FRIEND.
THAT'S HOW I KNEW ABOUT YOU TWO. I WAS IMAGINED TO KNOW THINGS ABOUT THE WORLD THAT JOY DOESN'T.
I DON'T WANT TO MAKE A BIG DEAL OF IT, KID, BUT WE CAN SEE YOUR IMAGINARY FRIEND.
IS THAT IMPOLITE OF US? EMBARRASSING FOR HIM?
AW, G'WAN.
BUT YOU MAY GET TO MEET AN UNDER-THE-BED MONSTER YET. SEE, I HAVE A MONSTER UNDER *MY* BED. A *REAL BAD* ONE TOO. AND THAT'S WHY I NEED YOUR HELP.
THEN IT'S TO THE BEDROOM!
NOT THE FIRST TIME YOU'VE MADE THAT TOAST, DARLING.

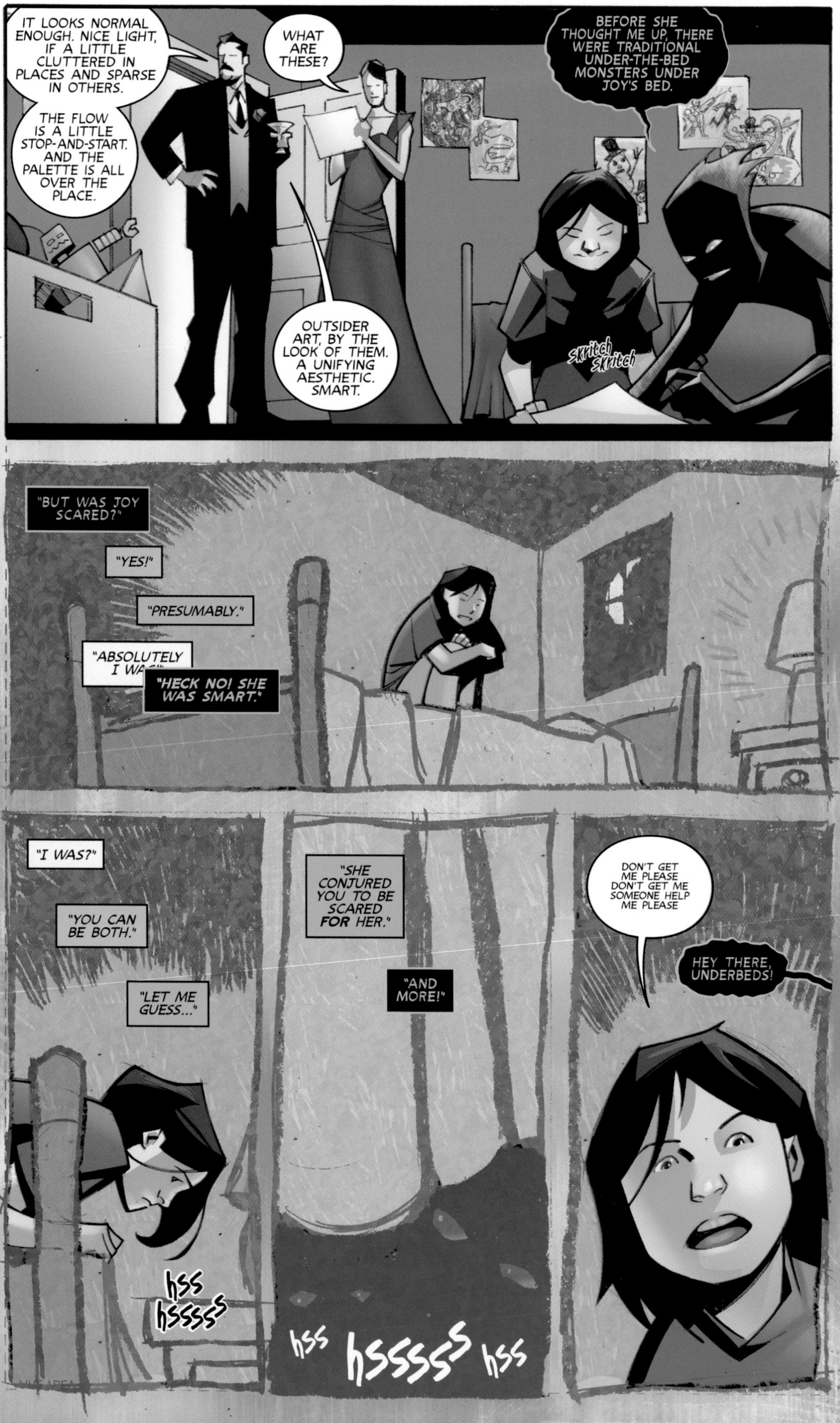
IT LOOKS NORMAL ENOUGH. NICE LIGHT, IF A LITTLE CLUTTERED IN PLACES AND SPARSE IN OTHERS.
THE FLOW IS A LITTLE STOP-AND-START. AND THE PALETTE IS ALL OVER THE PLACE.
WHAT ARE THESE?
OUTSIDER ART, BY THE LOOK OF THEM. A UNIFYING AESTHETIC. SMART.
BEFORE SHE THOUGHT ME UP, THERE WERE TRADITIONAL UNDER-THE-BED MONSTERS UNDER JOY'S BED.
SKRITCH SKRITCH
"BUT WAS JOY SCARED?"
"YES!"
"PRESUMABLY."
"ABSOLUTELY I WA
"HECK NO! SHE WAS SMART."
"I WAS?"
"YOU CAN BE BOTH."
"LET ME GUESS..."
hss hsssss
"SHE CONJURED YOU TO BE SCARED FOR HER."
"AND MORE!"
hss hsssss hss
DON'T GET ME PLEASE DON'T GET ME SOMEONE HELP ME PLEASE
HEY THERE, UNDERBEDS!

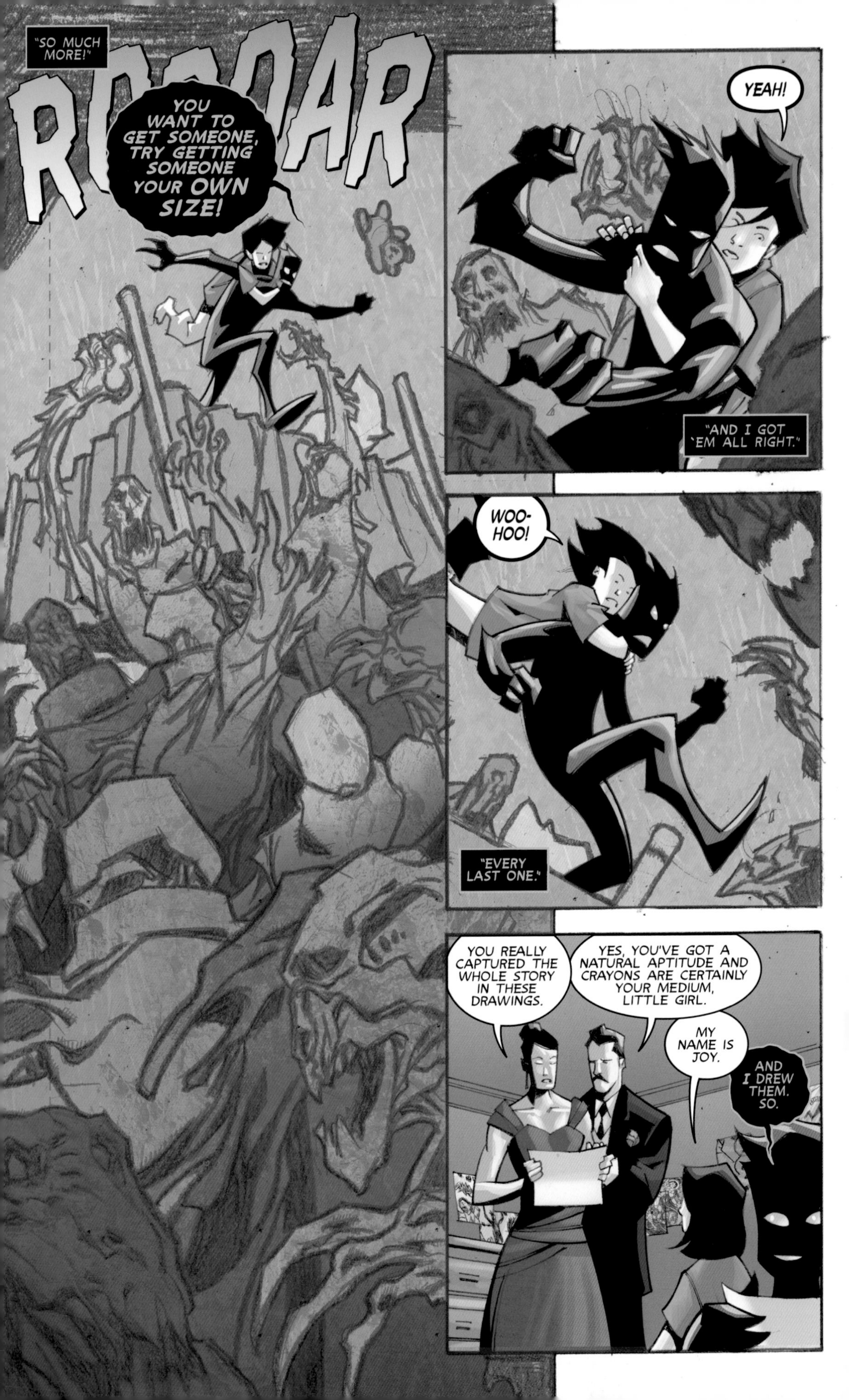
"SO MUCH MORE!"
ROOOAR
YOU WANT TO GET SOMEONE, TRY GETTING SOMEONE YOUR OWN SIZE!
YEAH!
"AND I GOT 'EM ALL RIGHT."
WOO-HOO!
"EVERY LAST ONE."
YOU REALLY CAPTURED THE WHOLE STORY IN THESE DRAWINGS.
YES, YOU'VE GOT A NATURAL APTITUDE AND CRAYONS ARE CERTAINLY YOUR MEDIUM, LITTLE GIRL.
MY NAME IS JOY.
AND I DREW THEM. SO.

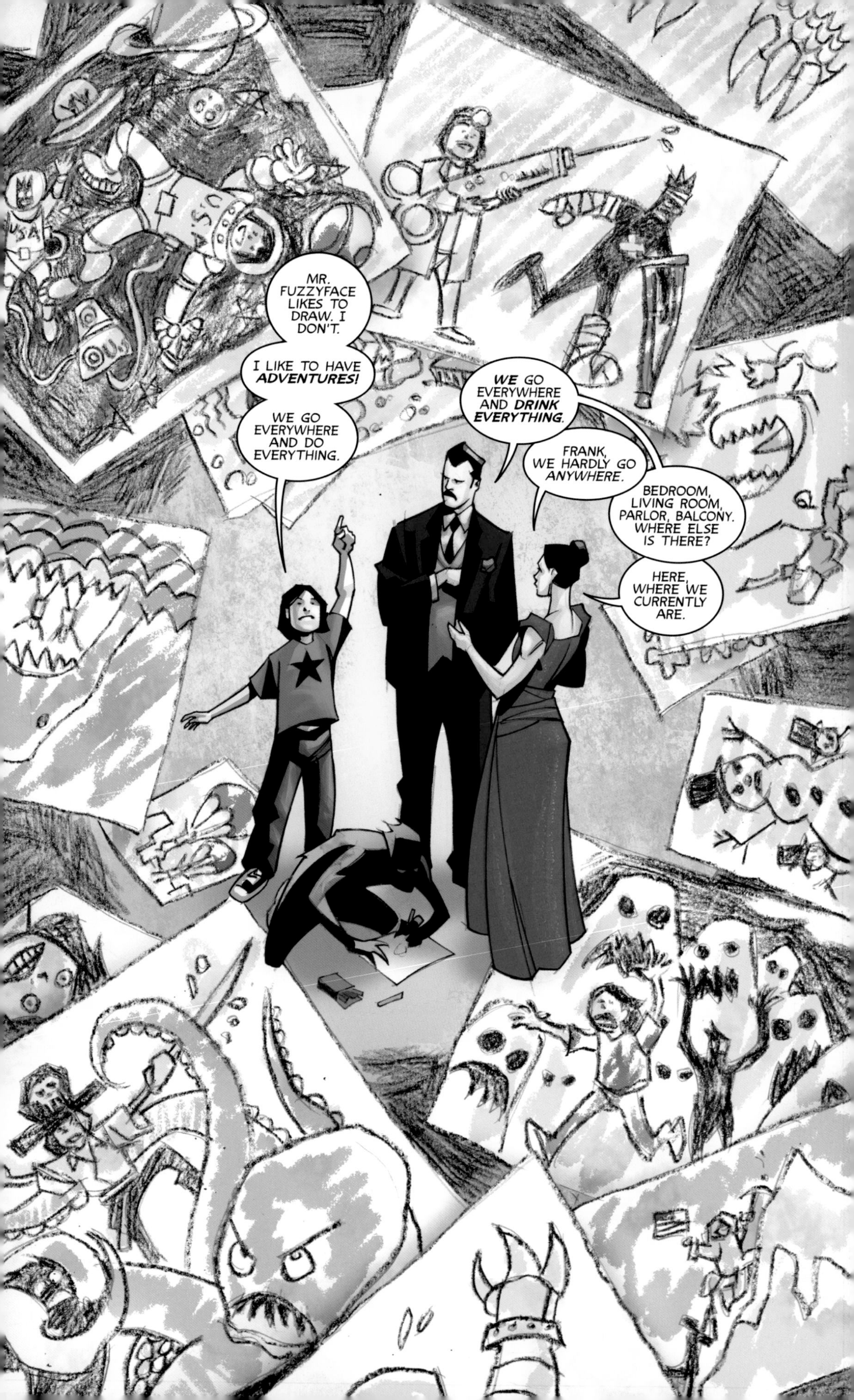
MR. FUZZYFACE LIKES TO DRAW. I DON'T.
I LIKE TO HAVE ***ADVENTURES!***
WE GO EVERYWHERE AND DO EVERYTHING.
WE GO EVERYWHERE AND ***DRINK EVERYTHING***.
FRANK, WE HARDLY GO *ANYWHERE*.
BEDROOM, LIVING ROOM, PARLOR, BALCONY. WHERE ELSE IS THERE?
HERE, WHERE WE CURRENTLY ARE.

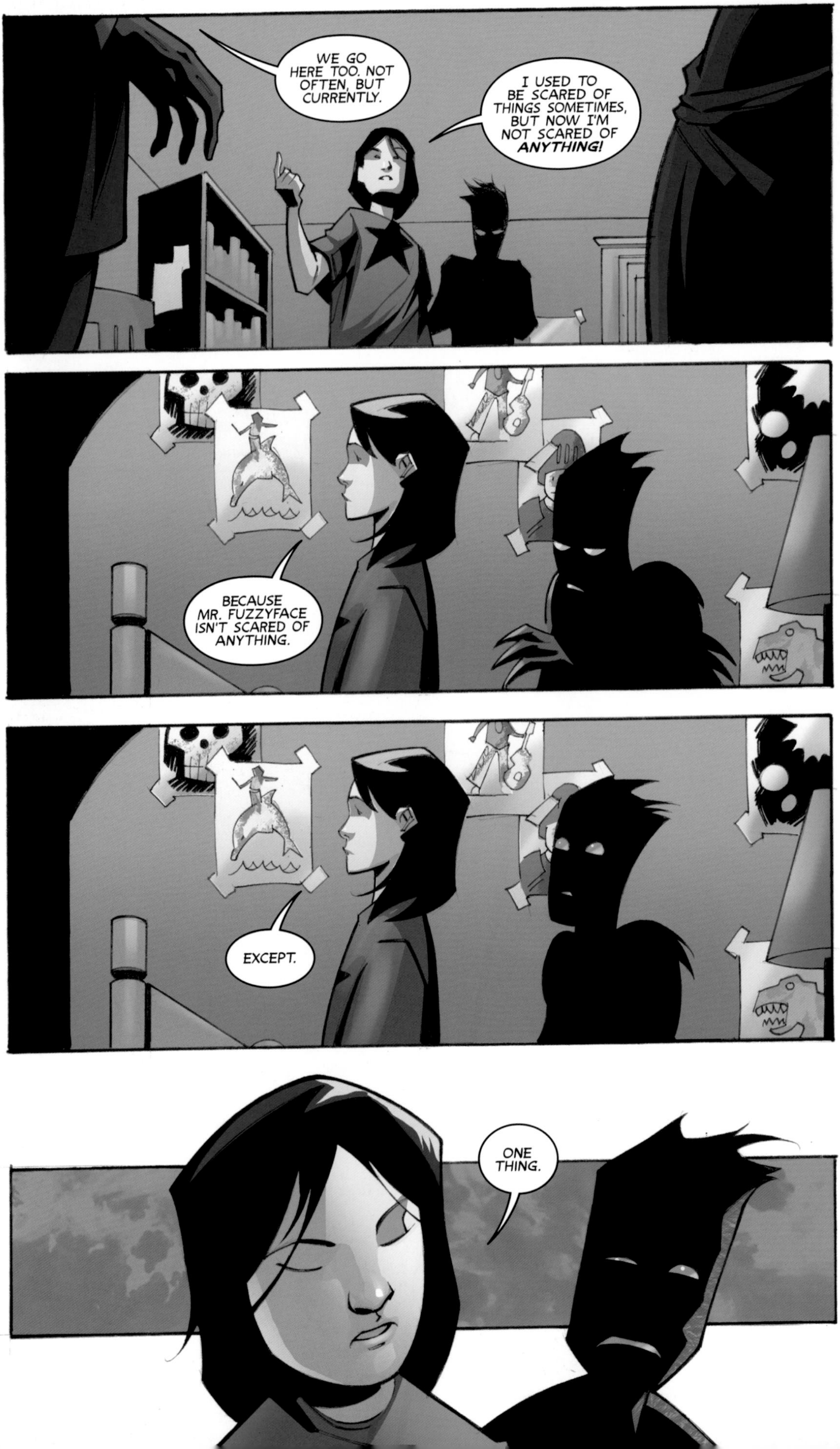
WE GO HERE TOO. NOT OFTEN, BUT CURRENTLY.
I USED TO BE SCARED OF THINGS SOMETIMES, BUT NOW I'M NOT SCARED OF ***ANYTHING!***
BECAUSE MR. FUZZYFACE ISN'T SCARED OF ANYTHING.
EXCEPT.
ONE THING.

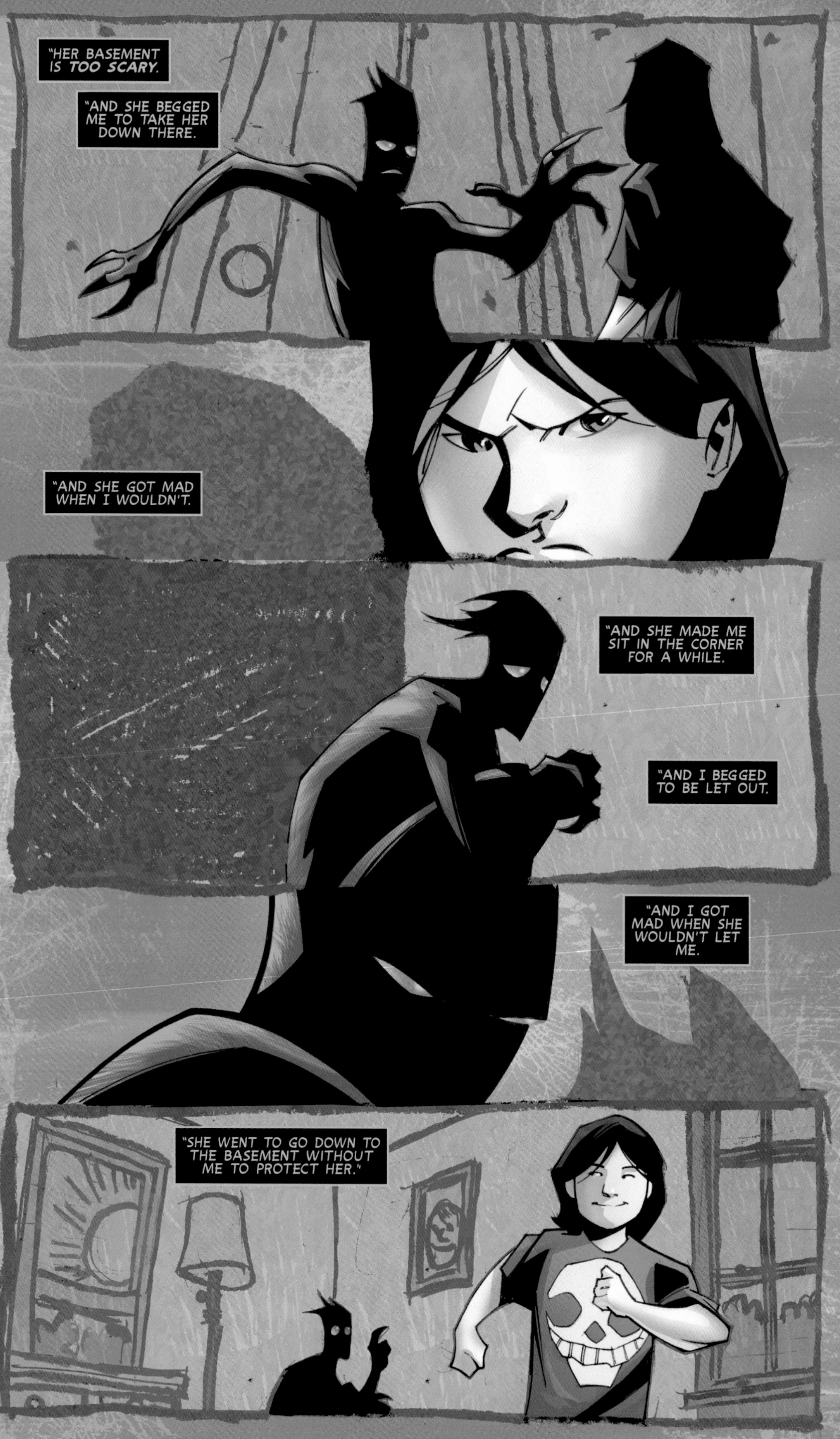
"HER BASEMENT IS TOO SCARY.
"AND SHE BEGGED ME TO TAKE HER DOWN THERE.
"AND SHE GOT MAD WHEN I WOULDN'T.
"AND SHE MADE ME SIT IN THE CORNER FOR A WHILE.
"AND I BEGGED TO BE LET OUT.
"AND I GOT MAD WHEN SHE WOULDN'T LET ME.
"SHE WENT TO GO DOWN TO THE BASEMENT WITHOUT ME TO PROTECT HER."

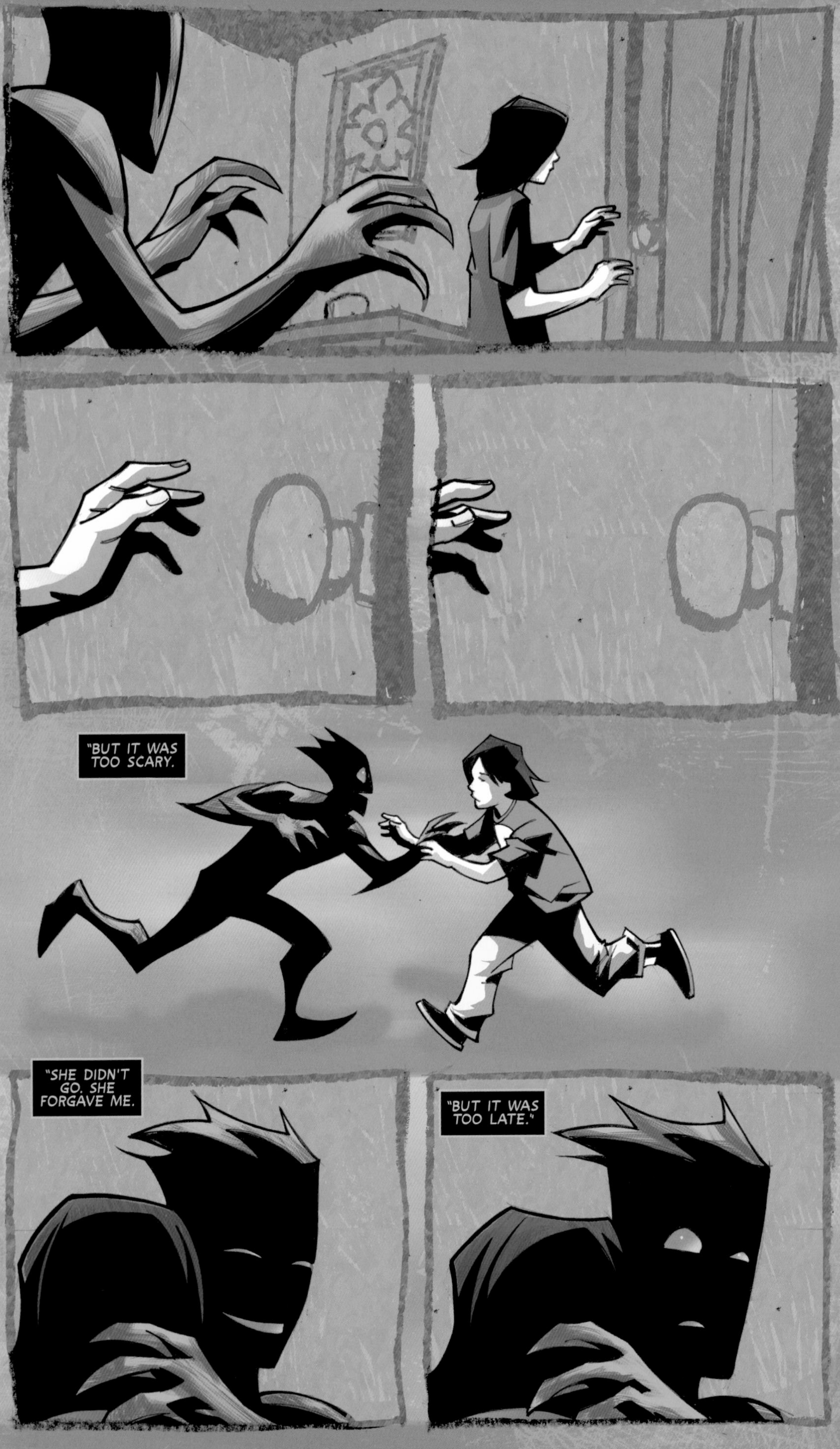
"BUT IT WAS TOO SCARY.
"SHE DIDN'T GO. SHE FORGAVE ME.
"BUT IT WAS TOO LATE."

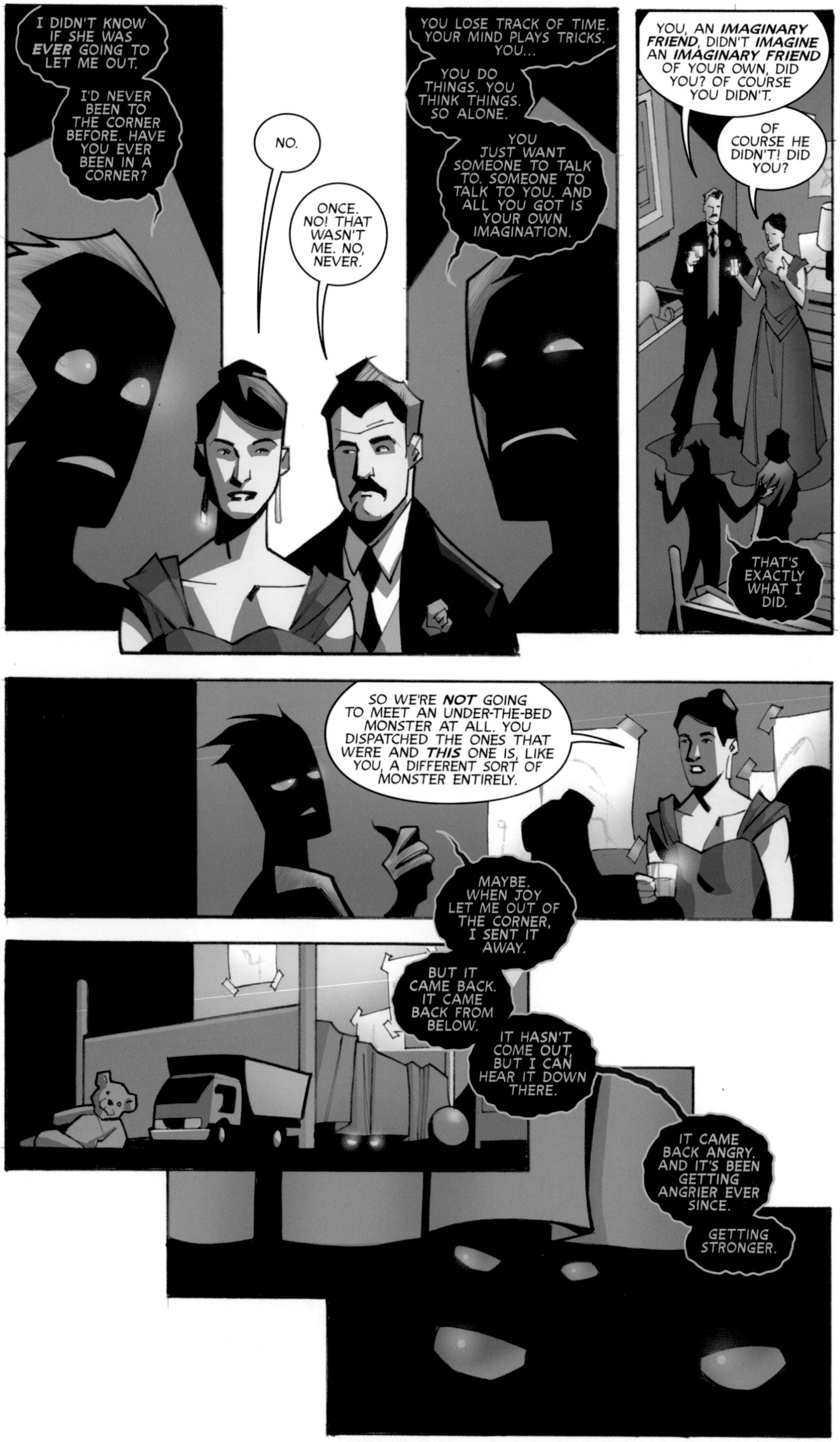
I DIDN'T KNOW IF SHE WAS **EVER** GOING TO LET ME OUT.
I'D NEVER BEEN TO THE CORNER BEFORE. HAVE YOU EVER BEEN IN A CORNER?
NO.
ONCE. NO! THAT WASN'T ME. NO, NEVER.
YOU LOSE TRACK OF TIME. YOUR MIND PLAYS TRICKS. YOU...
YOU DO THINGS. YOU THINK THINGS. SO ALONE.
YOU JUST WANT SOMEONE TO TALK TO. SOMEONE TO TALK TO YOU. AND ALL YOU GOT IS YOUR OWN IMAGINATION.
YOU, AN ***IMAGINARY FRIEND***, DIDN'T ***IMAGINE*** AN ***IMAGINARY FRIEND*** OF YOUR OWN, DID YOU? OF COURSE YOU DIDN'T.
OF COURSE HE DIDN'T! DID YOU?
THAT'S EXACTLY WHAT I DID.
SO WE'RE **NOT** GOING TO MEET AN UNDER-THE-BED MONSTER AT ALL. YOU DISPATCHED THE ONES THAT WERE AND **THIS** ONE IS, LIKE YOU, A DIFFERENT SORT OF MONSTER ENTIRELY.
MAYBE. WHEN JOY LET ME OUT OF THE CORNER, I SENT IT AWAY.
BUT IT CAME BACK. IT CAME BACK FROM BELOW.
IT HASN'T COME OUT, BUT I CAN HEAR IT DOWN THERE.
IT CAME BACK ANGRY. AND IT'S BEEN GETTING ANGRIER EVER SINCE.
GETTING STRONGER.

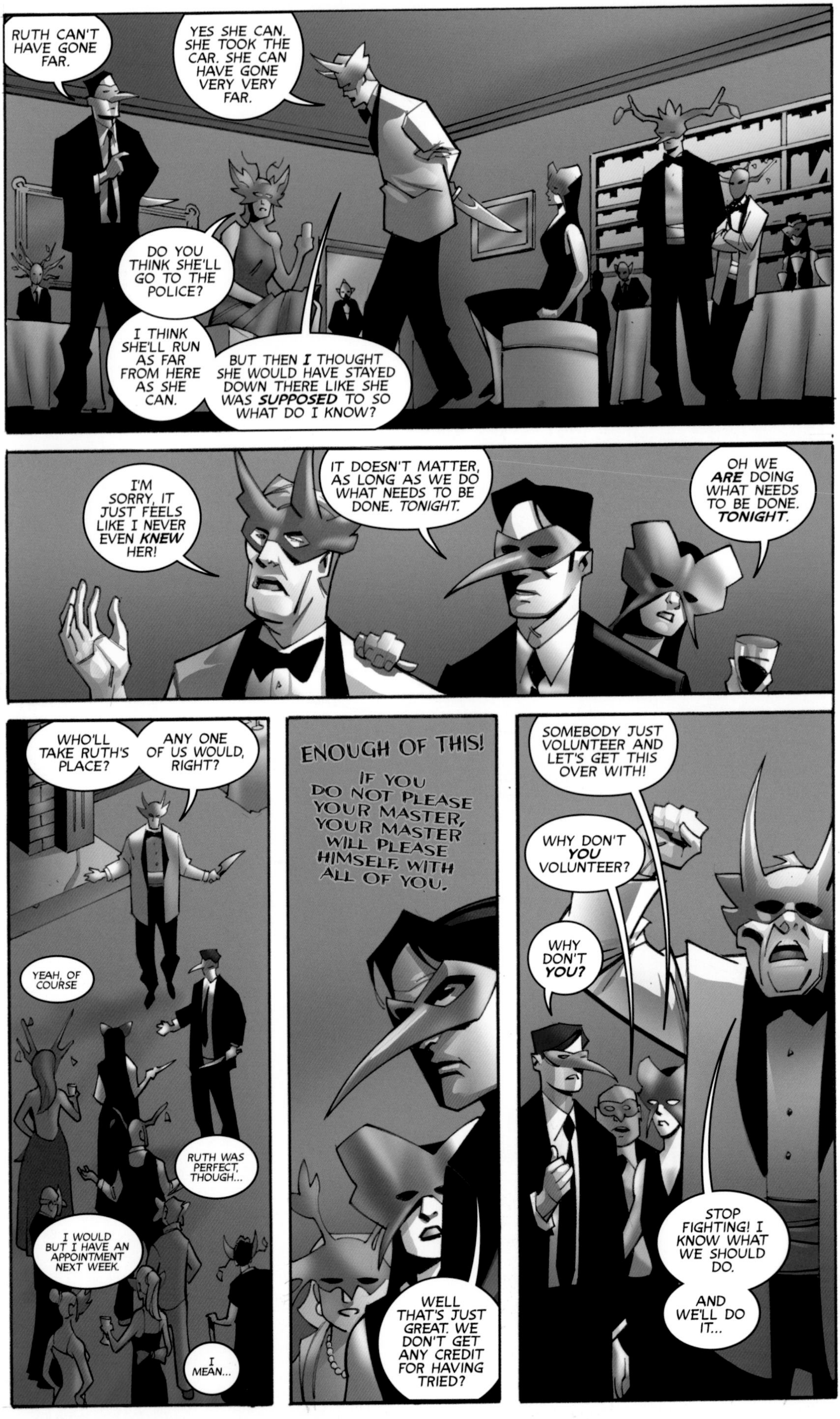
RUTH CAN'T HAVE GONE FAR.
YES SHE CAN. SHE TOOK THE CAR. SHE CAN HAVE GONE VERY VERY FAR.
DO YOU THINK SHE'LL GO TO THE POLICE?
I THINK SHE'LL RUN AS FAR FROM HERE AS SHE CAN.
BUT THEN I THOUGHT SHE WOULD HAVE STAYED DOWN THERE LIKE SHE WAS SUPPOSED TO SO WHAT DO I KNOW?
I'M SORRY, IT JUST FEELS LIKE I NEVER EVEN KNEW HER!
IT DOESN'T MATTER, AS LONG AS WE DO WHAT NEEDS TO BE DONE. TONIGHT.
OH WE ARE DOING WHAT NEEDS TO BE DONE. TONIGHT.
WHO'LL TAKE RUTH'S PLACE?
ANY ONE OF US WOULD, RIGHT?
YEAH, OF COURSE
RUTH WAS PERFECT, THOUGH...
I WOULD BUT I HAVE AN APPOINTMENT NEXT WEEK.
I MEAN...
ENOUGH OF THIS!
IF YOU DO NOT PLEASE YOUR MASTER, YOUR MASTER WILL PLEASE HIMSELF WITH ALL OF YOU.
WELL THAT'S JUST GREAT. WE DON'T GET ANY CREDIT FOR HAVING TRIED?
SOMEBODY JUST VOLUNTEER AND LET'S GET THIS OVER WITH!
WHY DON'T YOU VOLUNTEER?
WHY DON'T YOU?
STOP FIGHTING! I KNOW WHAT WE SHOULD DO.
AND WE'LL DO IT...

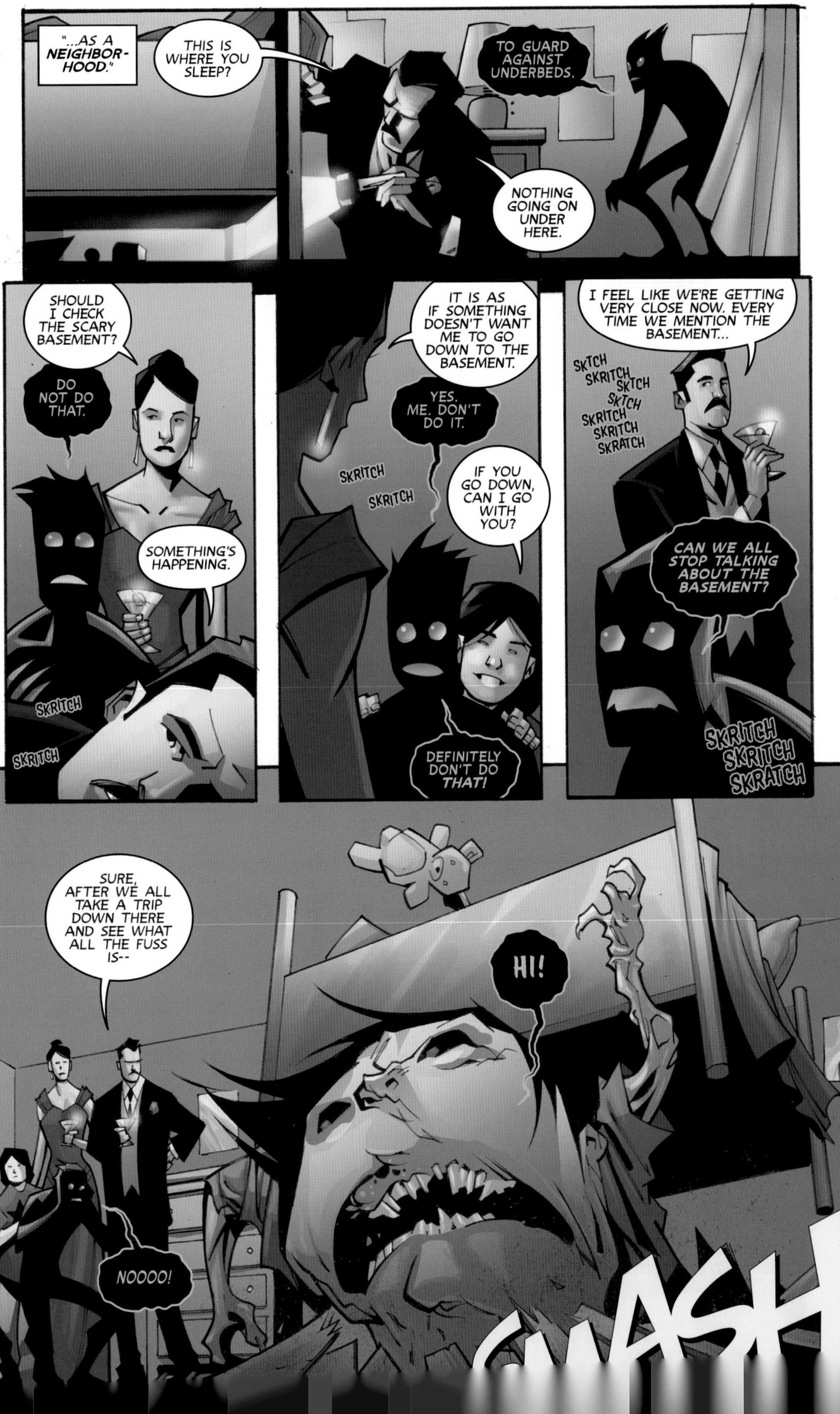
"...AS A NEIGHBORHOOD."
THIS IS WHERE YOU SLEEP?
TO GUARD AGAINST UNDERBEDS.
NOTHING GOING ON UNDER HERE.
SHOULD I CHECK THE SCARY BASEMENT?
DO NOT DO THAT.
SOMETHING'S HAPPENING.
SKRITCH
SKRITCH
IT IS AS IF SOMETHING DOESN'T WANT ME TO GO DOWN TO THE BASEMENT.
YES. ME. DON'T DO IT.
SKRITCH
SKRITCH
IF YOU GO DOWN, CAN I GO WITH YOU?
DEFINITELY DON'T DO THAT!
I FEEL LIKE WE'RE GETTING VERY CLOSE NOW. EVERY TIME WE MENTION THE BASEMENT...
SKTCH SKRITCH SKTCH SKTCH SKRITCH SKRITCH SKRATCH
CAN WE ALL STOP TALKING ABOUT THE BASEMENT?
SKRITCH SKRITCH SKRATCH
SURE, AFTER WE ALL TAKE A TRIP DOWN THERE AND SEE WHAT ALL THE FUSS IS--
HI!
NOOOO!

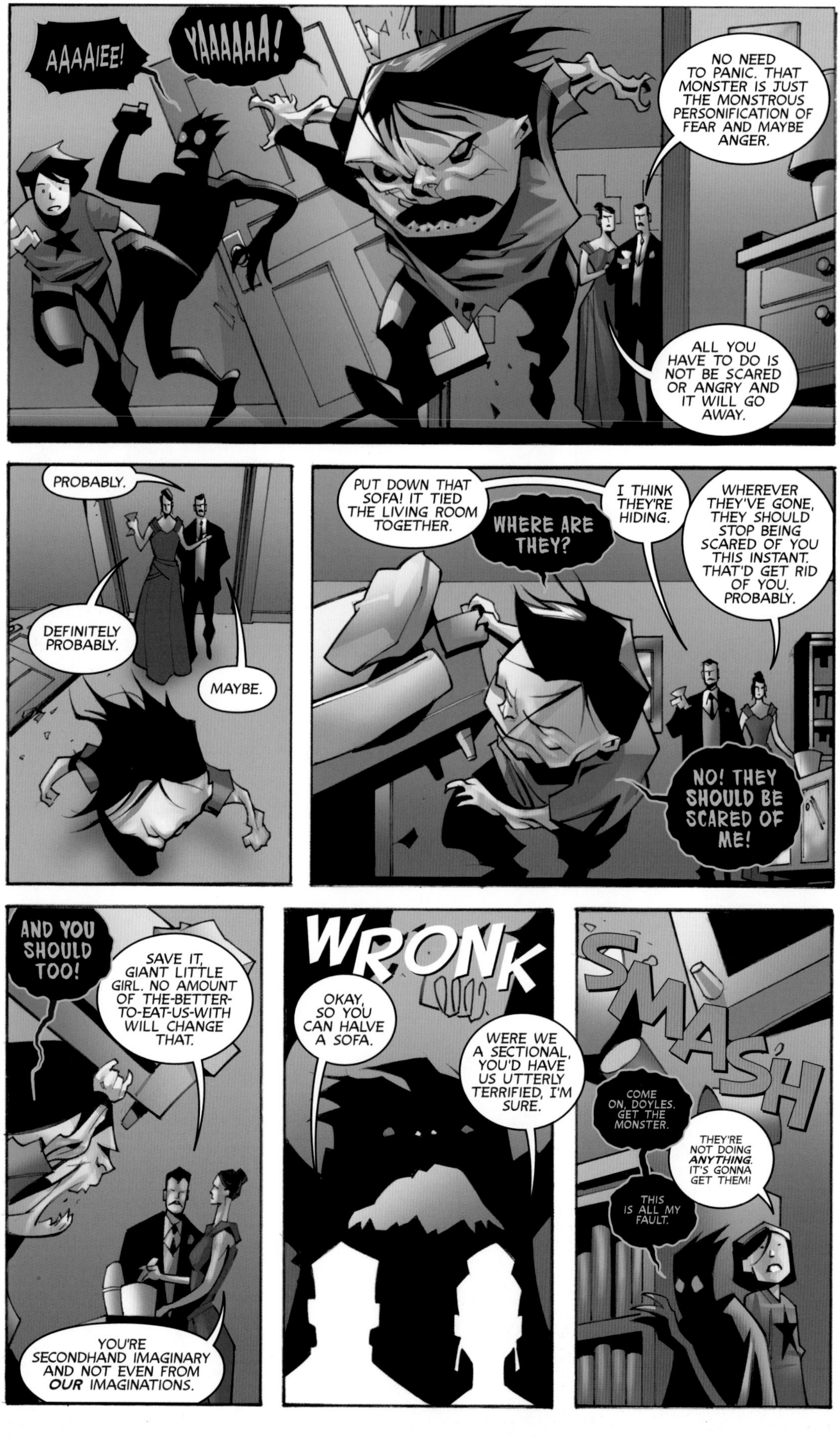
AAAAIEE!
YAAAAAA!
NO NEED TO PANIC. THAT MONSTER IS JUST THE MONSTROUS PERSONIFICATION OF FEAR AND MAYBE ANGER.
ALL YOU HAVE TO DO IS NOT BE SCARED OR ANGRY AND IT WILL GO AWAY.
PROBABLY.
DEFINITELY PROBABLY.
MAYBE.
PUT DOWN THAT SOFA! IT TIED THE LIVING ROOM TOGETHER.
WHERE ARE THEY?
I THINK THEY'RE HIDING.
WHEREVER THEY'VE GONE, THEY SHOULD STOP BEING SCARED OF YOU THIS INSTANT. THAT'D GET RID OF YOU. PROBABLY.
NO! THEY SHOULD BE SCARED OF ME!
AND YOU SHOULD TOO!
SAVE IT, GIANT LITTLE GIRL. NO AMOUNT OF THE-BETTER-TO-EAT-US-WITH WILL CHANGE THAT.
YOU'RE SECONDHAND IMAGINARY AND NOT EVEN FROM ***OUR*** IMAGINATIONS.
WRONK
OKAY, SO YOU CAN HALVE A SOFA.
WERE WE A SECTIONAL, YOU'D HAVE US UTTERLY TERRIFIED, I'M SURE.
SMASH
COME ON, DOYLES. GET THE MONSTER.
THEY'RE NOT DOING ***ANYTHING***. IT'S GONNA GET THEM!
THIS IS ALL MY FAULT.

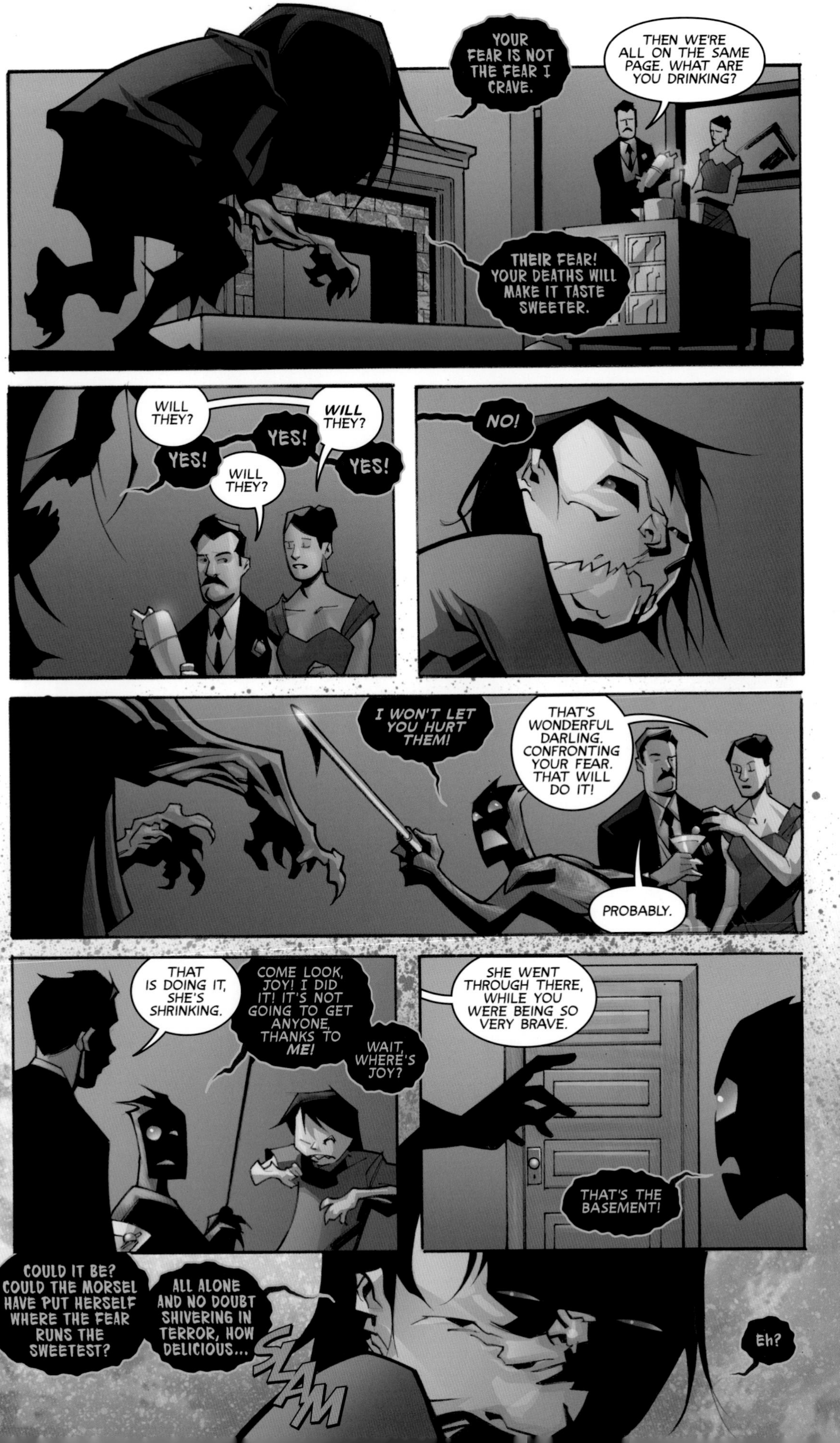

YOUR FEAR IS NOT THE FEAR I CRAVE.
THEN WE'RE ALL ON THE SAME PAGE. WHAT ARE YOU DRINKING?
THEIR FEAR! YOUR DEATHS WILL MAKE IT TASTE SWEETER.
WILL THEY?
WILL THEY?
YES!
YES!
WILL THEY?
YES!
NO!
I WON'T LET YOU HURT THEM!
THAT'S WONDERFUL DARLING. CONFRONTING YOUR FEAR. THAT WILL DO IT!
PROBABLY.
THAT IS DOING IT, SHE'S SHRINKING.
COME LOOK, JOY! I DID IT! IT'S NOT GOING TO GET ANYONE, THANKS TO ME!
WAIT, WHERE'S JOY?
SHE WENT THROUGH THERE, WHILE YOU WERE BEING SO VERY BRAVE.
THAT'S THE BASEMENT!
COULD IT BE? COULD THE MORSEL HAVE PUT HERSELF WHERE THE FEAR RUNS THE SWEETEST?
ALL ALONE AND NO DOUBT SHIVERING IN TERROR, HOW DELICIOUS...
SLAM
Eh?

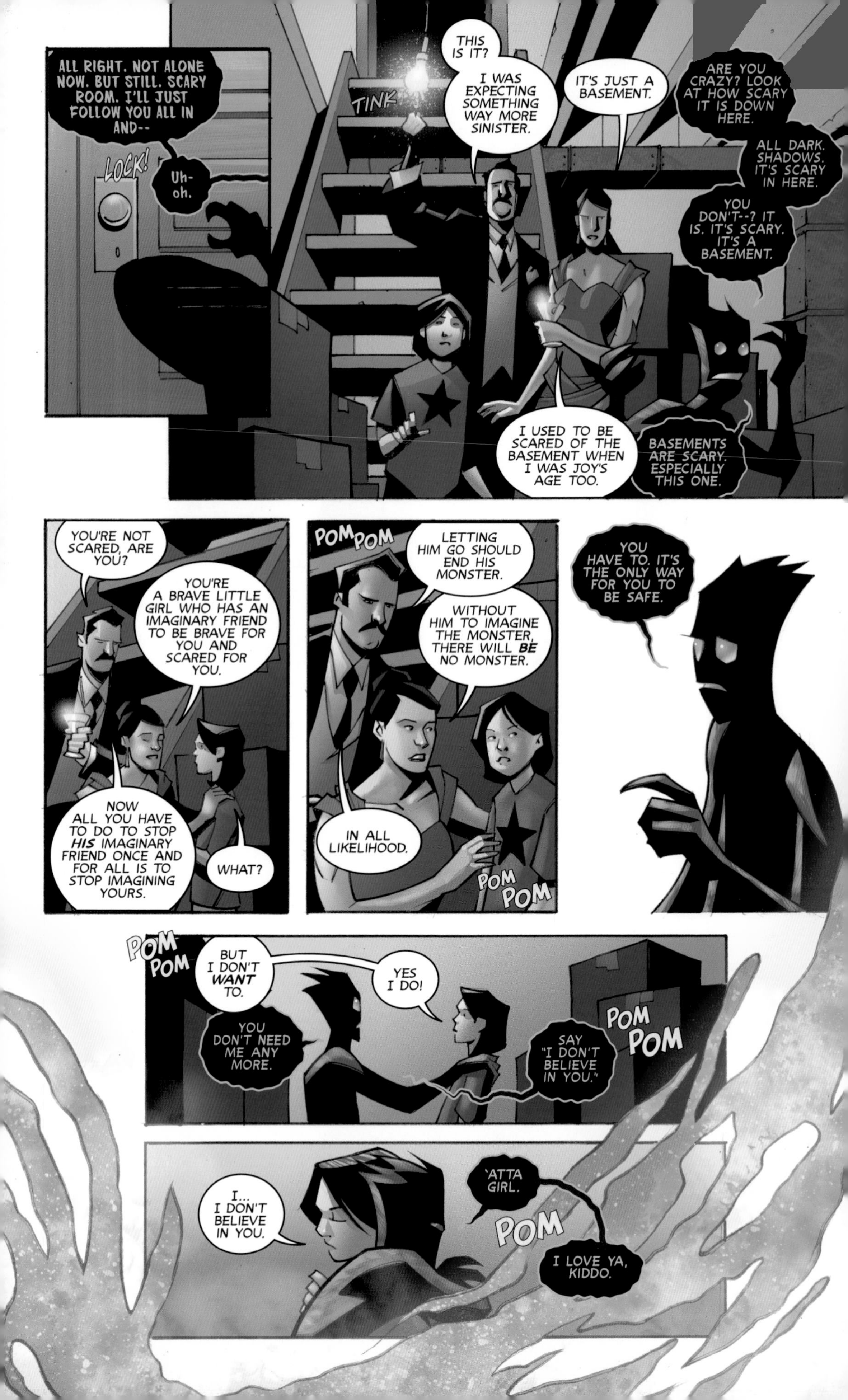
ALL RIGHT. NOT ALONE NOW. BUT STILL. SCARY ROOM. I'LL JUST FOLLOW YOU ALL IN AND--
LOCK!
Uh-oh.
TINK
THIS IS IT?
I WAS EXPECTING SOMETHING WAY MORE SINISTER.
IT'S JUST A BASEMENT.
ARE YOU CRAZY? LOOK AT HOW SCARY IT IS DOWN HERE.
ALL DARK. SHADOWS. IT'S SCARY IN HERE.
YOU DON'T--? IT IS. IT'S SCARY. IT'S A BASEMENT.
I USED TO BE SCARED OF THE BASEMENT WHEN I WAS JOY'S AGE TOO.
BASEMENTS ARE SCARY. ESPECIALLY THIS ONE.
YOU'RE NOT SCARED, ARE YOU?
YOU'RE A BRAVE LITTLE GIRL WHO HAS AN IMAGINARY FRIEND TO BE BRAVE FOR YOU AND SCARED FOR YOU.
NOW ALL YOU HAVE TO DO TO STOP HIS IMAGINARY FRIEND ONCE AND FOR ALL IS TO STOP IMAGINING YOURS.
WHAT?
POM POM
LETTING HIM GO SHOULD END HIS MONSTER.
WITHOUT HIM TO IMAGINE THE MONSTER, THERE WILL BE NO MONSTER.
IN ALL LIKELIHOOD.
POM POM
YOU HAVE TO. IT'S THE ONLY WAY FOR YOU TO BE SAFE.
POM POM
BUT I DON'T WANT TO.
YES I DO!
YOU DON'T NEED ME ANY MORE.
SAY "I DON'T BELIEVE IN YOU."
POM POM
I... I DON'T BELIEVE IN YOU.
'ATTA GIRL.
POM
I LOVE YA, KIDDO.

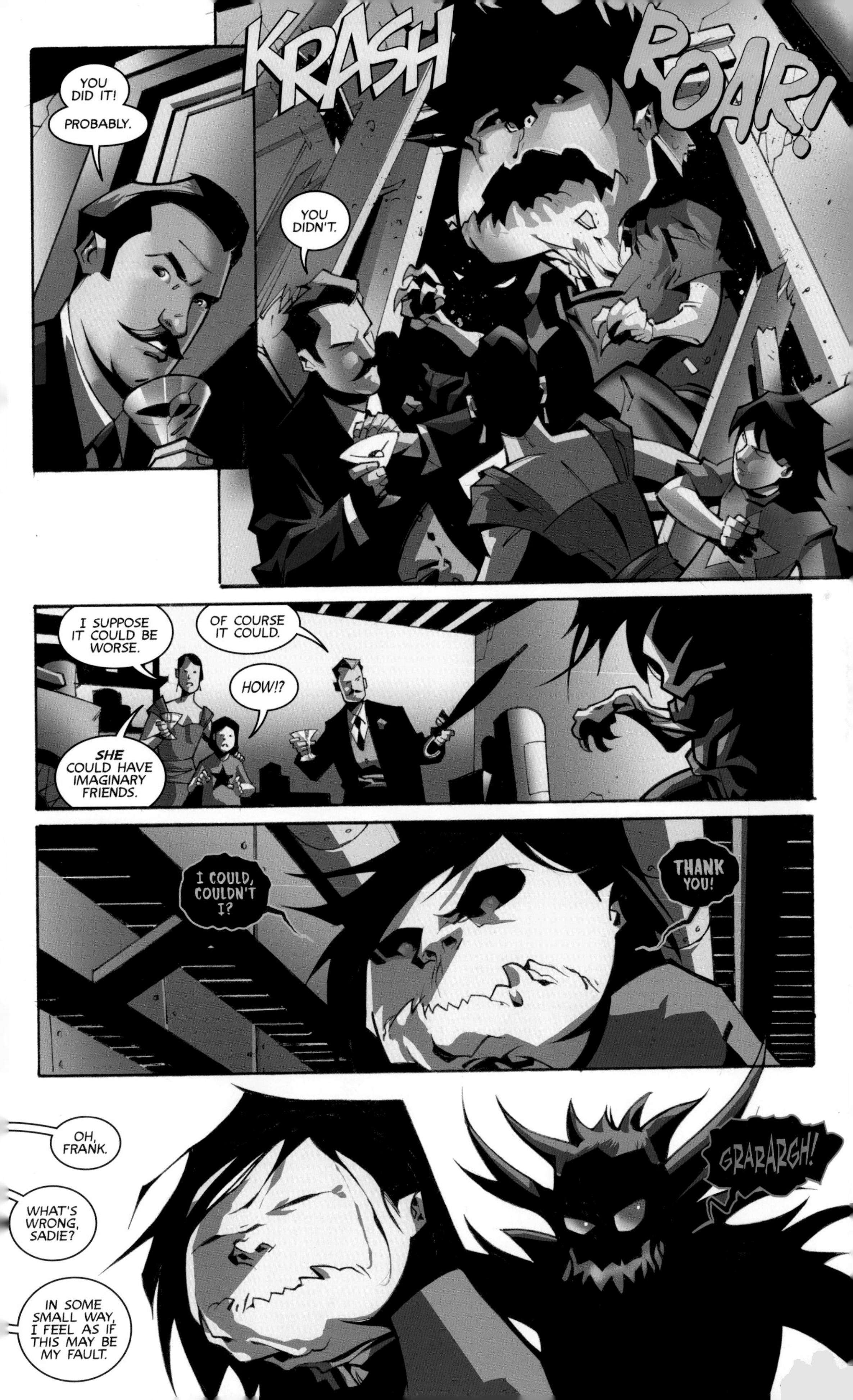
YOU DID IT!
PROBABLY.
KRASH
ROAR!
YOU DIDN'T.
I SUPPOSE IT COULD BE WORSE.
OF COURSE IT COULD.
HOW!?
SHE COULD HAVE IMAGINARY FRIENDS.
I COULD, COULDN'T I?
THANK YOU!
OH, FRANK.
WHAT'S WRONG, SADIE?
IN SOME SMALL WAY, I FEEL AS IF THIS MAY BE MY FAULT.
GRARARGH!

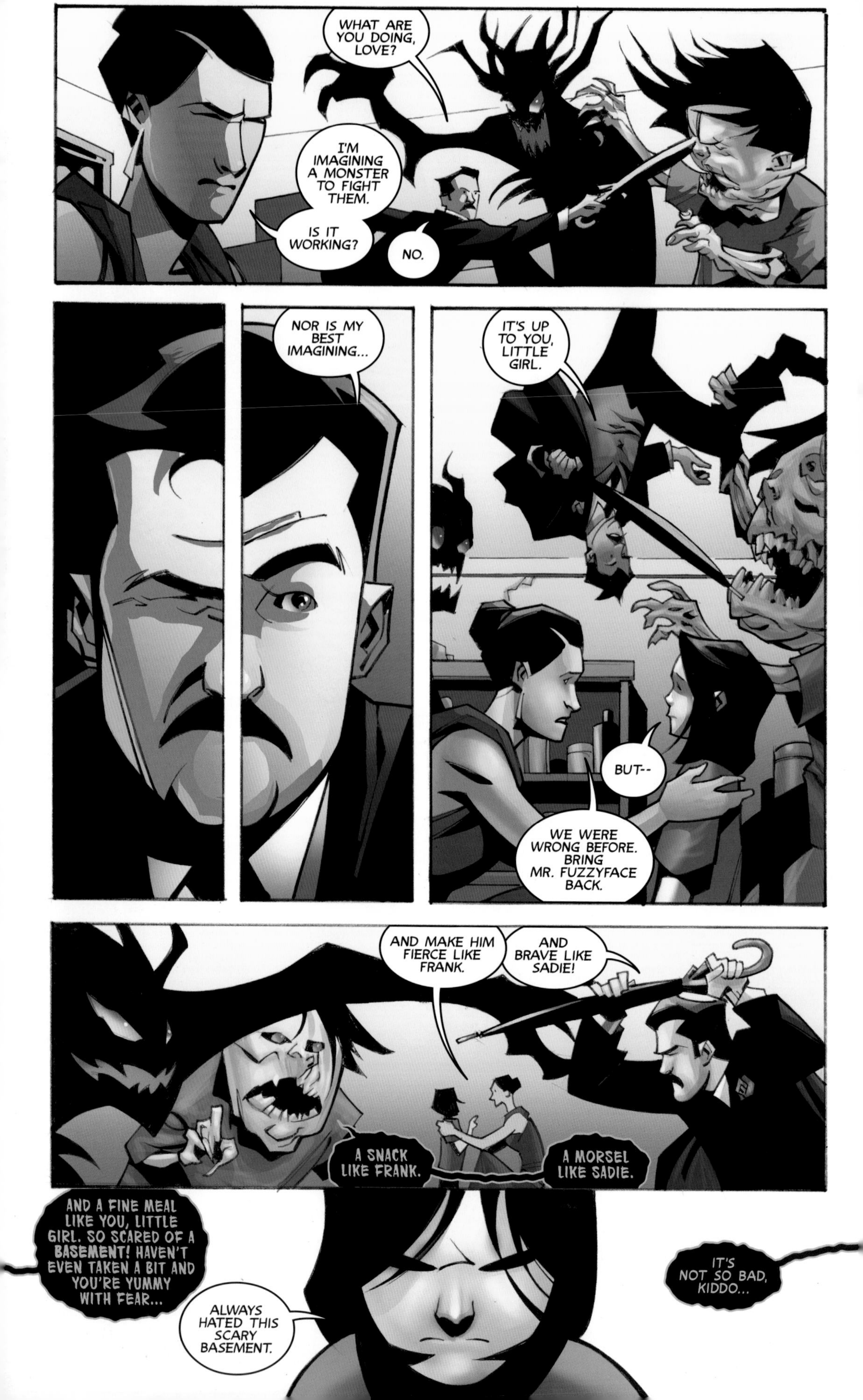

WHAT ARE YOU DOING, LOVE?
I'M IMAGINING A MONSTER TO FIGHT THEM.
IS IT WORKING?
NO.
NOR IS MY BEST IMAGINING...
IT'S UP TO YOU, LITTLE GIRL.
BUT--
WE WERE WRONG BEFORE. BRING MR. FUZZYFACE BACK.
AND MAKE HIM FIERCE LIKE FRANK.
AND BRAVE LIKE SADIE!
A SNACK LIKE FRANK.
A MORSEL LIKE SADIE.
AND A FINE MEAL LIKE YOU, LITTLE GIRL. SO SCARED OF A BASEMENT! HAVEN'T EVEN TAKEN A BIT AND YOU'RE YUMMY WITH FEAR...
ALWAYS HATED THIS SCARY BASEMENT.
IT'S NOT SO BAD, KIDDO...

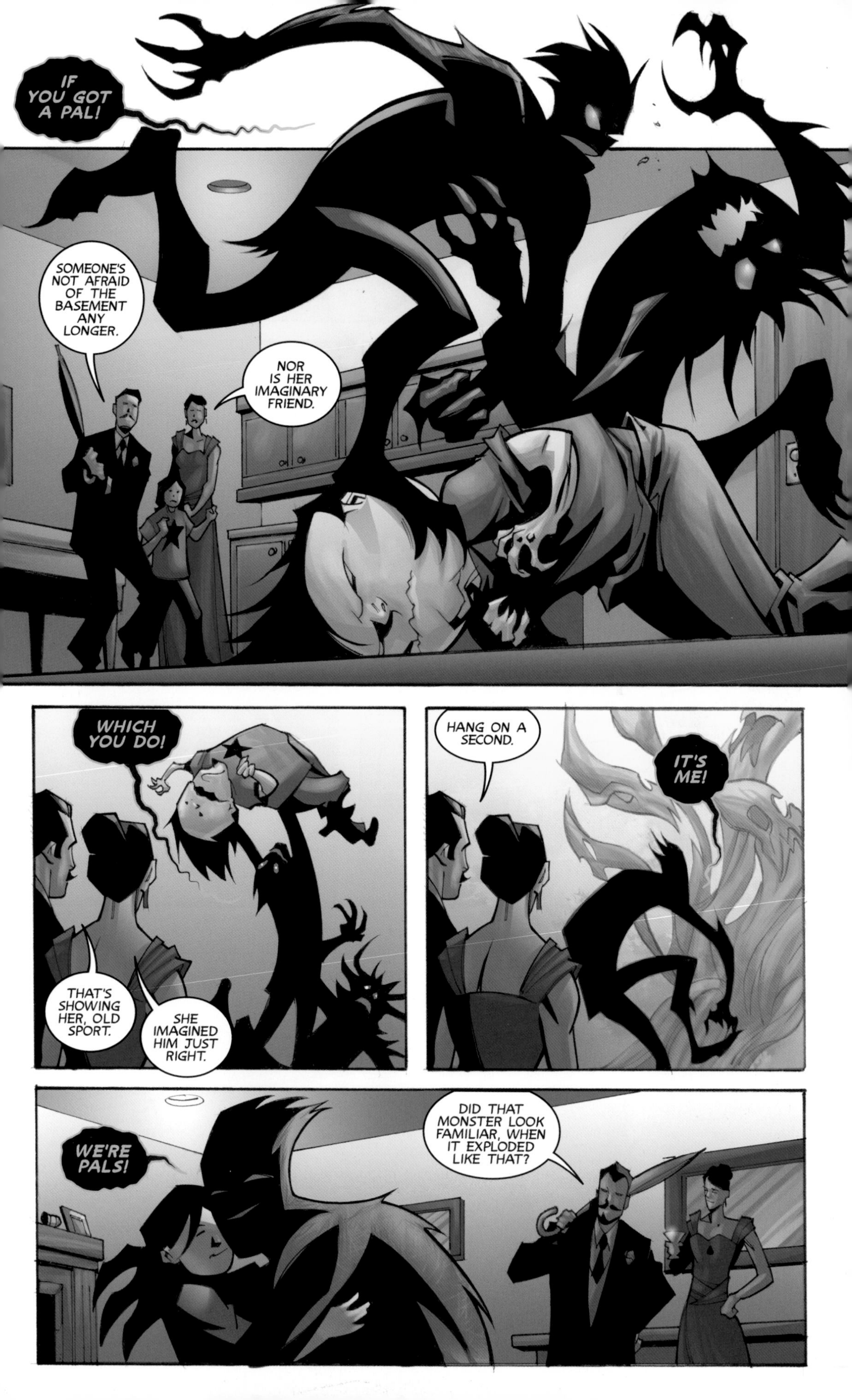
IF YOU GOT A PAL!
SOMEONE'S NOT AFRAID OF THE BASEMENT ANY LONGER.
NOR IS HER IMAGINARY FRIEND.
WHICH YOU DO!
THAT'S SHOWING HER, OLD SPORT.
SHE IMAGINED HIM JUST RIGHT.
HANG ON A SECOND.
IT'S ME!
WE'RE PALS!
DID THAT MONSTER LOOK FAMILIAR, WHEN IT EXPLODED LIKE THAT?

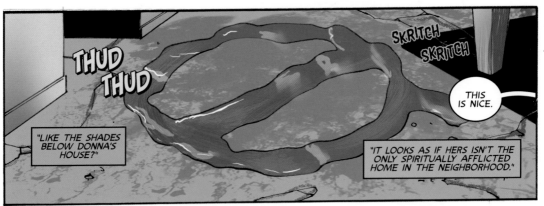

THUD THUD

SKRITCH SKRITCH

THIS IS NICE.

"LIKE THE SHADES BELOW DONNA'S HOUSE?"

"IT LOOKS AS IF HERS ISN'T THE ONLY SPIRITUALLY AFFLICTED HOME IN THE NEIGHBORHOOD."

"WHO KNOWS HOW FAR IT SPREADS AND JUST OF WHAT THEY'RE AFTER."

A NICE HOUSE IN A NICE NEIGHBORHOOD. I CAN BARELY HEAR THE MONSTERS UNDER THE HOUSE.

MAYBE IT'S THE WINE, MAYBE IT'S THE BREEZE, BUT I HAVE A FEELING EVERYTHING'S GONNA BE PRETTY GREAT FROM HERE ON OUT. I SHOULD SEND FRANK AND SADIE A THANK YOU CARD.

NO, THAT'S NOT RIGHT. WHAT DO YOU SEND SOMEONE FOR CLEANING SPIRITS OUT OF YOUR HOUSE? HM. WELL, A BOTTLE OF SOMETHING IS A GOOD GIFT FOR THOSE--

KNOCK KNOCK KNOCK

OF WHAT THEY'RE CAPABLE.

DONNA DONNER?

YES?

"WELL..."

WHAT IS--

WHY ARE YOU--

...COSTUMES?

THE TREE WOULD LIKE TO MEET YOU.

YEAH, THE...

WAIT, WHAT?

"AT LEAST DONNA'S SAFE."

Chapter

THREE

The Last House on the Left... Right?

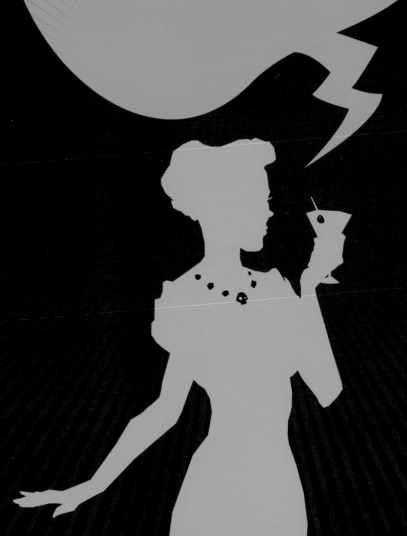

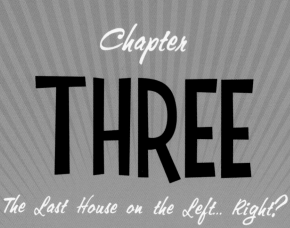

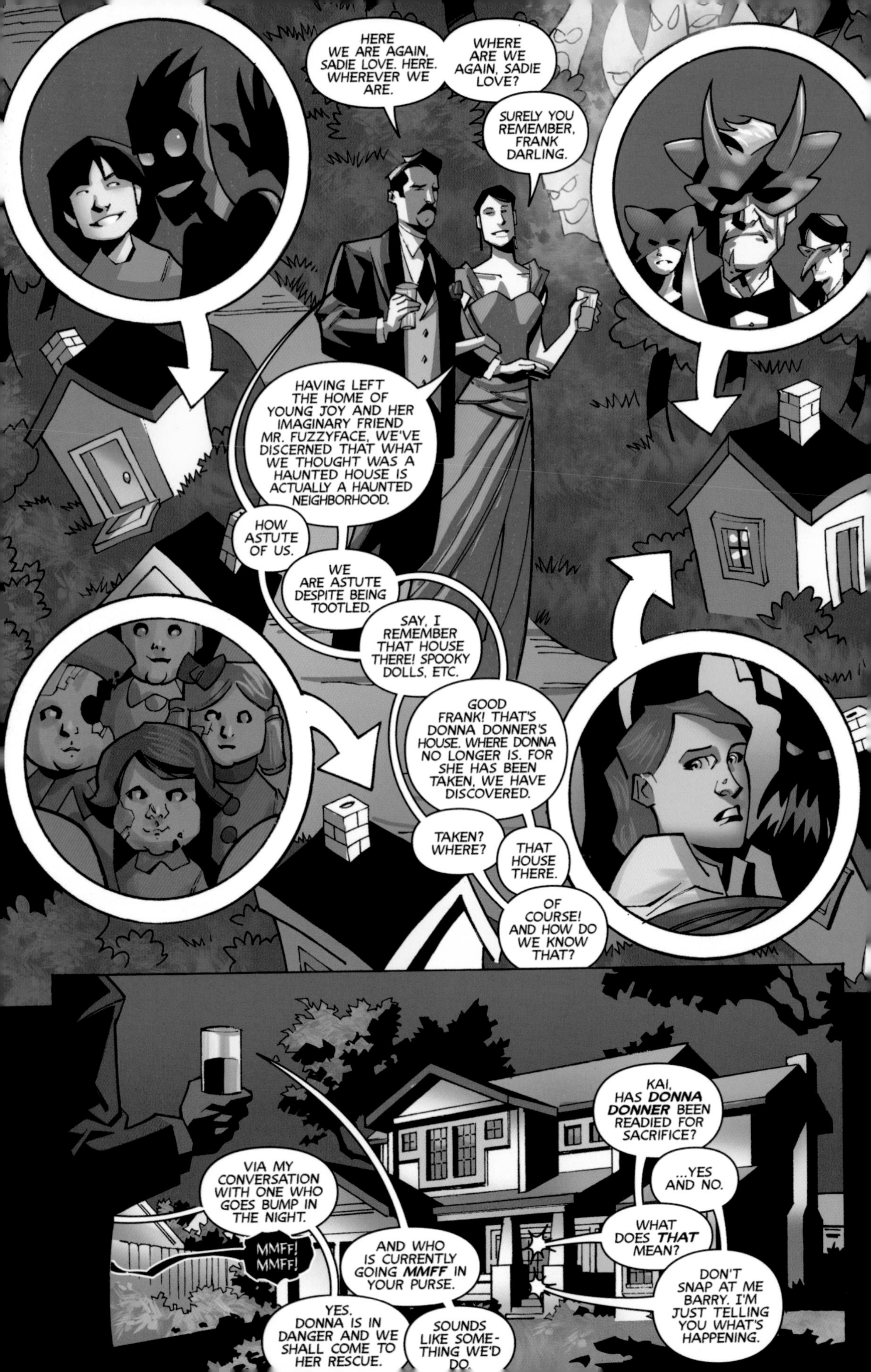
HERE WE ARE AGAIN, SADIE LOVE. HERE. WHEREVER WE ARE.
WHERE ARE WE AGAIN, SADIE LOVE?
SURELY YOU REMEMBER, FRANK DARLING.
HAVING LEFT THE HOME OF YOUNG JOY AND HER IMAGINARY FRIEND MR. FUZZYFACE, WE'VE DISCERNED THAT WHAT WE THOUGHT WAS A HAUNTED HOUSE IS ACTUALLY A HAUNTED NEIGHBORHOOD.
HOW ASTUTE OF US.
WE ARE ASTUTE DESPITE BEING TOOTLED.
SAY, I REMEMBER THAT HOUSE THERE! SPOOKY DOLLS, ETC.
GOOD FRANK! THAT'S DONNA DONNER'S HOUSE. WHERE DONNA NO LONGER IS. FOR SHE HAS BEEN TAKEN, WE HAVE DISCOVERED.
TAKEN? WHERE?
THAT HOUSE THERE.
OF COURSE! AND HOW DO WE KNOW THAT?
VIA MY CONVERSATION WITH ONE WHO GOES BUMP IN THE NIGHT.
MMFF! MMFF!
AND WHO IS CURRENTLY GOING ***MMFF*** IN YOUR PURSE.
YES. DONNA IS IN DANGER AND WE SHALL COME TO HER RESCUE.
SOUNDS LIKE SOME-THING WE'D DO.
KAI, HAS ***DONNA DONNER*** BEEN READIED FOR SACRIFICE?
...YES AND NO.
WHAT DOES ***THAT*** MEAN?
DON'T SNAP AT ME BARRY. I'M JUST TELLING YOU WHAT'S HAPPENING.

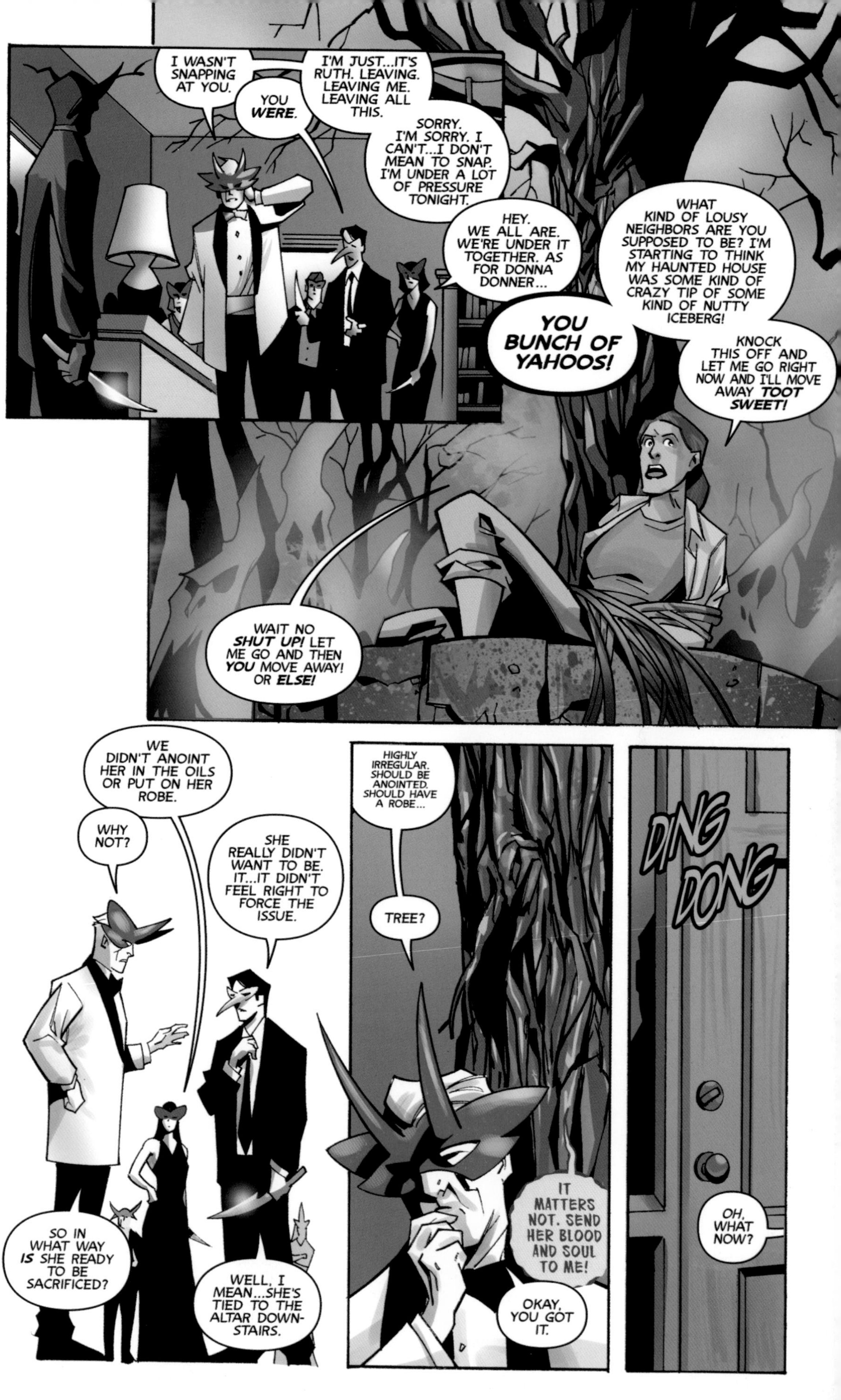
I WASN'T SNAPPING AT YOU.
YOU *WERE*.
I'M JUST...IT'S RUTH. LEAVING. LEAVING ME. LEAVING ALL THIS.
SORRY. I'M SORRY. I CAN'T...I DON'T MEAN TO SNAP. I'M UNDER A LOT OF PRESSURE TONIGHT.
HEY. WE ALL ARE. WE'RE UNDER IT TOGETHER. AS FOR DONNA DONNER...
WHAT KIND OF LOUSY NEIGHBORS ARE YOU SUPPOSED TO BE? I'M STARTING TO THINK MY HAUNTED HOUSE WAS SOME KIND OF CRAZY TIP OF SOME KIND OF NUTTY ICEBERG!
YOU BUNCH OF YAHOOS!
KNOCK THIS OFF AND LET ME GO RIGHT NOW AND I'LL MOVE AWAY ***TOOT SWEET!***
WAIT NO ***SHUT UP!*** LET ME GO AND THEN ***YOU*** MOVE AWAY! OR ***ELSE!***
WE DIDN'T ANOINT HER IN THE OILS OR PUT ON HER ROBE.
WHY NOT?
SHE REALLY DIDN'T WANT TO BE. IT...IT DIDN'T FEEL RIGHT TO FORCE THE ISSUE.
SO IN WHAT WAY ***IS*** SHE READY TO BE SACRIFICED?
WELL, I MEAN...SHE'S TIED TO THE ALTAR DOWN-STAIRS.
HIGHLY IRREGULAR. SHOULD BE ANOINTED. SHOULD HAVE A ROBE...
TREE?
IT MATTERS NOT. SEND HER BLOOD AND SOUL TO ME!
OKAY, YOU GOT IT.
DING DONG
OH, WHAT NOW?

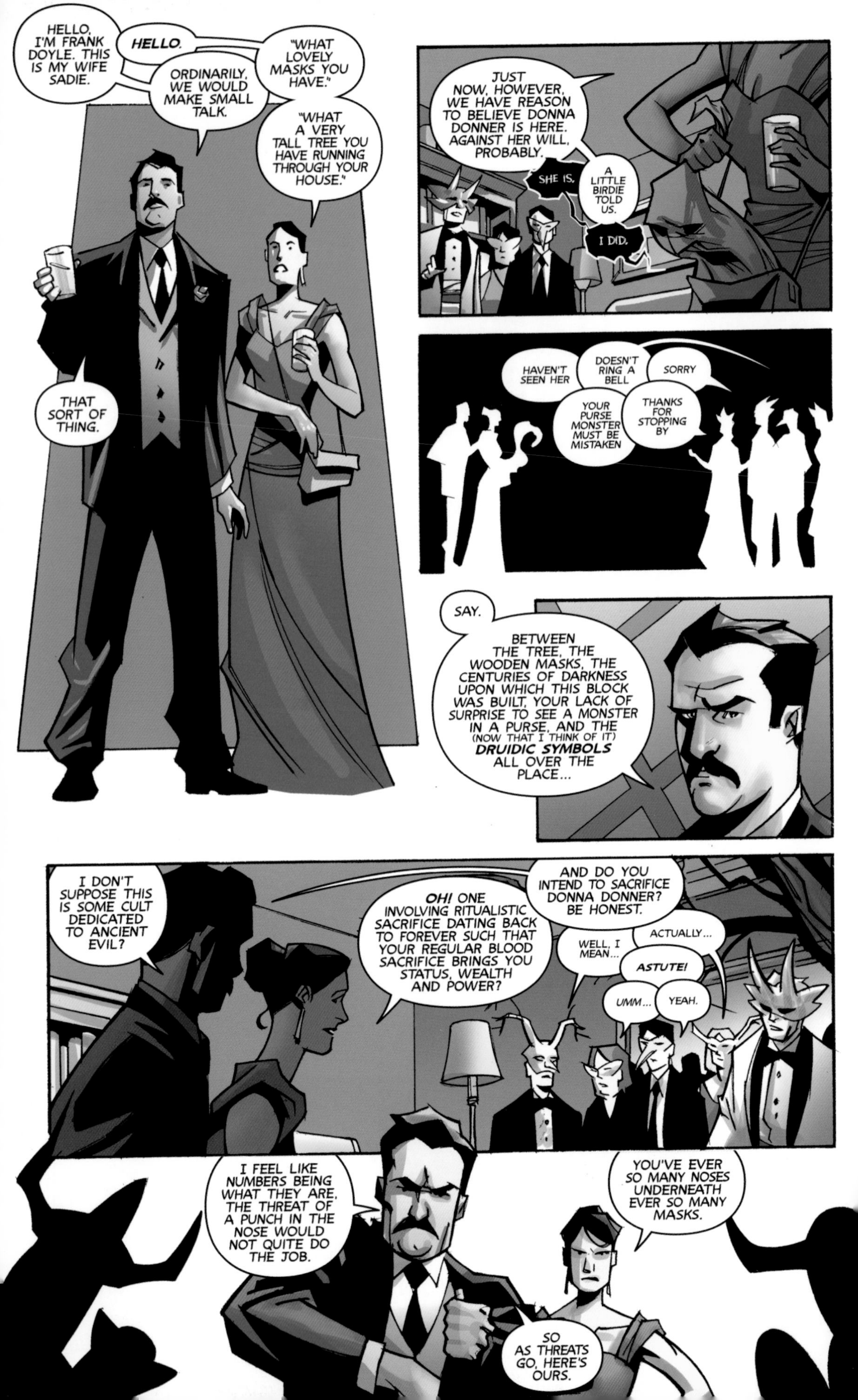
HELLO, I'M FRANK DOYLE. THIS IS MY WIFE SADIE.
HELLO.
"WHAT LOVELY MASKS YOU HAVE."
ORDINARILY, WE WOULD MAKE SMALL TALK.
"WHAT A VERY TALL TREE YOU HAVE RUNNING THROUGH YOUR HOUSE."
THAT SORT OF THING.
JUST NOW, HOWEVER, WE HAVE REASON TO BELIEVE DONNA DONNER IS HERE. AGAINST HER WILL, PROBABLY.
SHE IS.
A LITTLE BIRDIE TOLD US.
I DID.
HAVEN'T SEEN HER
DOESN'T RING A BELL
SORRY
YOUR PURSE MONSTER MUST BE MISTAKEN
THANKS FOR STOPPING BY
SAY.
BETWEEN THE TREE, THE WOODEN MASKS, THE CENTURIES OF DARKNESS UPON WHICH THIS BLOCK WAS BUILT, YOUR LACK OF SURPRISE TO SEE A MONSTER IN A PURSE, AND THE (NOW THAT I THINK OF IT) DRUIDIC SYMBOLS ALL OVER THE PLACE...
I DON'T SUPPOSE THIS IS SOME CULT DEDICATED TO ANCIENT EVIL?
OH! ONE INVOLVING RITUALISTIC SACRIFICE DATING BACK TO FOREVER SUCH THAT YOUR REGULAR BLOOD SACRIFICE BRINGS YOU STATUS, WEALTH AND POWER?
AND DO YOU INTEND TO SACRIFICE DONNA DONNER? BE HONEST.
WELL, I MEAN...
ACTUALLY...
ASTUTE!
UMM...
YEAH.
I FEEL LIKE NUMBERS BEING WHAT THEY ARE, THE THREAT OF A PUNCH IN THE NOSE WOULD NOT QUITE DO THE JOB.
YOU'VE EVER SO MANY NOSES UNDERNEATH EVER SO MANY MASKS.
SO AS THREATS GO, HERE'S OURS.

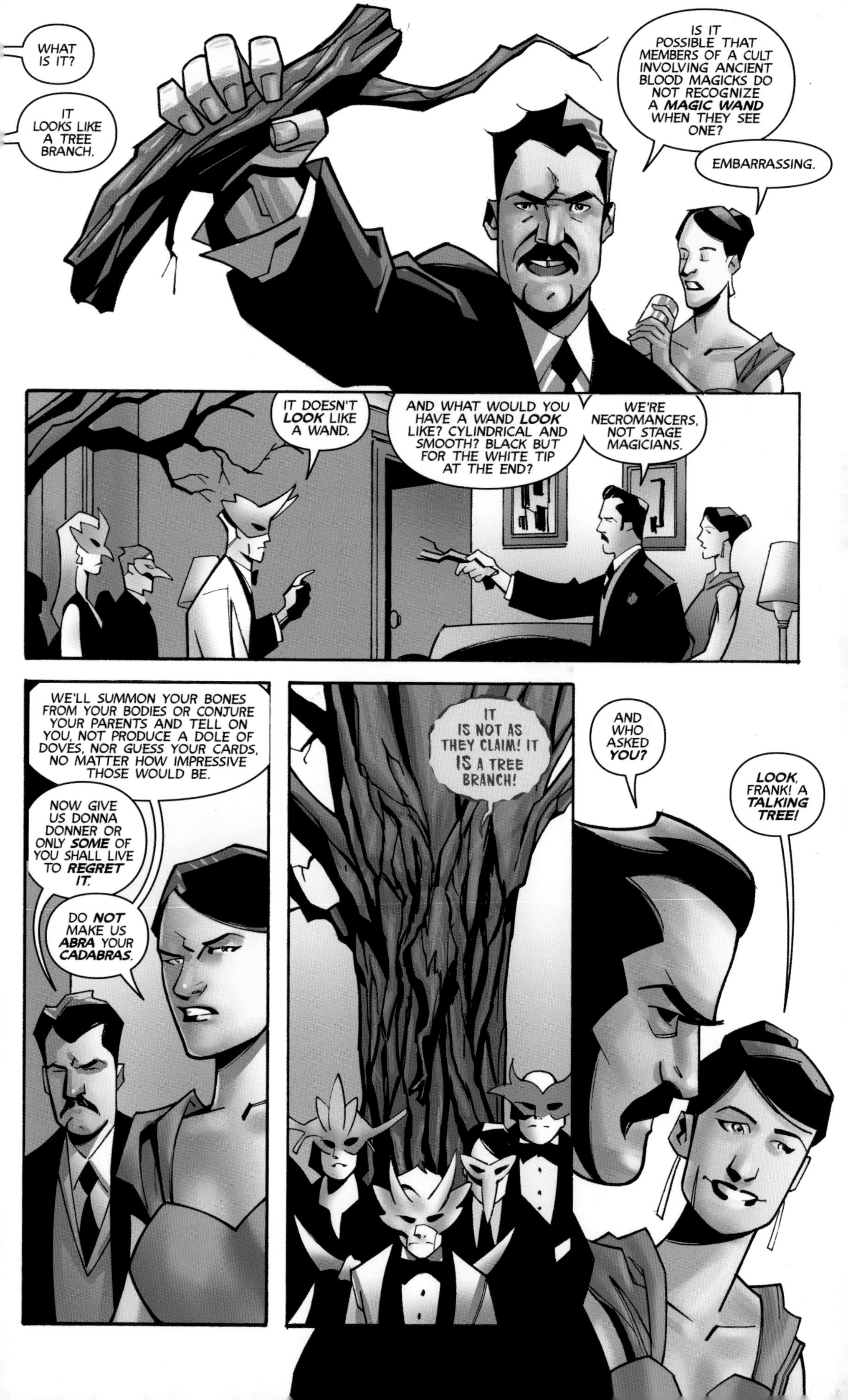

WHAT IS IT?
IT LOOKS LIKE A TREE BRANCH.
IS IT POSSIBLE THAT MEMBERS OF A CULT INVOLVING ANCIENT BLOOD MAGICKS DO NOT RECOGNIZE A MAGIC WAND WHEN THEY SEE ONE?
EMBARRASSING.
IT DOESN'T LOOK LIKE A WAND.
AND WHAT WOULD YOU HAVE A WAND LOOK LIKE? CYLINDRICAL AND SMOOTH? BLACK BUT FOR THE WHITE TIP AT THE END?
WE'RE NECROMANCERS, NOT STAGE MAGICIANS.
WE'LL SUMMON YOUR BONES FROM YOUR BODIES OR CONJURE YOUR PARENTS AND TELL ON YOU, NOT PRODUCE A DOLE OF DOVES, NOR GUESS YOUR CARDS, NO MATTER HOW IMPRESSIVE THOSE WOULD BE.
NOW GIVE US DONNA DONNER OR ONLY SOME OF YOU SHALL LIVE TO REGRET IT.
DO NOT MAKE US ABRA YOUR CADABRAS.
IT IS NOT AS THEY CLAIM! IT IS A TREE BRANCH!
AND WHO ASKED YOU?
LOOK, FRANK! A TALKING TREE!

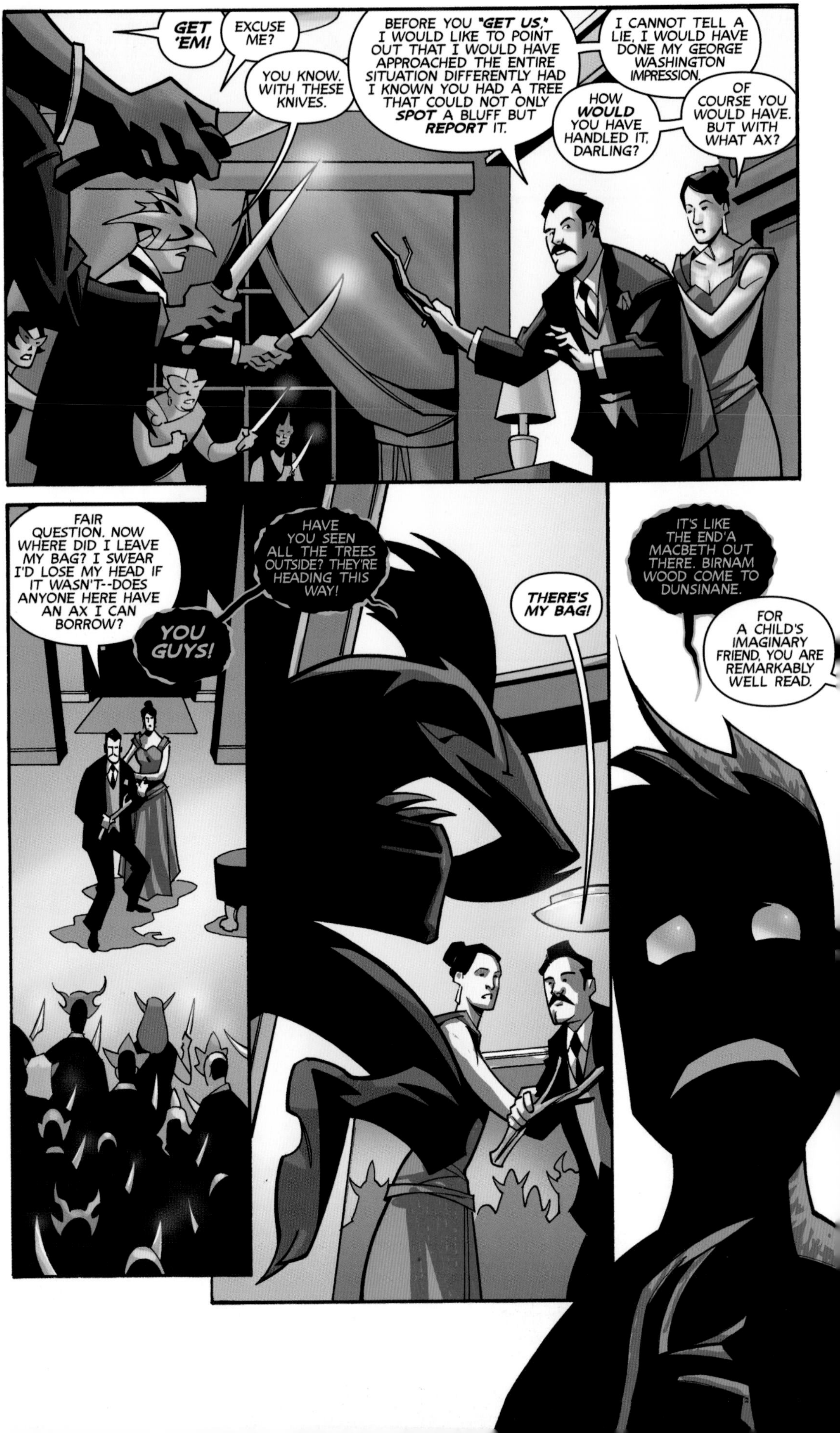
GET 'EM!
EXCUSE ME?
YOU KNOW. WITH THESE KNIVES.
BEFORE YOU "GET US," I WOULD LIKE TO POINT OUT THAT I WOULD HAVE APPROACHED THE ENTIRE SITUATION DIFFERENTLY HAD I KNOWN YOU HAD A TREE THAT COULD NOT ONLY SPOT A BLUFF BUT REPORT IT.
I CANNOT TELL A LIE, I WOULD HAVE DONE MY GEORGE WASHINGTON IMPRESSION.
HOW WOULD YOU HAVE HANDLED IT, DARLING?
OF COURSE YOU WOULD HAVE. BUT WITH WHAT AX?
FAIR QUESTION. NOW WHERE DID I LEAVE MY BAG? I SWEAR I'D LOSE MY HEAD IF IT WASN'T--DOES ANYONE HERE HAVE AN AX I CAN BORROW?
YOU GUYS!
HAVE YOU SEEN ALL THE TREES OUTSIDE? THEY'RE HEADING THIS WAY!
THERE'S MY BAG!
IT'S LIKE THE END'A MACBETH OUT THERE. BIRNAM WOOD COME TO DUNSINANE.
FOR A CHILD'S IMAGINARY FRIEND, YOU ARE REMARKABLY WELL READ.

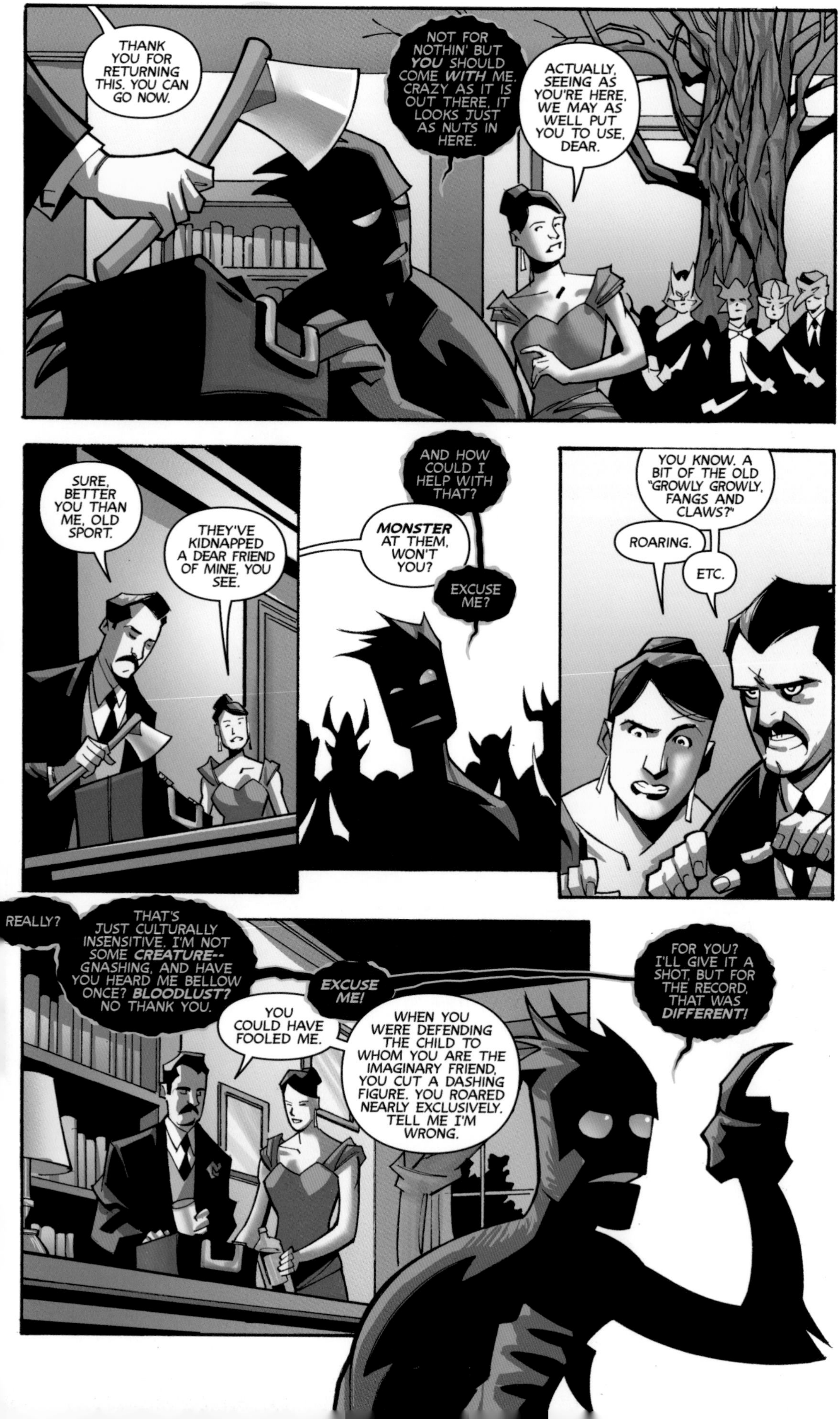

THANK YOU FOR RETURNING THIS. YOU CAN GO NOW.
NOT FOR NOTHIN' BUT YOU SHOULD COME WITH ME. CRAZY AS IT IS OUT THERE, IT LOOKS JUST AS NUTS IN HERE.
ACTUALLY, SEEING AS YOU'RE HERE, WE MAY AS WELL PUT YOU TO USE, DEAR.
SURE, BETTER YOU THAN ME, OLD SPORT.
THEY'VE KIDNAPPED A DEAR FRIEND OF MINE, YOU SEE.
AND HOW COULD I HELP WITH THAT?
MONSTER AT THEM, WON'T YOU?
EXCUSE ME?
YOU KNOW. A BIT OF THE OLD "GROWLY GROWLY, FANGS AND CLAWS?"
ROARING.
ETC.
REALLY?
THAT'S JUST CULTURALLY INSENSITIVE. I'M NOT SOME CREATURE-- GNASHING, AND HAVE YOU HEARD ME BELLOW ONCE? BLOODLUST? NO THANK YOU.
YOU COULD HAVE FOOLED ME.
EXCUSE ME!
WHEN YOU WERE DEFENDING THE CHILD TO WHOM YOU ARE THE IMAGINARY FRIEND, YOU CUT A DASHING FIGURE. YOU ROARED NEARLY EXCLUSIVELY. TELL ME I'M WRONG.
FOR YOU? I'LL GIVE IT A SHOT, BUT FOR THE RECORD, THAT WAS DIFFERENT!

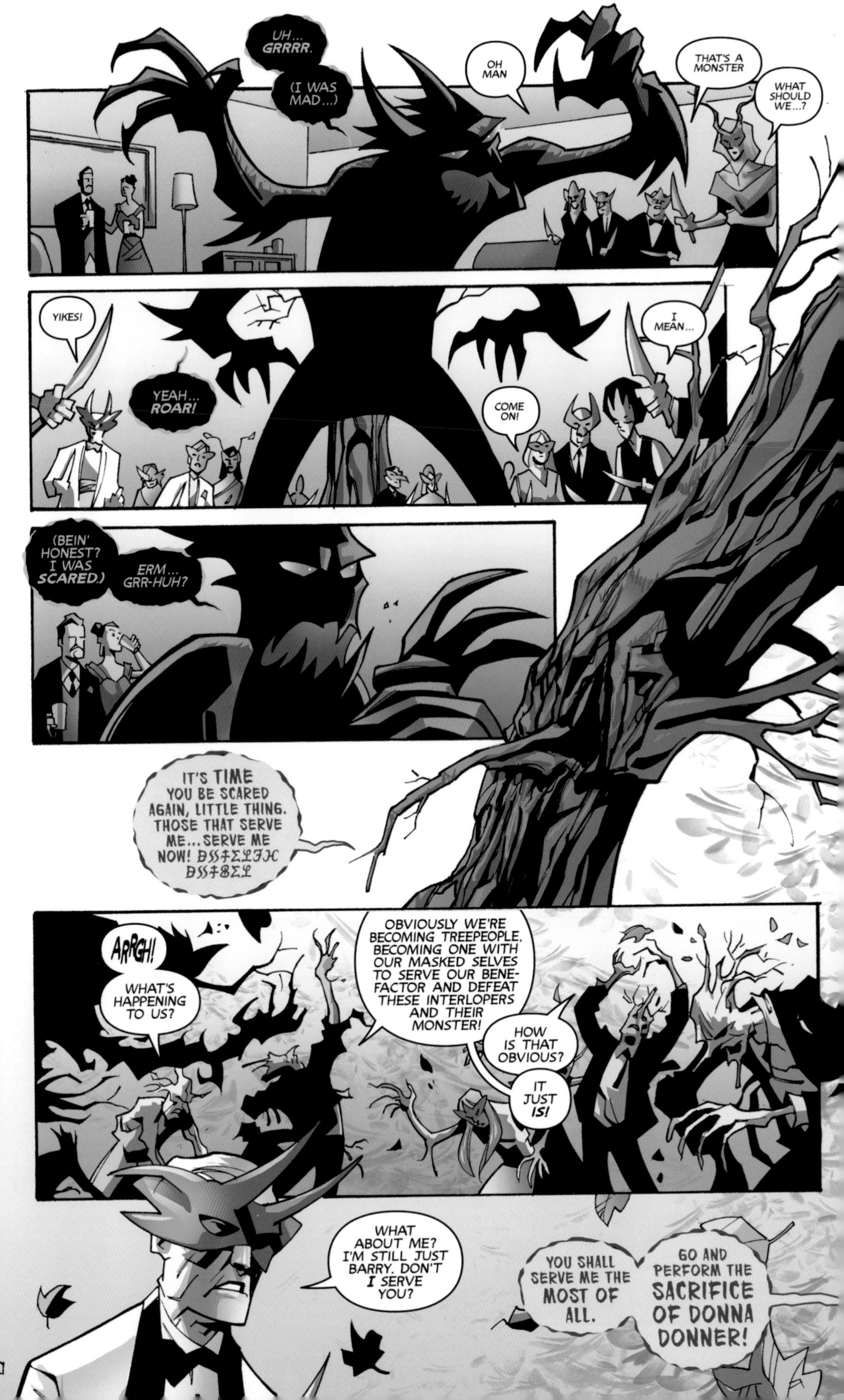
UH... GRRRR.
(I WAS MAD...)
OH MAN
THAT'S A MONSTER
WHAT SHOULD WE...?
YIKES!
YEAH... ROAR!
COME ON!
I MEAN...
(BEIN' HONEST? I WAS SCARED.)
ERM... GRR-HUH?
IT'S TIME YOU BE SCARED AGAIN, LITTLE THING. THOSE THAT SERVE ME... SERVE ME NOW!
ARRGH!
WHAT'S HAPPENING TO US?
OBVIOUSLY WE'RE BECOMING TREEPEOPLE, BECOMING ONE WITH OUR MASKED SELVES TO SERVE OUR BENEFACTOR AND DEFEAT THESE INTERLOPERS AND THEIR MONSTER!
HOW IS THAT OBVIOUS?
IT JUST IS!
WHAT ABOUT ME? I'M STILL JUST BARRY. DON'T I SERVE YOU?
YOU SHALL SERVE ME THE MOST OF ALL.
GO AND PERFORM THE SACRIFICE OF DONNA DONNER!

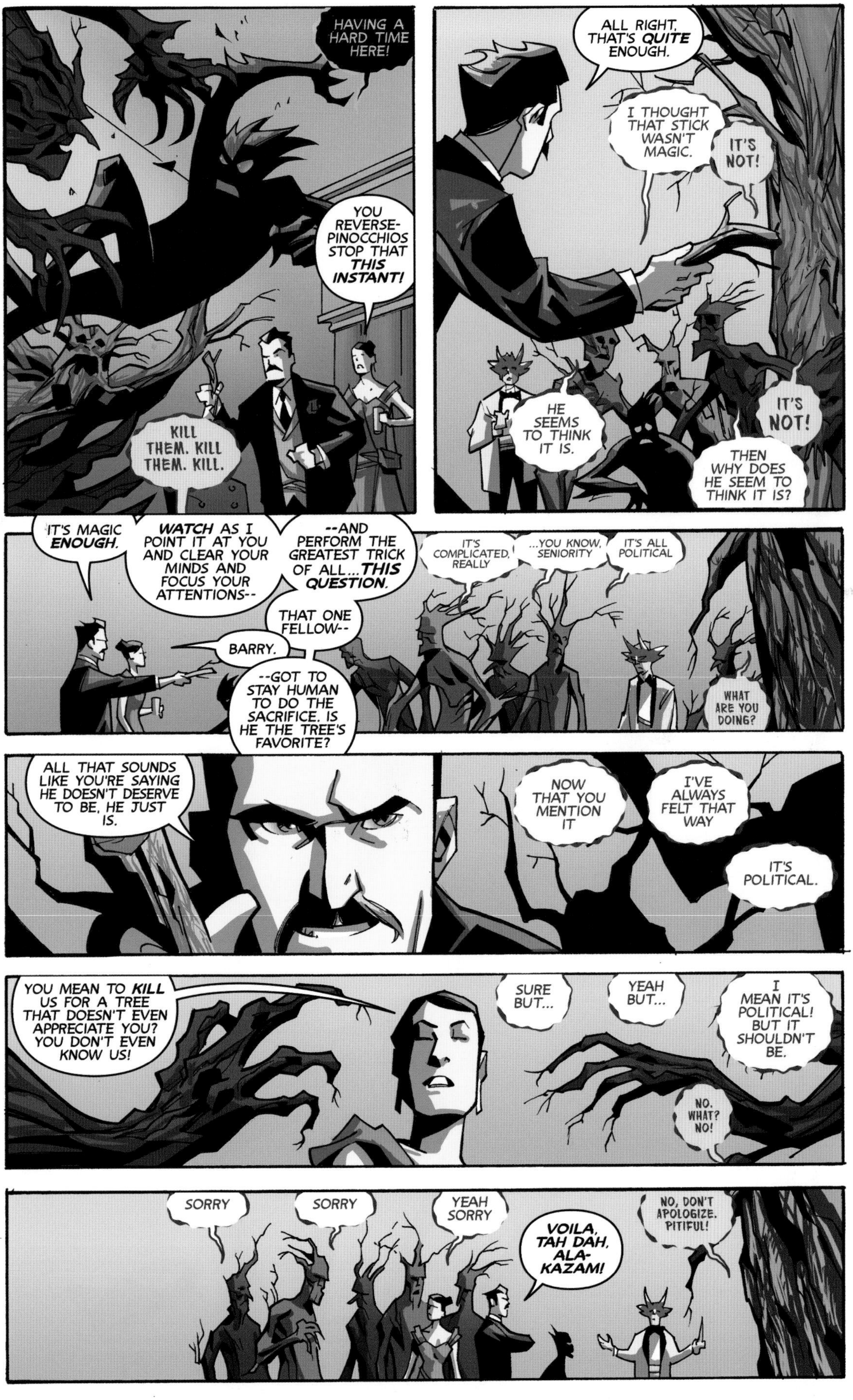
HAVING A HARD TIME HERE!
YOU REVERSE-PINOCCHIOS STOP THAT THIS INSTANT!
KILL THEM. KILL THEM. KILL.
ALL RIGHT, THAT'S QUITE ENOUGH.
I THOUGHT THAT STICK WASN'T MAGIC.
IT'S NOT!
HE SEEMS TO THINK IT IS.
IT'S NOT!
THEN WHY DOES HE SEEM TO THINK IT IS?
IT'S MAGIC ENOUGH.
WATCH AS I POINT IT AT YOU AND CLEAR YOUR MINDS AND FOCUS YOUR ATTENTIONS--
--AND PERFORM THE GREATEST TRICK OF ALL...THIS QUESTION.
THAT ONE FELLOW--
BARRY.
--GOT TO STAY HUMAN TO DO THE SACRIFICE. IS HE THE TREE'S FAVORITE?
IT'S COMPLICATED, REALLY
...YOU KNOW, SENIORITY
IT'S ALL POLITICAL
WHAT ARE YOU DOING?
ALL THAT SOUNDS LIKE YOU'RE SAYING HE DOESN'T DESERVE TO BE, HE JUST IS.
NOW THAT YOU MENTION IT
I'VE ALWAYS FELT THAT WAY
IT'S POLITICAL.
YOU MEAN TO KILL US FOR A TREE THAT DOESN'T EVEN APPRECIATE YOU? YOU DON'T EVEN KNOW US!
SURE BUT...
YEAH BUT...
I MEAN IT'S POLITICAL! BUT IT SHOULDN'T BE.
NO. WHAT? NO!
SORRY
SORRY
YEAH SORRY
VOILA, TAH DAH, ALA-KAZAM!
NO, DON'T APOLOGIZE. PITIFUL!

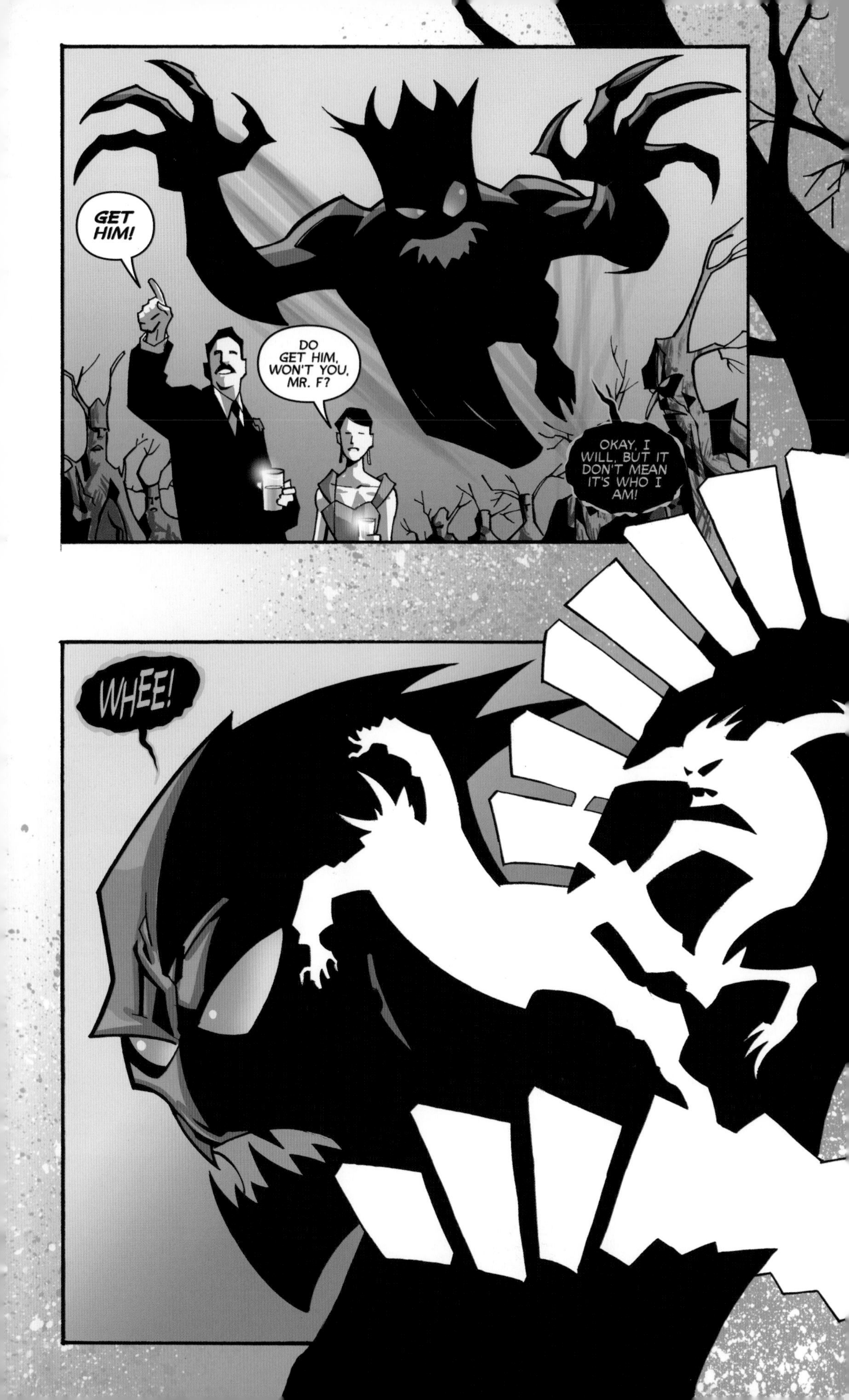
GET HIM!
DO GET HIM, WON'T YOU, MR. F?
OKAY, I WILL, BUT IT DON'T MEAN IT'S WHO I AM!
WHEE!

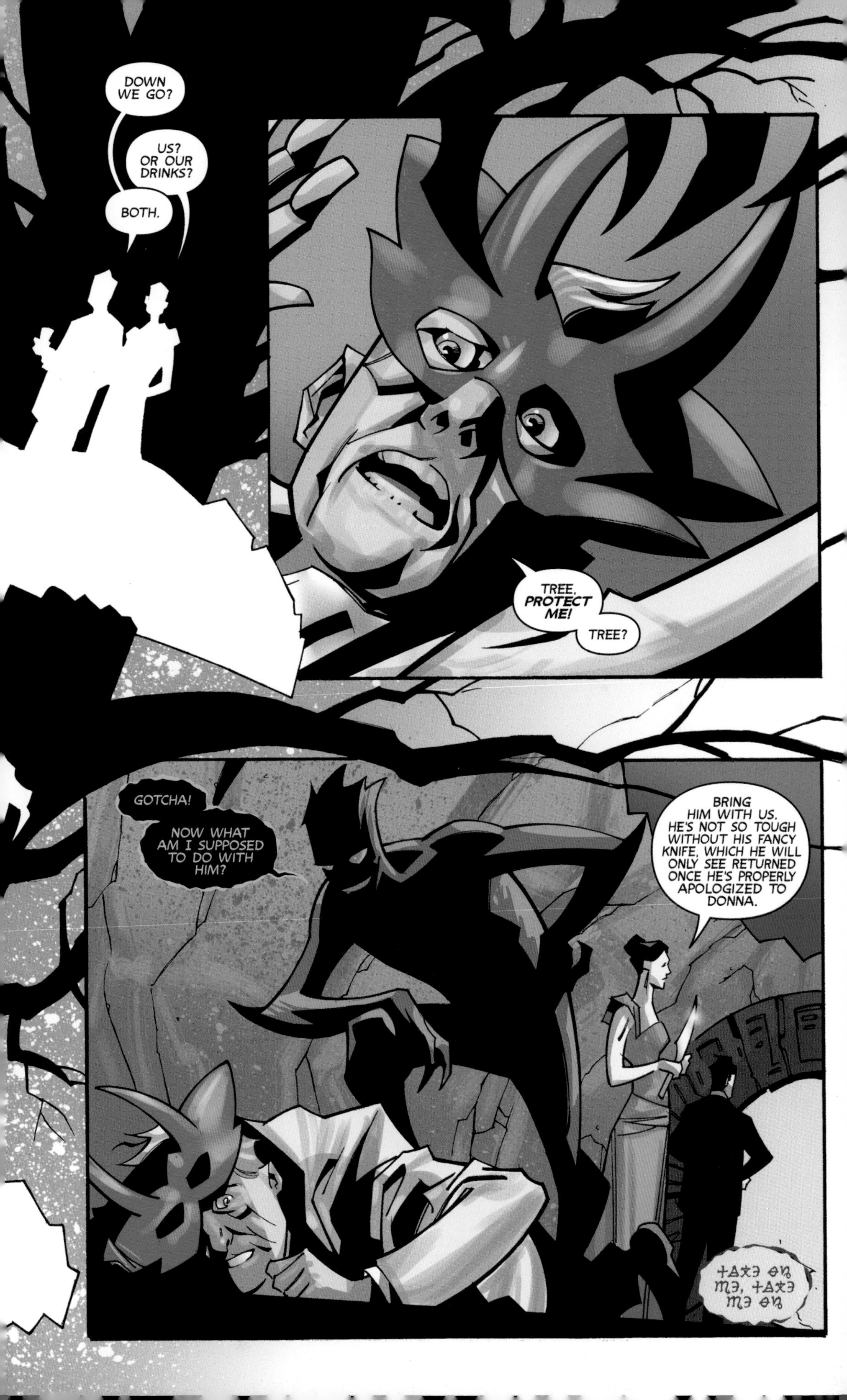
DOWN WE GO?
US? OR OUR DRINKS?
BOTH.
TREE, PROTECT ME!
TREE?
GOTCHA!
NOW WHAT AM I SUPPOSED TO DO WITH HIM?
BRING HIM WITH US. HE'S NOT SO TOUGH WITHOUT HIS FANCY KNIFE, WHICH HE WILL ONLY SEE RETURNED ONCE HE'S PROPERLY APOLOGIZED TO DONNA.

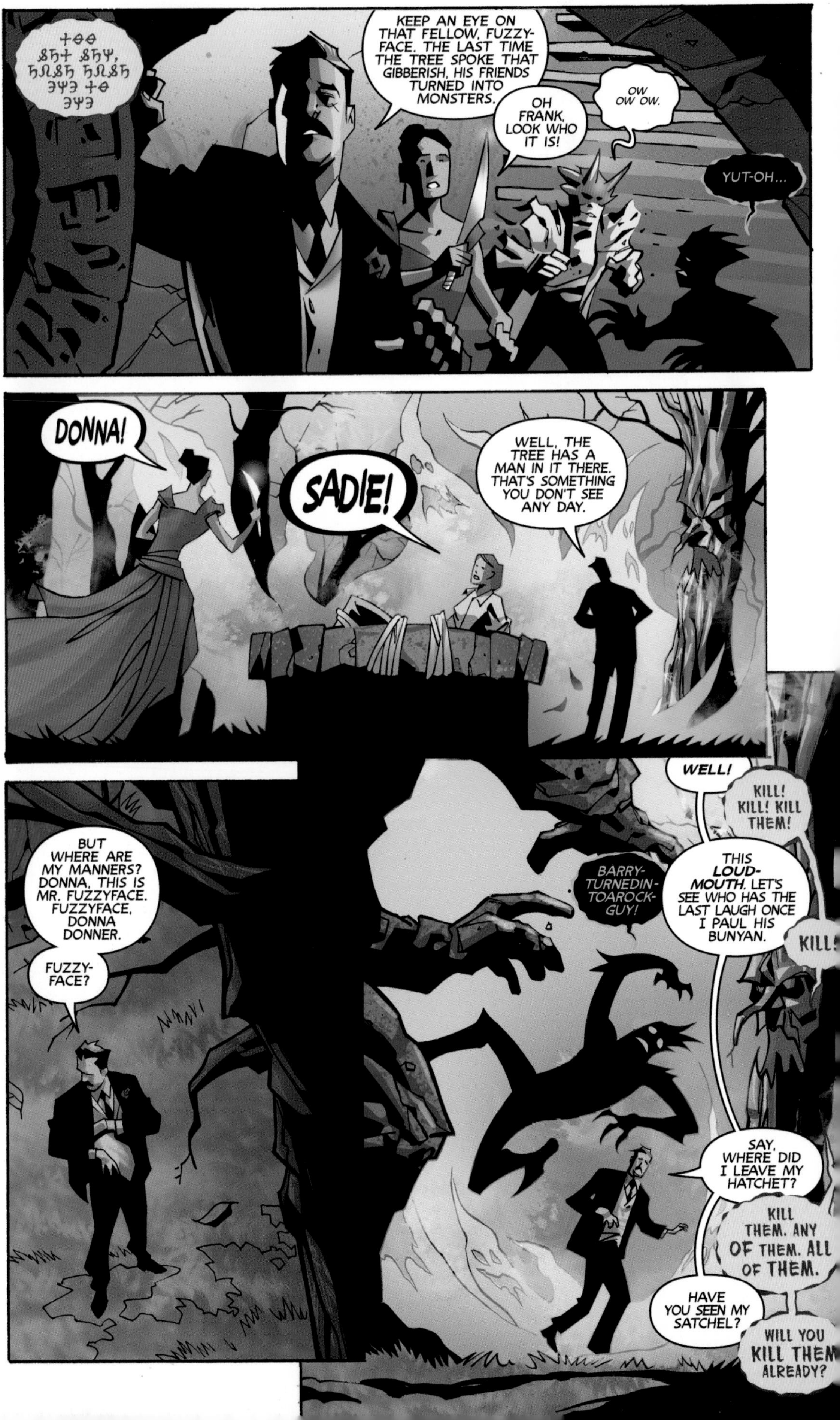
KEEP AN EYE ON THAT FELLOW, FUZZY-FACE. THE LAST TIME THE TREE SPOKE THAT GIBBERISH, HIS FRIENDS TURNED INTO MONSTERS.
OH FRANK, LOOK WHO IT IS!
OW OW OW.
YUT-OH...
DONNA!
SADIE!
WELL, THE TREE HAS A MAN IN IT THERE. THAT'S SOMETHING YOU DON'T SEE ANY DAY.
BUT WHERE ARE MY MANNERS? DONNA, THIS IS MR. FUZZYFACE. FUZZYFACE, DONNA DONNER.
FUZZY-FACE?
BARRY-TURNEDIN-TOAROCK-GUY!
WELL!
KILL! KILL! KILL THEM!
THIS LOUD-MOUTH, LET'S SEE WHO HAS THE LAST LAUGH ONCE I PAUL HIS BUNYAN.
KILL!
SAY, WHERE DID I LEAVE MY HATCHET?
KILL THEM. ANY OF THEM. ALL OF THEM.
HAVE YOU SEEN MY SATCHEL?
WILL YOU KILL THEM ALREADY?

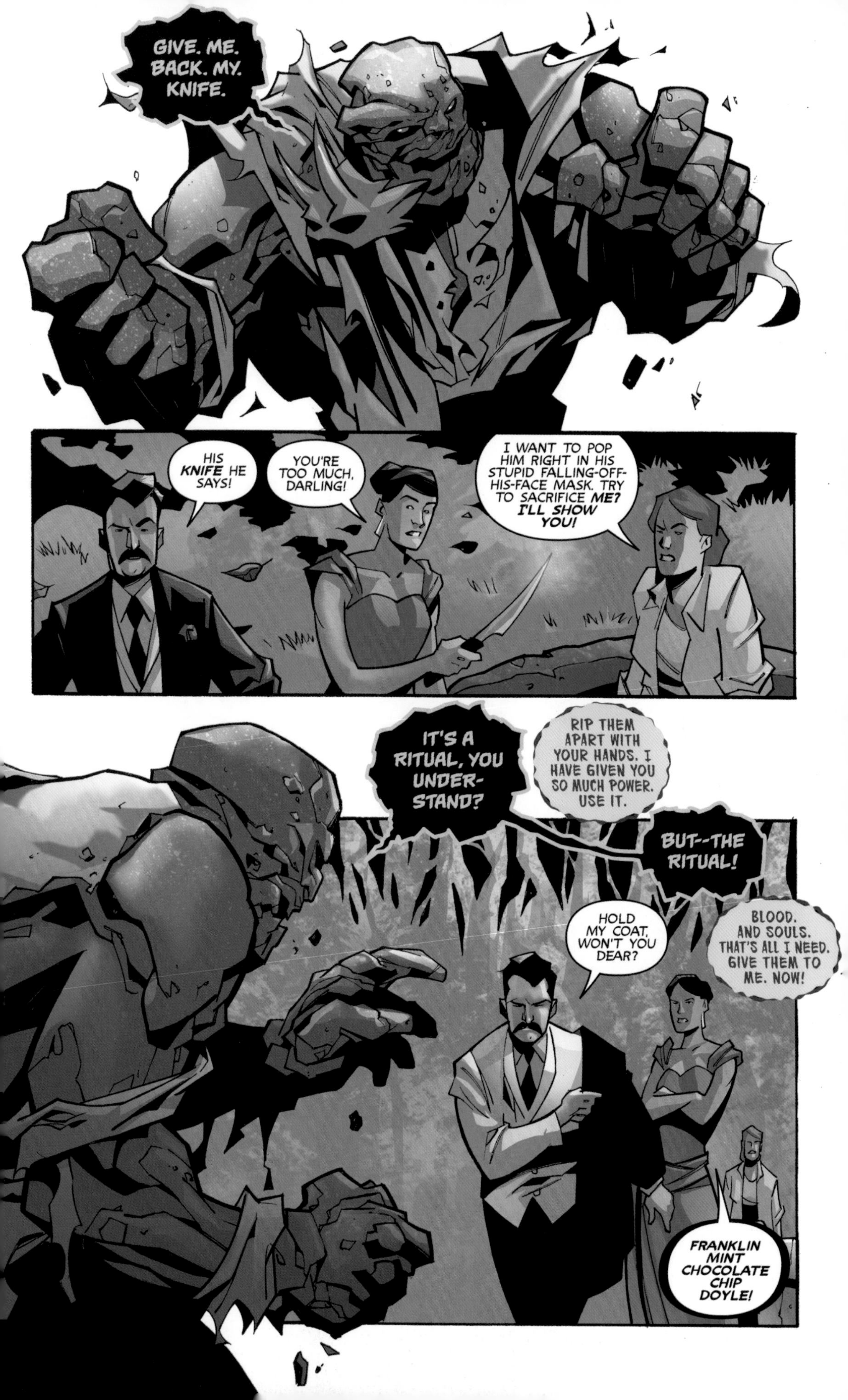
GIVE. ME. BACK. MY. KNIFE.
HIS KNIFE HE SAYS!
YOU'RE TOO MUCH, DARLING!
I WANT TO POP HIM RIGHT IN HIS STUPID FALLING-OFF-HIS-FACE MASK. TRY TO SACRIFICE ME? I'LL SHOW YOU!
IT'S A RITUAL, YOU UNDER-STAND?
RIP THEM APART WITH YOUR HANDS. I HAVE GIVEN YOU SO MUCH POWER. USE IT.
BUT--THE RITUAL!
HOLD MY COAT, WON'T YOU DEAR?
BLOOD. AND SOULS. THAT'S ALL I NEED. GIVE THEM TO ME. NOW!
FRANKLIN MINT CHOCOLATE CHIP DOYLE!

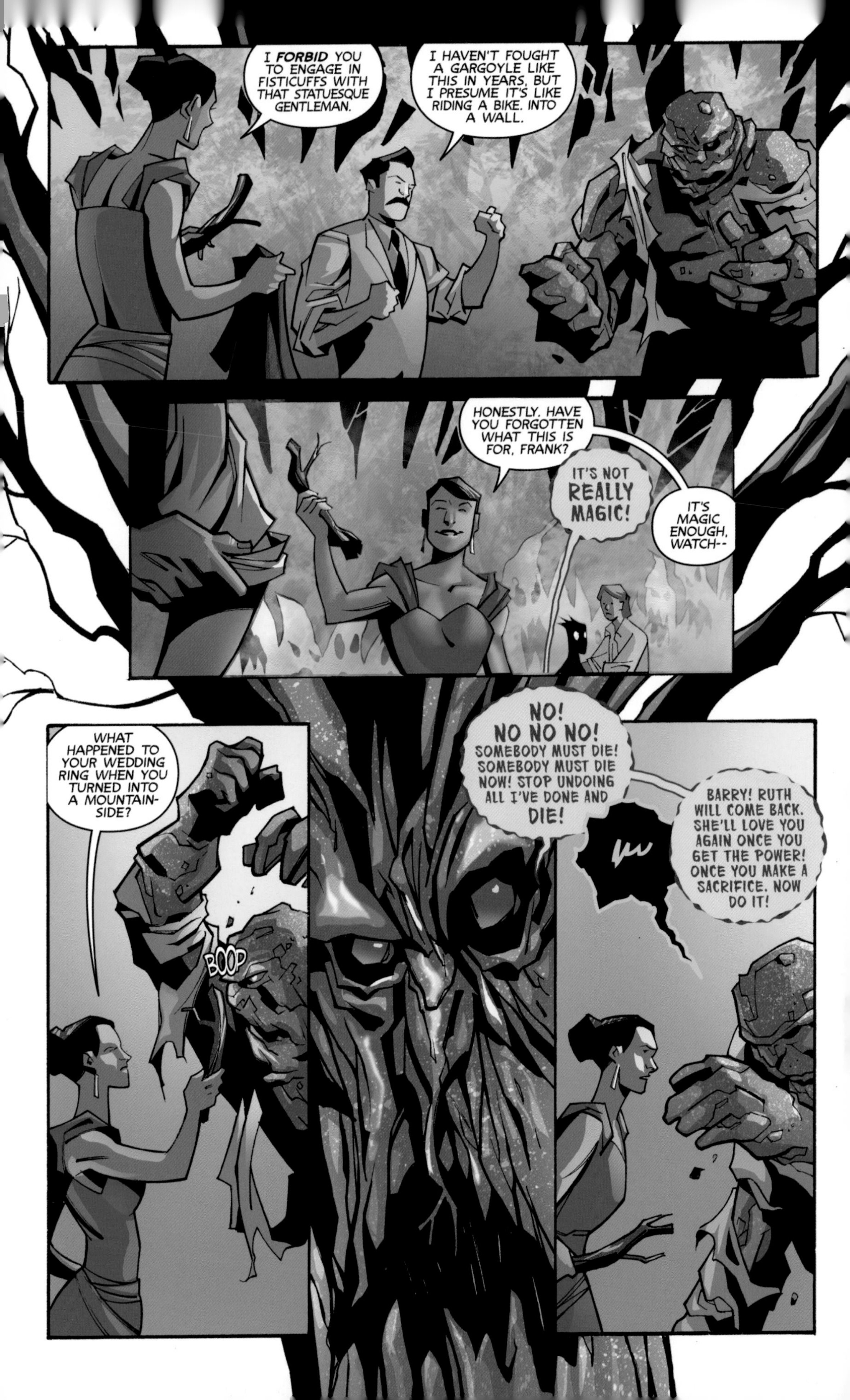
I FORBID YOU TO ENGAGE IN FISTICUFFS WITH THAT STATUESQUE GENTLEMAN.
I HAVEN'T FOUGHT A GARGOYLE LIKE THIS IN YEARS, BUT I PRESUME IT'S LIKE RIDING A BIKE. INTO A WALL.
HONESTLY. HAVE YOU FORGOTTEN WHAT THIS IS FOR, FRANK?
IT'S NOT REALLY MAGIC!
IT'S MAGIC ENOUGH, WATCH--
WHAT HAPPENED TO YOUR WEDDING RING WHEN YOU TURNED INTO A MOUNTAIN-SIDE?
BOOP
NO! NO NO NO! SOMEBODY MUST DIE! SOMEBODY MUST DIE NOW! STOP UNDOING ALL I'VE DONE AND DIE!
BARRY! RUTH WILL COME BACK. SHE'LL LOVE YOU AGAIN ONCE YOU GET THE POWER! ONCE YOU MAKE A SACRIFICE. NOW DO IT!

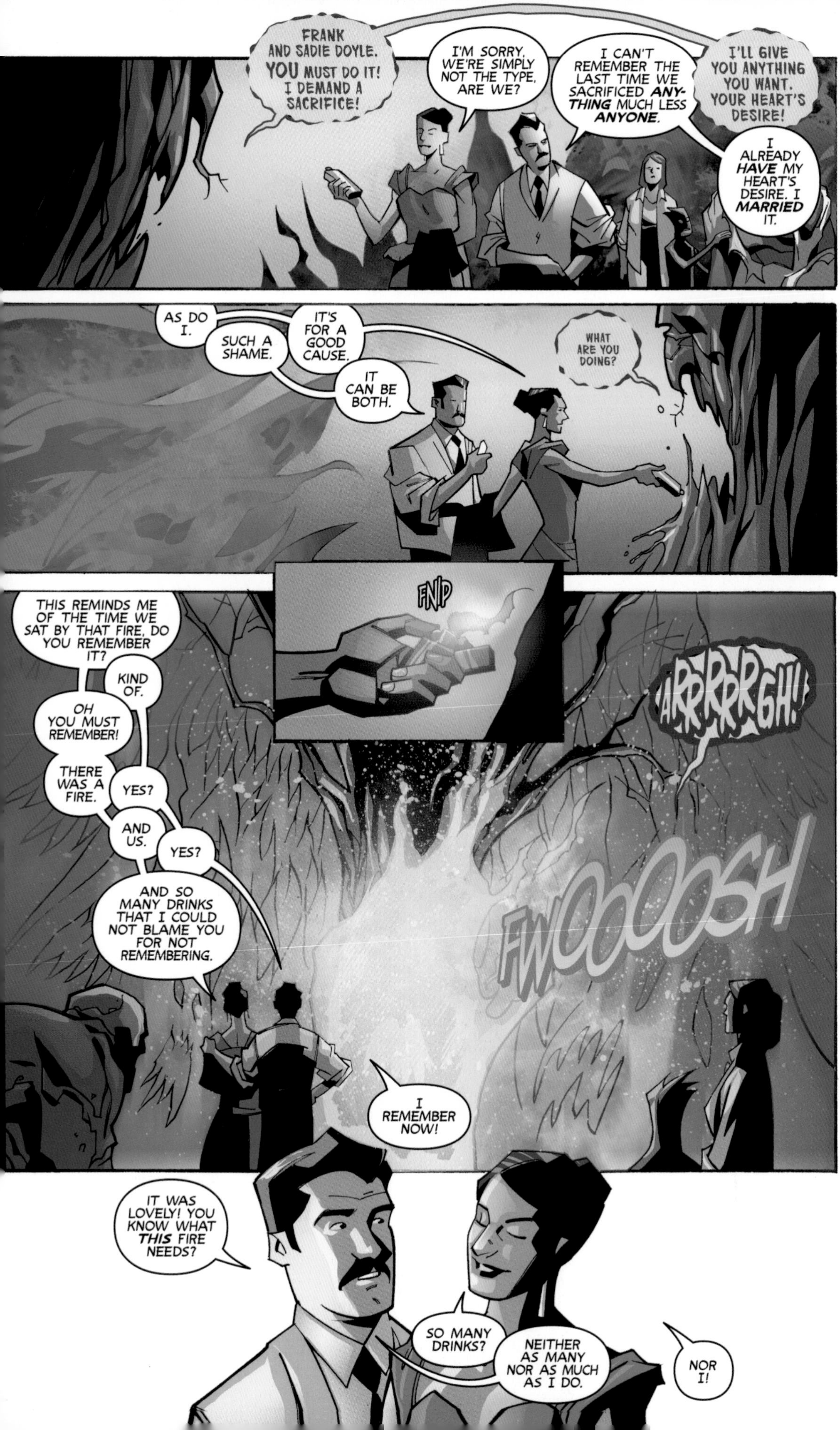
FRANK AND SADIE DOYLE. YOU MUST DO IT! I DEMAND A SACRIFICE!
I'M SORRY, WE'RE SIMPLY NOT THE TYPE, ARE WE?
I CAN'T REMEMBER THE LAST TIME WE SACRIFICED ANY-THING MUCH LESS ANYONE.
I'LL GIVE YOU ANYTHING YOU WANT. YOUR HEART'S DESIRE!
I ALREADY HAVE MY HEART'S DESIRE. I MARRIED IT.
AS DO I.
SUCH A SHAME.
IT'S FOR A GOOD CAUSE.
IT CAN BE BOTH.
WHAT ARE YOU DOING?
FNIP
THIS REMINDS ME OF THE TIME WE SAT BY THAT FIRE, DO YOU REMEMBER IT?
KIND OF.
OH YOU MUST REMEMBER!
THERE WAS A FIRE.
YES?
AND US.
YES?
AND SO MANY DRINKS THAT I COULD NOT BLAME YOU FOR NOT REMEMBERING.
ARRRRRGH!
FWOOOOSH
I REMEMBER NOW!
IT WAS LOVELY! YOU KNOW WHAT THIS FIRE NEEDS?
SO MANY DRINKS?
NEITHER AS MANY NOR AS MUCH AS I DO.
NOR I!

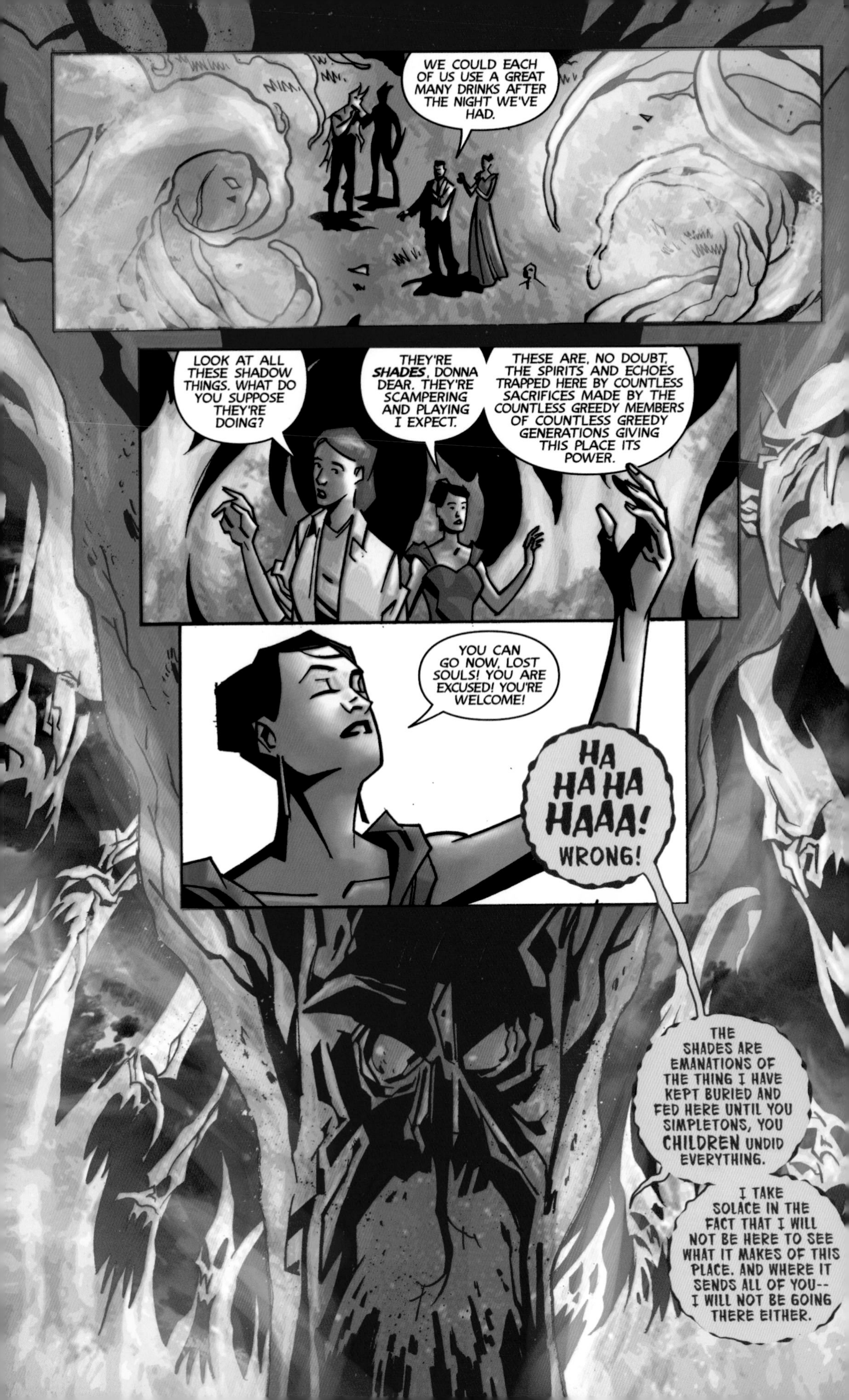
WE COULD EACH OF US USE A GREAT MANY DRINKS AFTER THE NIGHT WE'VE HAD.
LOOK AT ALL THESE SHADOW THINGS. WHAT DO YOU SUPPOSE THEY'RE DOING?
THEY'RE *SHADES*, DONNA DEAR. THEY'RE SCAMPERING AND PLAYING I EXPECT.
THESE ARE, NO DOUBT, THE SPIRITS AND ECHOES TRAPPED HERE BY COUNTLESS SACRIFICES MADE BY THE COUNTLESS GREEDY MEMBERS OF COUNTLESS GREEDY GENERATIONS GIVING THIS PLACE ITS POWER.
YOU CAN GO NOW, LOST SOULS! YOU ARE EXCUSED! YOU'RE WELCOME!
HA HA HA HAAA! WRONG!
THE SHADES ARE EMANATIONS OF THE THING I HAVE KEPT BURIED AND FED HERE UNTIL YOU SIMPLETONS, YOU CHILDREN UNDID EVERYTHING.
I TAKE SOLACE IN THE FACT THAT I WILL NOT BE HERE TO SEE WHAT IT MAKES OF THIS PLACE. AND WHERE IT SENDS ALL OF YOU-- I WILL NOT BE GOING THERE EITHER.

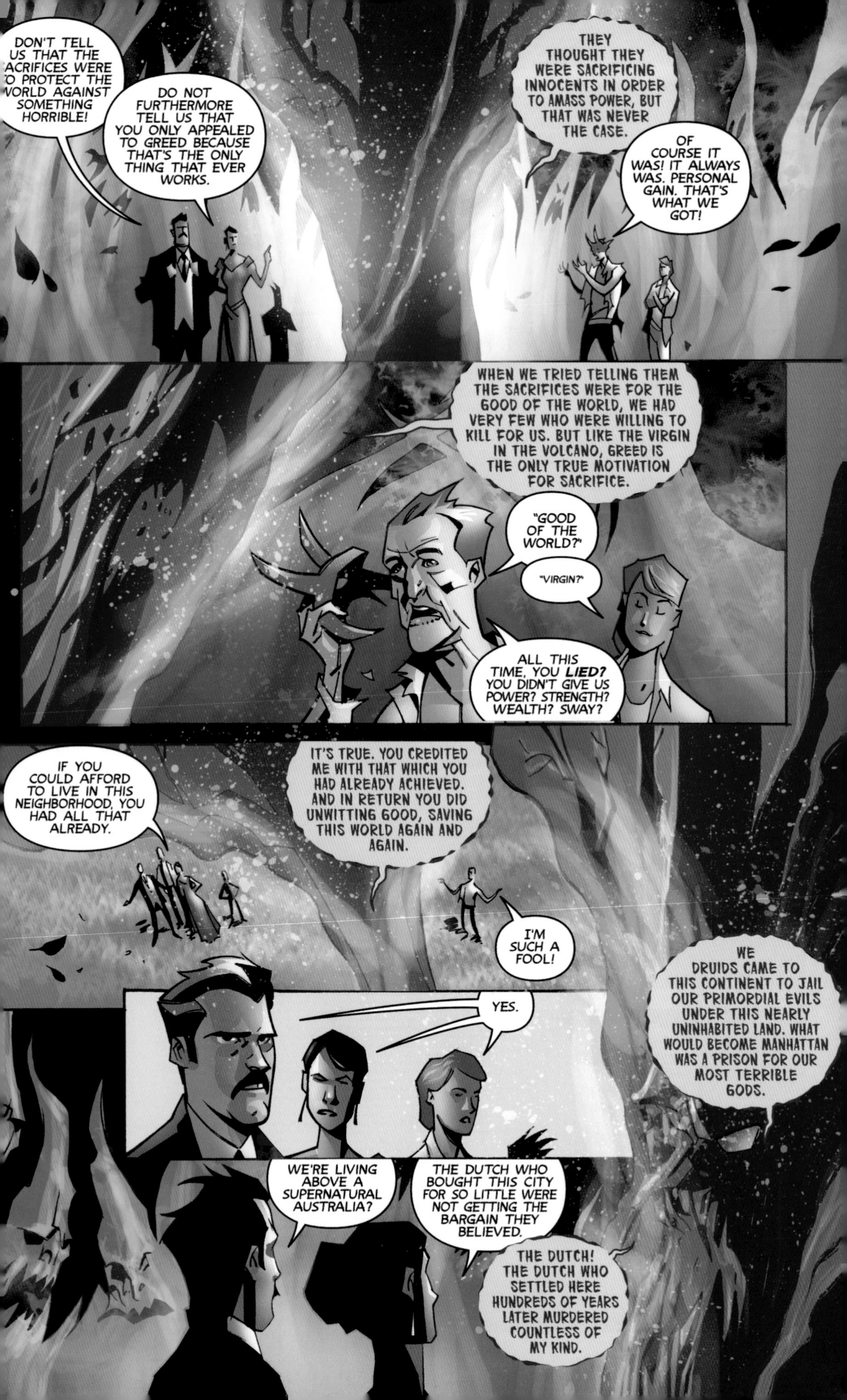
DON'T TELL US THAT THE SACRIFICES WERE TO PROTECT THE WORLD AGAINST SOMETHING HORRIBLE!
DO NOT FURTHERMORE TELL US THAT YOU ONLY APPEALED TO GREED BECAUSE THAT'S THE ONLY THING THAT EVER WORKS.
THEY THOUGHT THEY WERE SACRIFICING INNOCENTS IN ORDER TO AMASS POWER, BUT THAT WAS NEVER THE CASE.
OF COURSE IT WAS! IT ALWAYS WAS. PERSONAL GAIN. THAT'S WHAT WE GOT!
WHEN WE TRIED TELLING THEM THE SACRIFICES WERE FOR THE GOOD OF THE WORLD, WE HAD VERY FEW WHO WERE WILLING TO KILL FOR US. BUT LIKE THE VIRGIN IN THE VOLCANO, GREED IS THE ONLY TRUE MOTIVATION FOR SACRIFICE.
"GOOD OF THE WORLD?"
"VIRGIN?"
ALL THIS TIME, YOU ***LIED?*** YOU DIDN'T GIVE US POWER? STRENGTH? WEALTH? SWAY?
IF YOU COULD AFFORD TO LIVE IN THIS NEIGHBORHOOD, YOU HAD ALL THAT ALREADY.
IT'S TRUE. YOU CREDITED ME WITH THAT WHICH YOU HAD ALREADY ACHIEVED. AND IN RETURN YOU DID UNWITTING GOOD, SAVING THIS WORLD AGAIN AND AGAIN.
I'M SUCH A FOOL!
YES.
WE DRUIDS CAME TO THIS CONTINENT TO JAIL OUR PRIMORDIAL EVILS UNDER THIS NEARLY UNINHABITED LAND. WHAT WOULD BECOME MANHATTAN WAS A PRISON FOR OUR MOST TERRIBLE GODS.
WE'RE LIVING ABOVE A SUPERNATURAL AUSTRALIA?
THE DUTCH WHO BOUGHT THIS CITY FOR SO LITTLE WERE NOT GETTING THE BARGAIN THEY BELIEVED.
THE DUTCH! THE DUTCH WHO SETTLED HERE HUNDREDS OF YEARS LATER MURDERED COUNTLESS OF MY KIND.

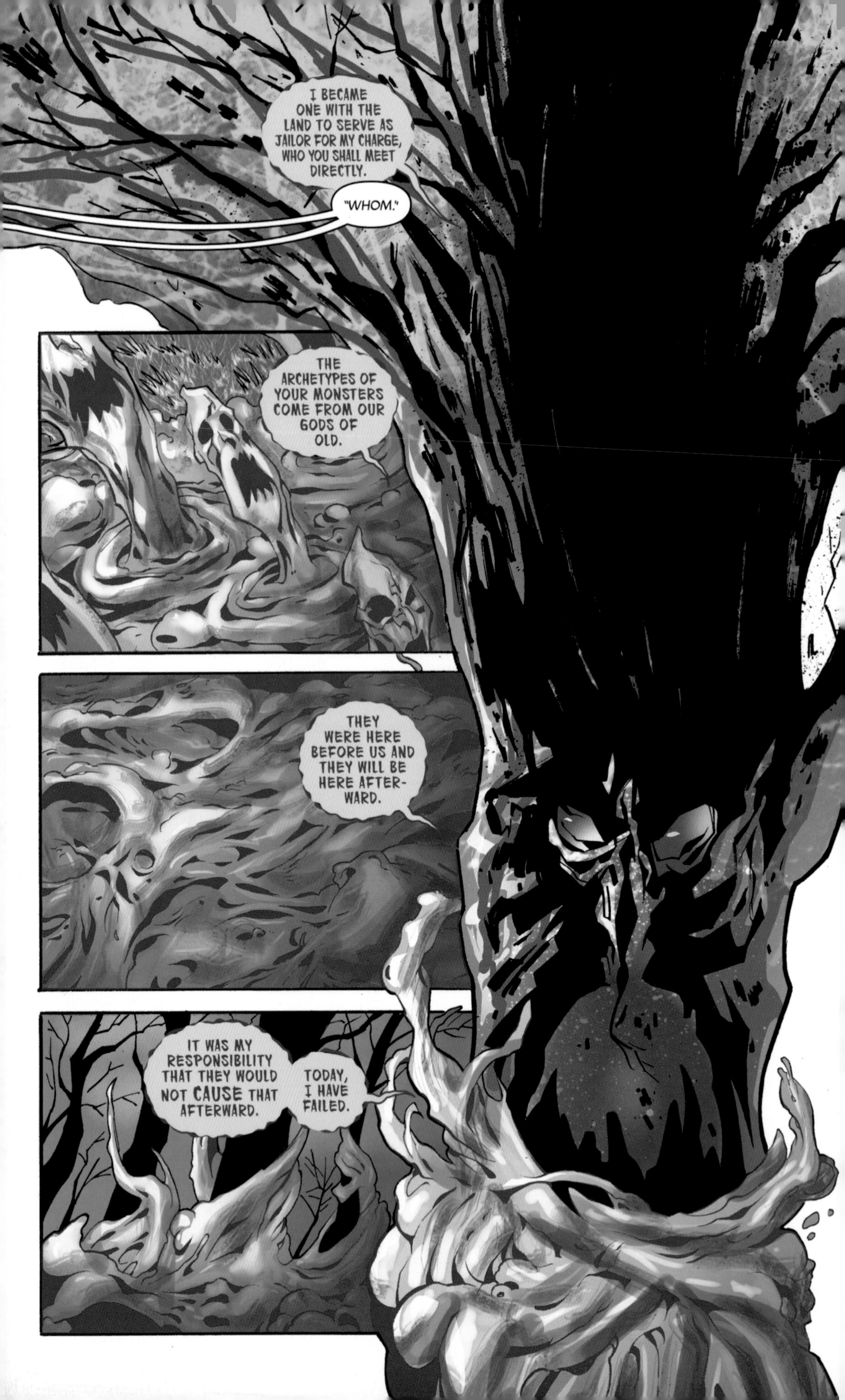
I BECAME ONE WITH THE LAND TO SERVE AS JAILOR FOR MY CHARGE, WHO YOU SHALL MEET DIRECTLY.
"WHOM."
THE ARCHETYPES OF YOUR MONSTERS COME FROM OUR GODS OF OLD.
THEY WERE HERE BEFORE US AND THEY WILL BE HERE AFTER-WARD.
IT WAS MY RESPONSIBILITY THAT THEY WOULD NOT CAUSE THAT AFTERWARD.
TODAY, I HAVE FAILED.

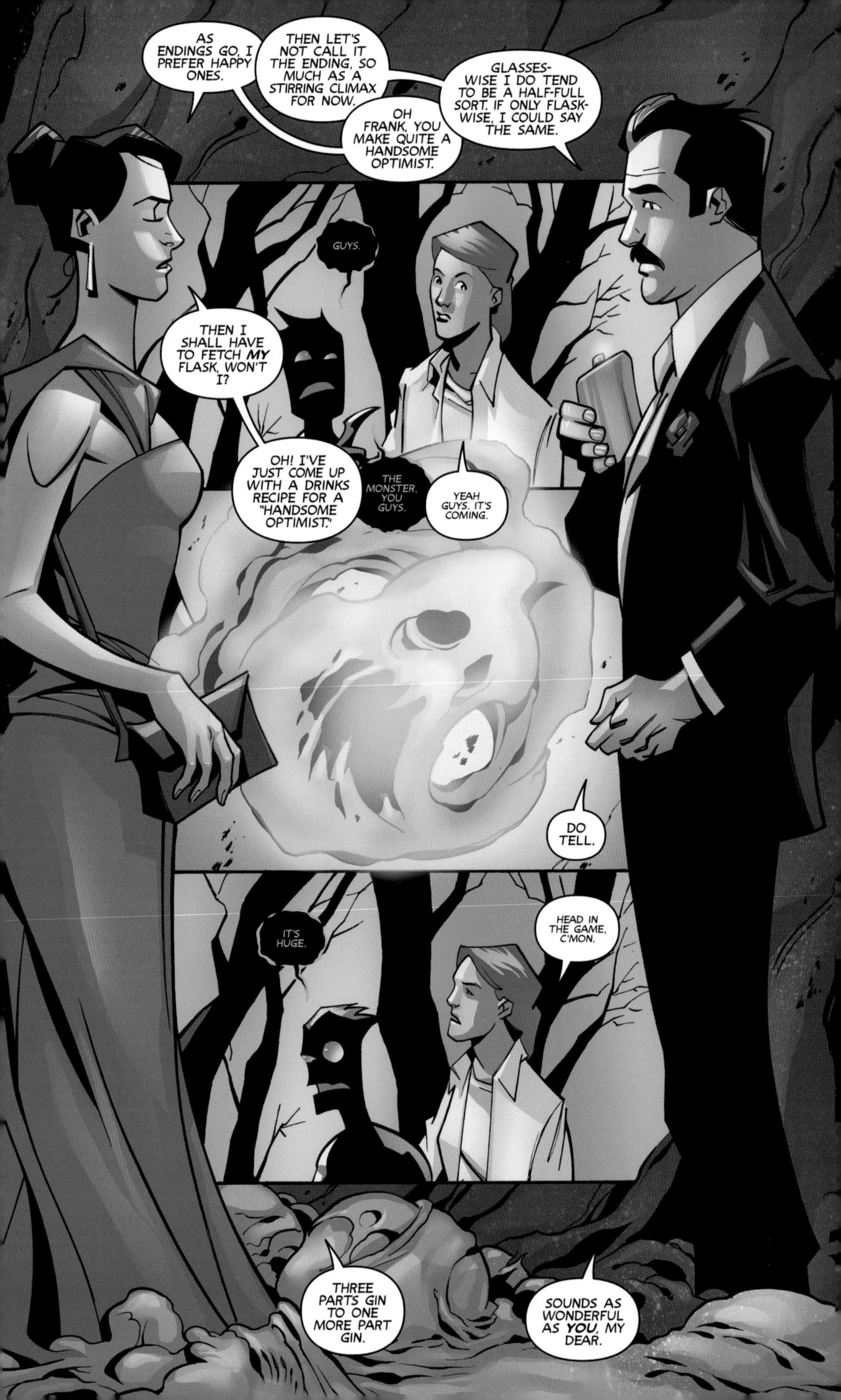
AS ENDINGS GO, I PREFER HAPPY ONES.
THEN LET'S NOT CALL IT THE ENDING, SO MUCH AS A STIRRING CLIMAX FOR NOW.
OH FRANK, YOU MAKE QUITE A HANDSOME OPTIMIST.
GLASSES-WISE I DO TEND TO BE A HALF-FULL SORT. IF ONLY FLASK-WISE, I COULD SAY THE SAME.
GUYS.
THEN I SHALL HAVE TO FETCH **MY** FLASK, WON'T I?
OH! I'VE JUST COME UP WITH A DRINKS RECIPE FOR A "HANDSOME OPTIMIST."
THE MONSTER, YOU GUYS.
YEAH GUYS, IT'S COMING.
DO TELL.
IT'S HUGE.
HEAD IN THE GAME, C'MON.
THREE PARTS GIN TO ONE MORE PART GIN.
SOUNDS AS WONDERFUL AS **YOU**, MY DEAR.

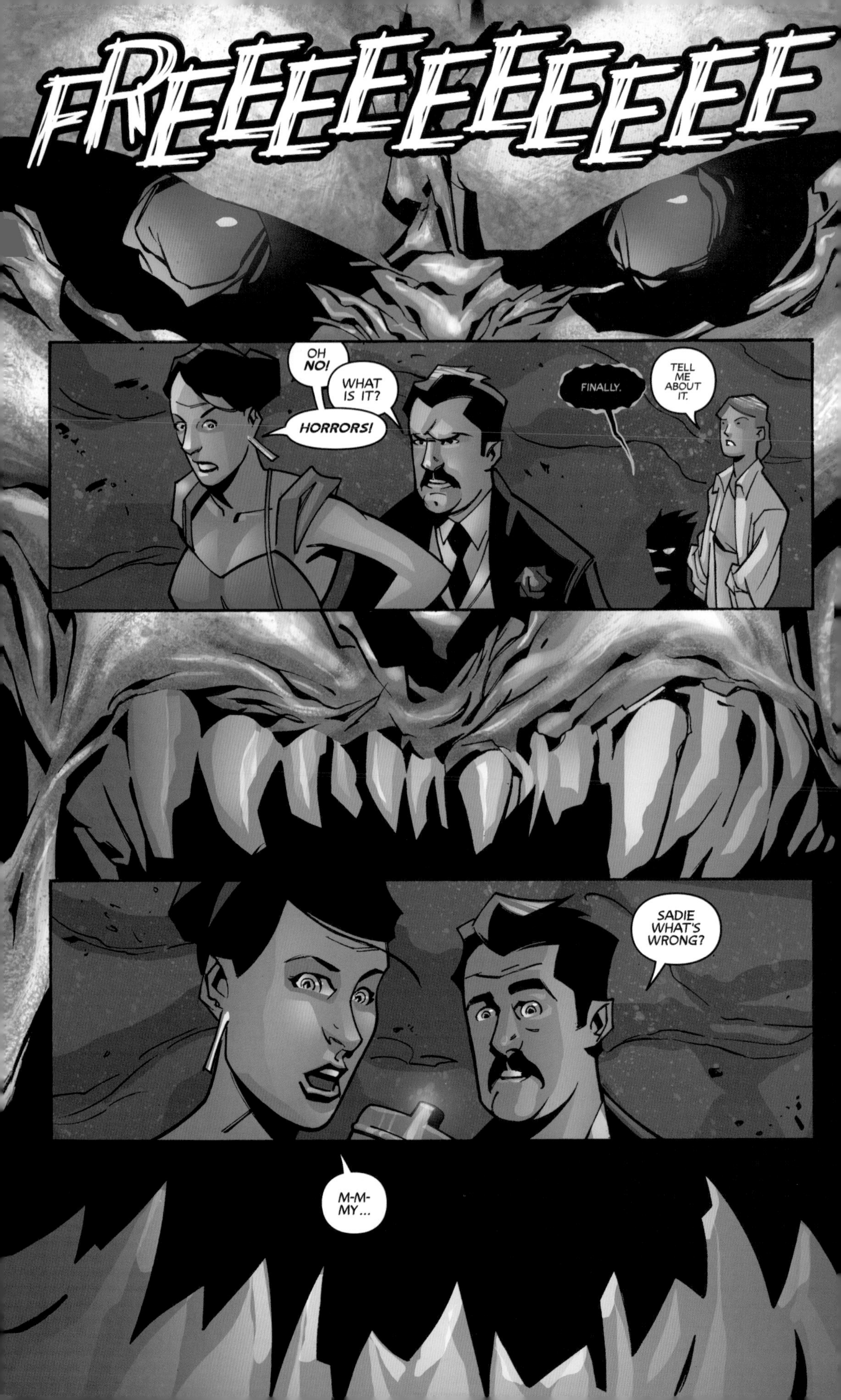
FREEEEEEEEEEEE
OH NO!
WHAT IS IT?
HORRORS!
FINALLY.
TELL ME ABOUT IT.
SADIE WHAT'S WRONG?
M-M-MY...

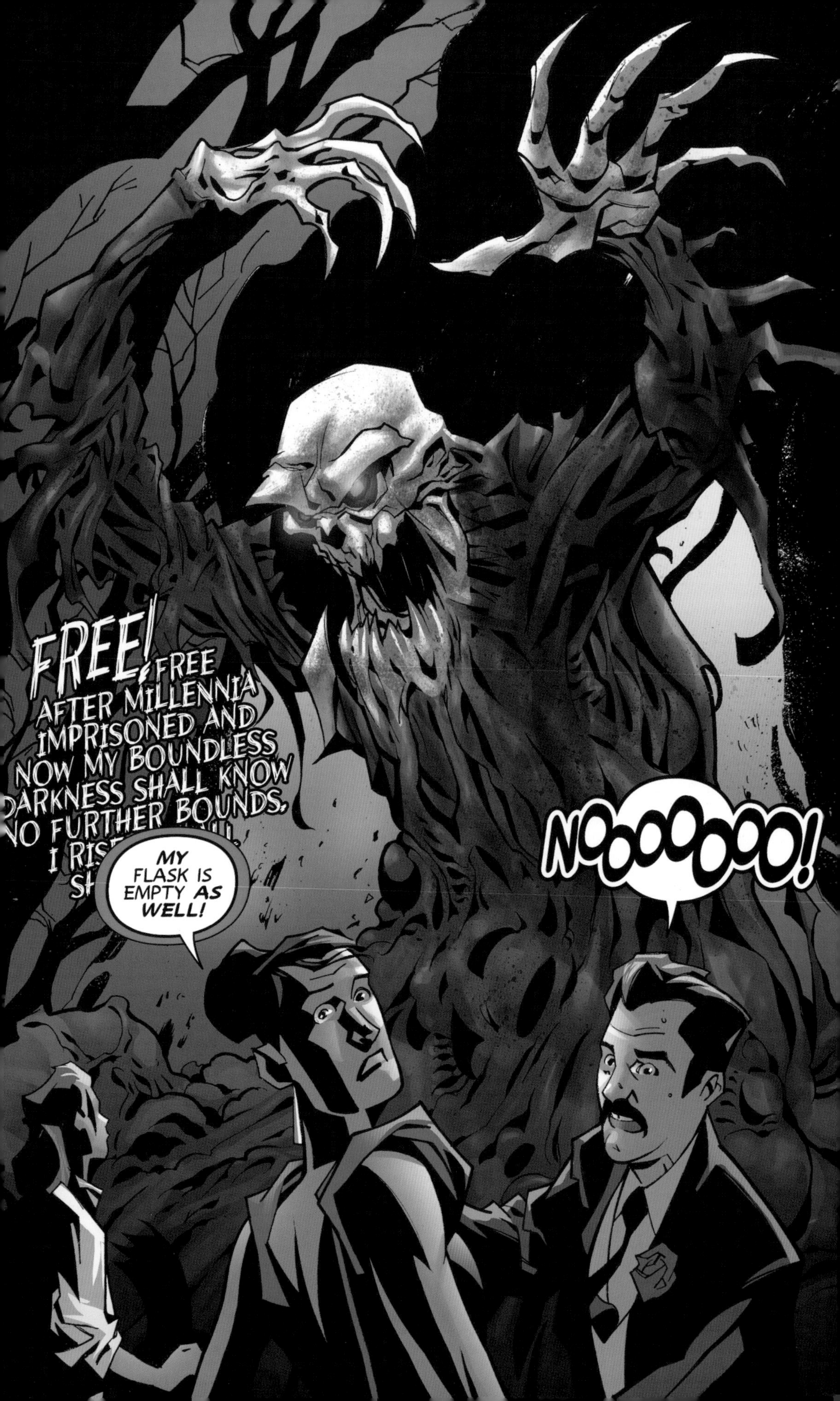
FREE! FREE
AFTER MILLENNIA IMPRISONED AND NOW MY BOUNDLESS DARKNESS SHALL KNOW NO FURTHER BOUNDS. I RISE
MY FLASK IS EMPTY AS WELL!
NOOOOOOOO!

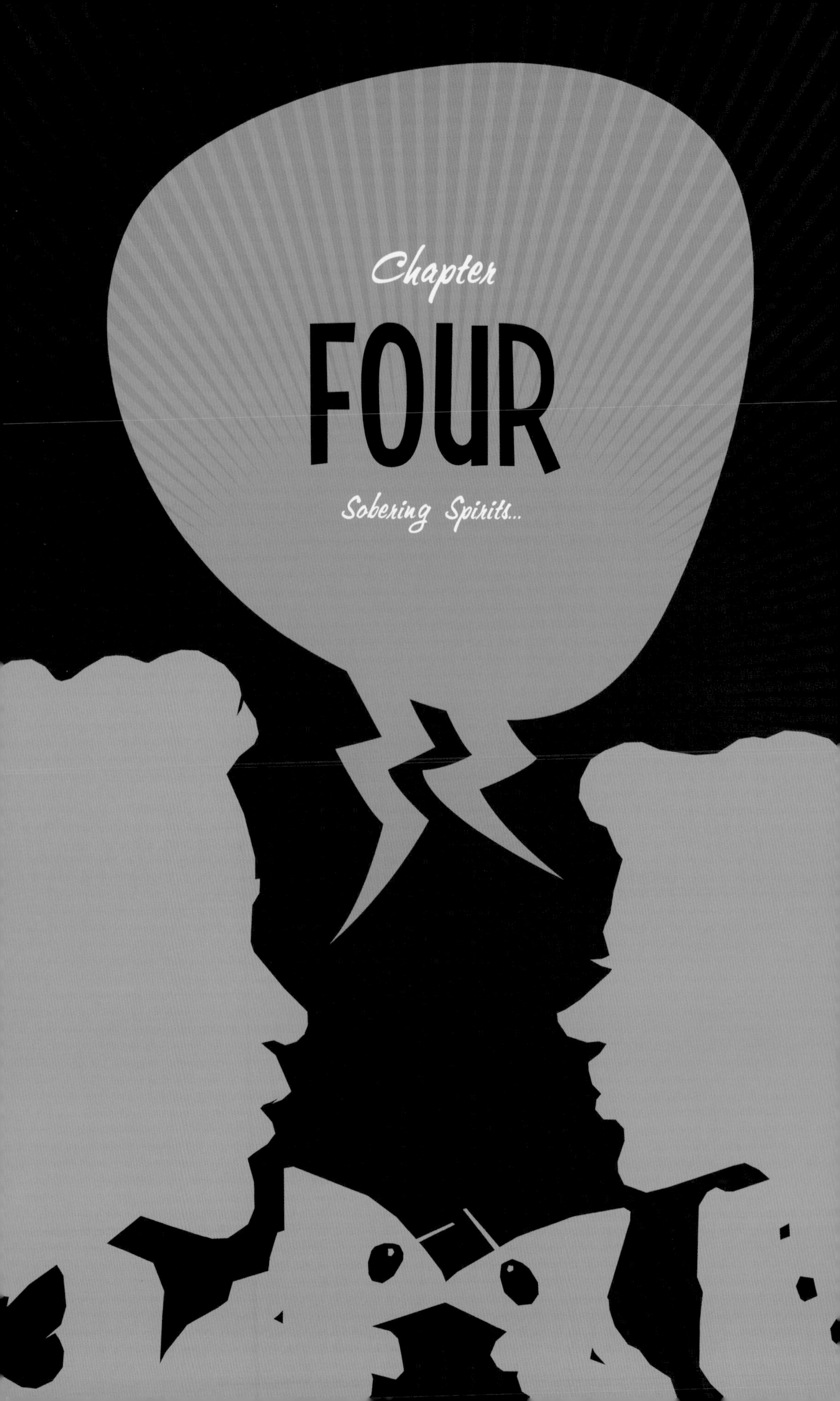
Chapter
FOUR
Sobering Spirits...

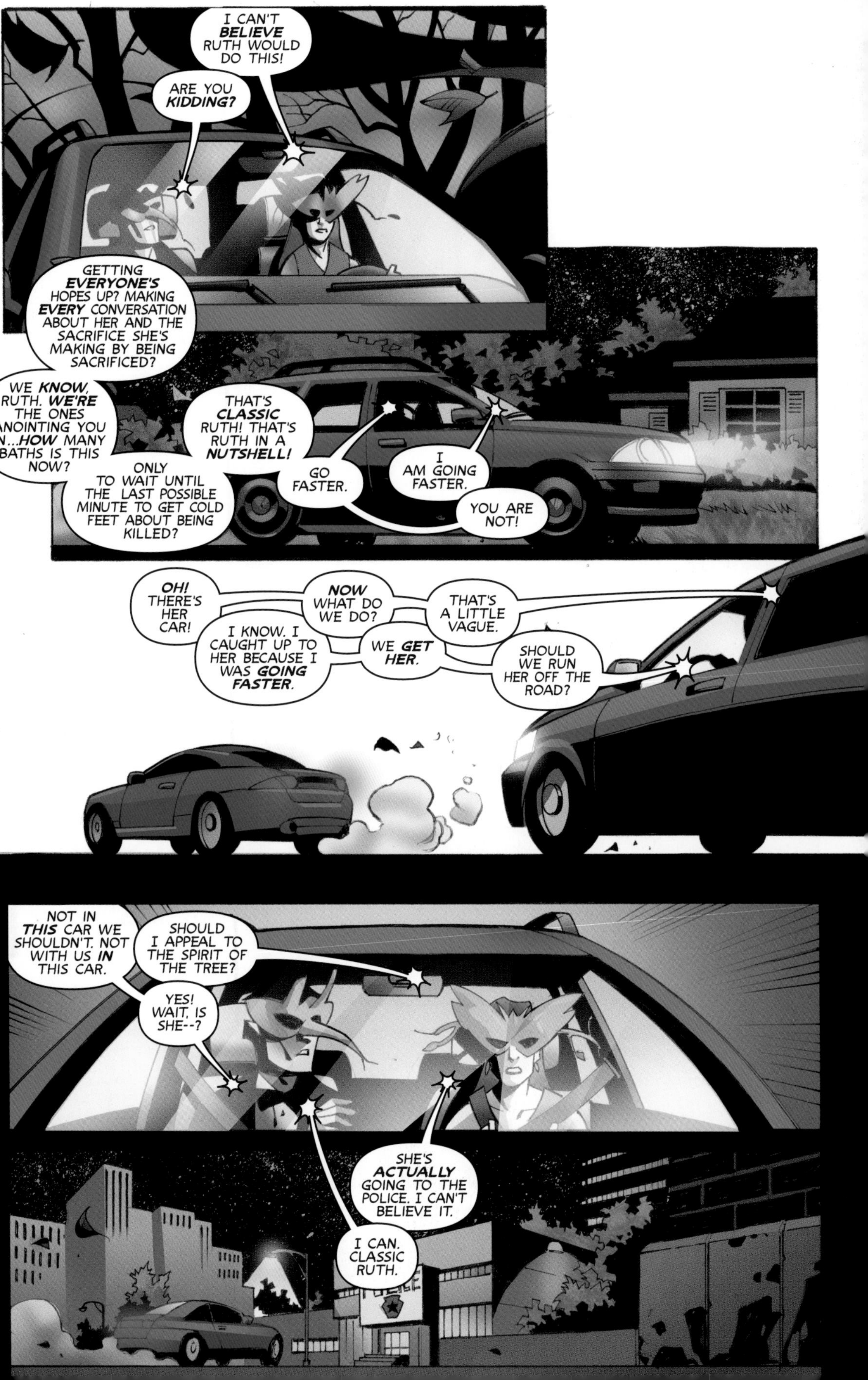
ARE YOU KIDDING?
I CAN'T BELIEVE RUTH WOULD DO THIS!
GETTING EVERYONE'S HOPES UP? MAKING EVERY CONVERSATION ABOUT HER AND THE SACRIFICE SHE'S MAKING BY BEING SACRIFICED?
WE KNOW, RUTH. WE'RE THE ONES ANOINTING YOU IN...HOW MANY BATHS IS THIS NOW?
ONLY TO WAIT UNTIL THE LAST POSSIBLE MINUTE TO GET COLD FEET ABOUT BEING KILLED?
THAT'S CLASSIC RUTH! THAT'S RUTH IN A NUTSHELL!
GO FASTER.
I AM GOING FASTER.
YOU ARE NOT!
OH! THERE'S HER CAR!
I KNOW. I CAUGHT UP TO HER BECAUSE I WAS GOING FASTER.
NOW WHAT DO WE DO?
WE GET HER.
THAT'S A LITTLE VAGUE.
SHOULD WE RUN HER OFF THE ROAD?
NOT IN THIS CAR WE SHOULDN'T. NOT WITH US IN THIS CAR.
SHOULD I APPEAL TO THE SPIRIT OF THE TREE?
YES! WAIT, IS SHE--?
SHE'S ACTUALLY GOING TO THE POLICE. I CAN'T BELIEVE IT.
I CAN. CLASSIC RUTH.

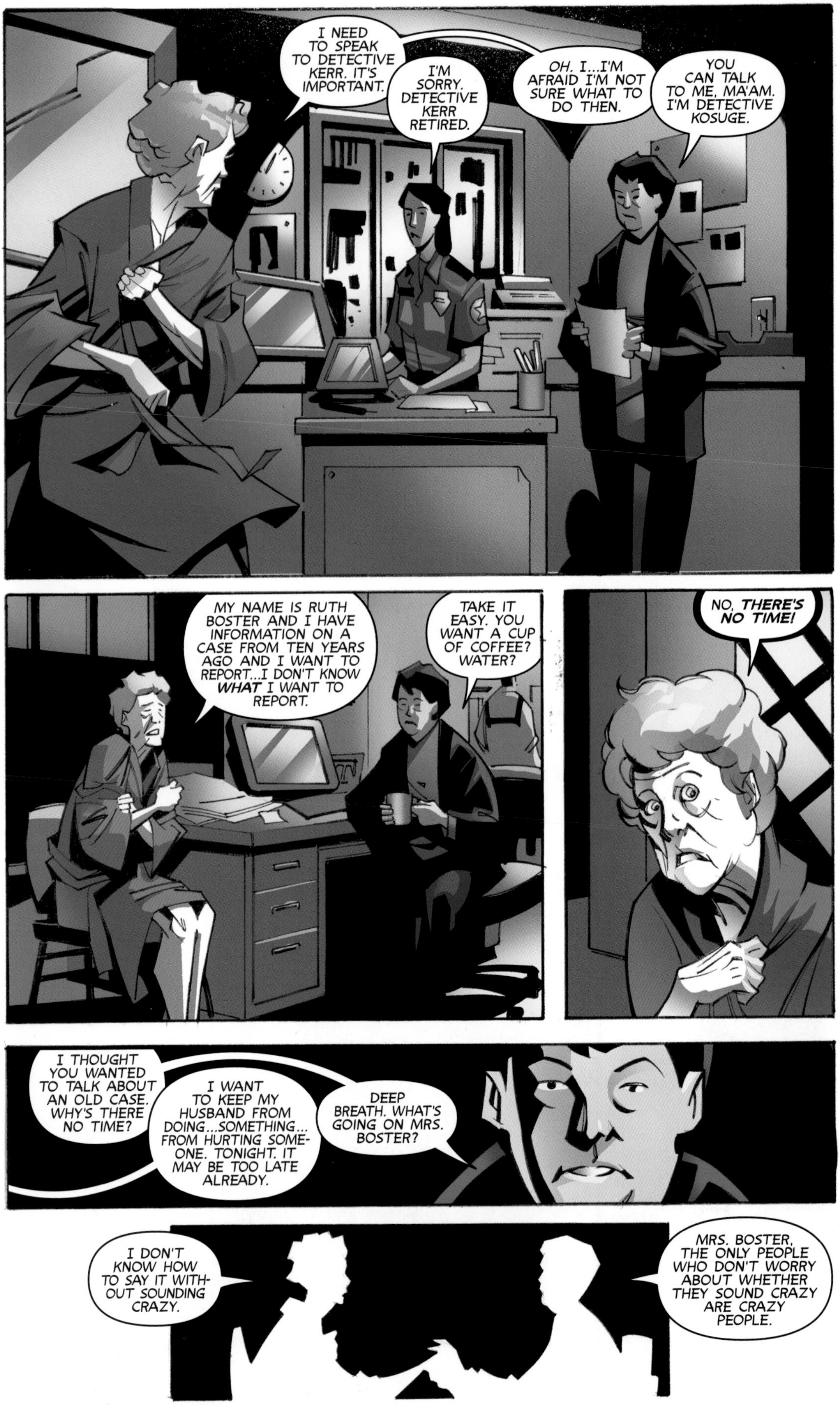
I NEED TO SPEAK TO DETECTIVE KERR. IT'S IMPORTANT.
I'M SORRY. DETECTIVE KERR RETIRED.
OH. I...I'M AFRAID I'M NOT SURE WHAT TO DO THEN.
YOU CAN TALK TO ME, MA'AM. I'M DETECTIVE KOSUGE.
MY NAME IS RUTH BOSTER AND I HAVE INFORMATION ON A CASE FROM TEN YEARS AGO AND I WANT TO REPORT...I DON'T KNOW WHAT I WANT TO REPORT.
TAKE IT EASY. YOU WANT A CUP OF COFFEE? WATER?
NO, THERE'S NO TIME!
I THOUGHT YOU WANTED TO TALK ABOUT AN OLD CASE. WHY'S THERE NO TIME?
I WANT TO KEEP MY HUSBAND FROM DOING...SOMETHING... FROM HURTING SOME-ONE. TONIGHT. IT MAY BE TOO LATE ALREADY.
DEEP BREATH. WHAT'S GOING ON MRS. BOSTER?
I DON'T KNOW HOW TO SAY IT WITH-OUT SOUNDING CRAZY.
MRS. BOSTER, THE ONLY PEOPLE WHO DON'T WORRY ABOUT WHETHER THEY SOUND CRAZY ARE CRAZY PEOPLE.

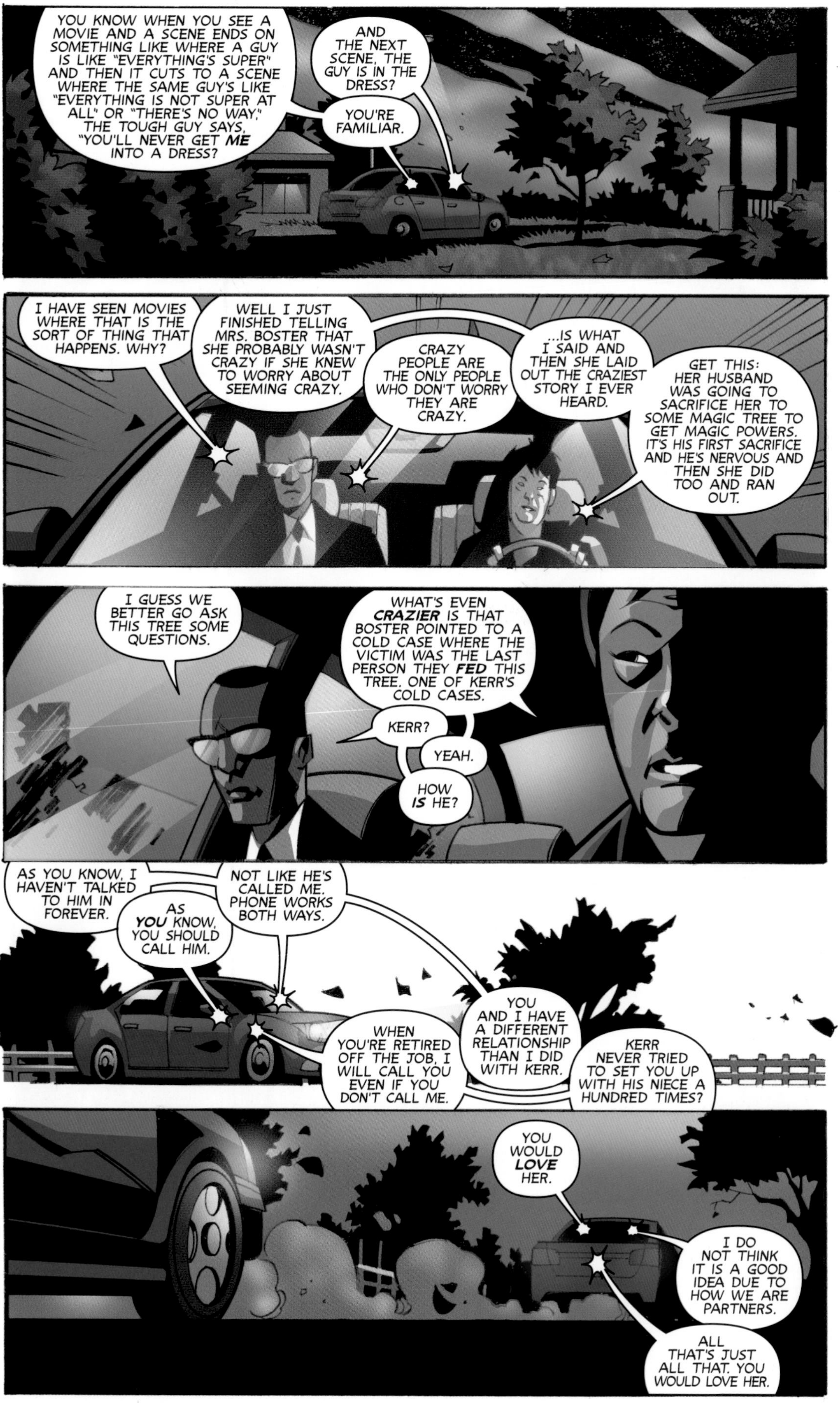
YOU KNOW WHEN YOU SEE A MOVIE AND A SCENE ENDS ON SOMETHING LIKE WHERE A GUY IS LIKE "EVERYTHING'S SUPER" AND THEN IT CUTS TO A SCENE WHERE THE SAME GUY'S LIKE "EVERYTHING IS NOT SUPER AT ALL" OR "THERE'S NO WAY," THE TOUGH GUY SAYS, "YOU'LL NEVER GET **ME** INTO A DRESS?
AND THE NEXT SCENE, THE GUY IS IN THE DRESS?
YOU'RE FAMILIAR.
I HAVE SEEN MOVIES WHERE THAT IS THE SORT OF THING THAT HAPPENS. WHY?
WELL I JUST FINISHED TELLING MRS. BOSTER THAT SHE PROBABLY WASN'T CRAZY IF SHE KNEW TO WORRY ABOUT SEEMING CRAZY.
CRAZY PEOPLE ARE THE ONLY PEOPLE WHO DON'T WORRY THEY ARE CRAZY.
...IS WHAT I SAID AND THEN SHE LAID OUT THE CRAZIEST STORY I EVER HEARD.
GET THIS: HER HUSBAND WAS GOING TO SACRIFICE HER TO SOME MAGIC TREE TO GET MAGIC POWERS. IT'S HIS FIRST SACRIFICE AND HE'S NERVOUS AND THEN SHE DID TOO AND RAN OUT.
I GUESS WE BETTER GO ASK THIS TREE SOME QUESTIONS.
WHAT'S EVEN **CRAZIER** IS THAT BOSTER POINTED TO A COLD CASE WHERE THE VICTIM WAS THE LAST PERSON THEY **FED** THIS TREE. ONE OF KERR'S COLD CASES.
KERR?
YEAH.
HOW **IS** HE?
AS YOU KNOW, I HAVEN'T TALKED TO HIM IN FOREVER.
NOT LIKE HE'S CALLED ME. PHONE WORKS BOTH WAYS.
AS **YOU** KNOW, YOU SHOULD CALL HIM.
YOU AND I HAVE A DIFFERENT RELATIONSHIP THAN I DID WITH KERR.
WHEN YOU'RE RETIRED OFF THE JOB, I WILL CALL YOU EVEN IF YOU DON'T CALL ME.
KERR NEVER TRIED TO SET YOU UP WITH HIS NIECE A HUNDRED TIMES?
YOU WOULD **LOVE** HER.
I DO NOT THINK IT IS A GOOD IDEA DUE TO HOW WE ARE PARTNERS.
ALL THAT'S JUST ALL THAT. YOU WOULD LOVE HER.

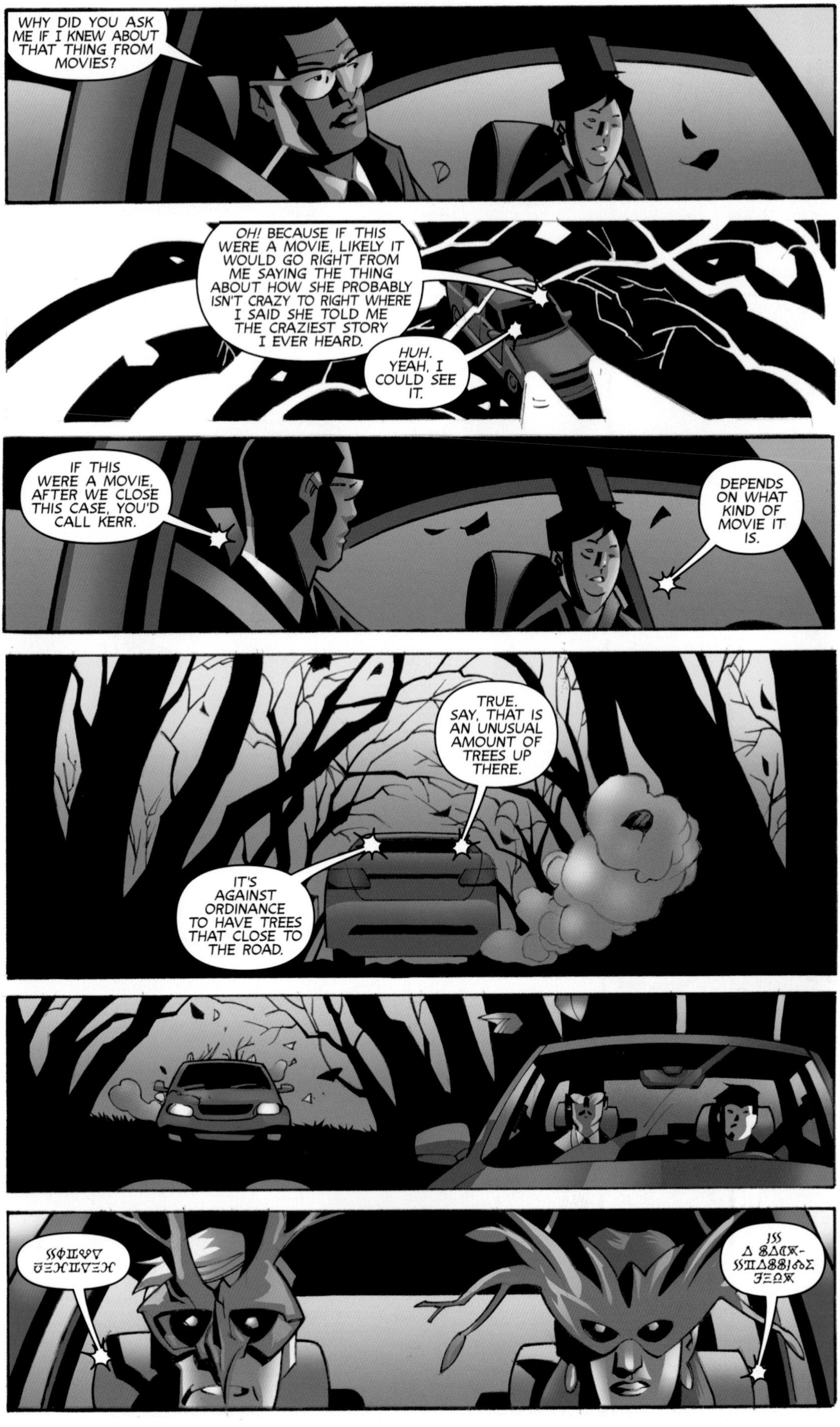
WHY DID YOU ASK ME IF I KNEW ABOUT THAT THING FROM MOVIES?
OH! BECAUSE IF THIS WERE A MOVIE, LIKELY IT WOULD GO RIGHT FROM ME SAYING THE THING ABOUT HOW SHE PROBABLY ISN'T CRAZY TO RIGHT WHERE I SAID SHE TOLD ME THE CRAZIEST STORY I EVER HEARD.
HUH. YEAH, I COULD SEE IT.
IF THIS WERE A MOVIE, AFTER WE CLOSE THIS CASE, YOU'D CALL KERR.
DEPENDS ON WHAT KIND OF MOVIE IT IS.
TRUE. SAY, THAT IS AN UNUSUAL AMOUNT OF TREES UP THERE.
IT'S AGAINST ORDINANCE TO HAVE TREES THAT CLOSE TO THE ROAD.

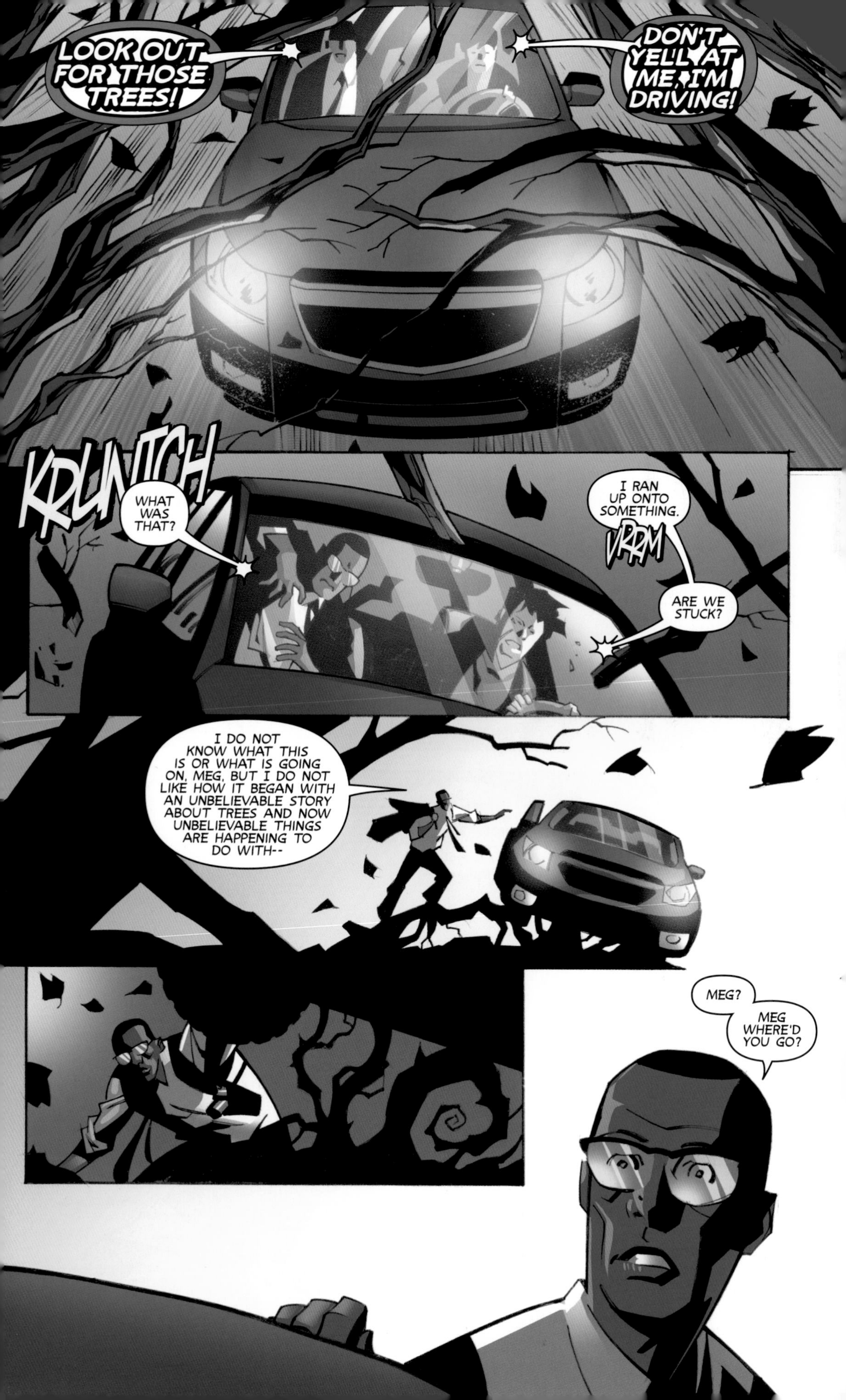
LOOK OUT FOR THOSE TREES!
DON'T YELL AT ME. I'M DRIVING!
KRUNTCH
WHAT WAS THAT?
I RAN UP ONTO SOMETHING.
VRRM
ARE WE STUCK?
I DO NOT KNOW WHAT THIS IS OR WHAT IS GOING ON, MEG, BUT I DO NOT LIKE HOW IT BEGAN WITH AN UNBELIEVABLE STORY ABOUT TREES AND NOW UNBELIEVABLE THINGS ARE HAPPENING TO DO WITH--
MEG?
MEG WHERE'D YOU GO?

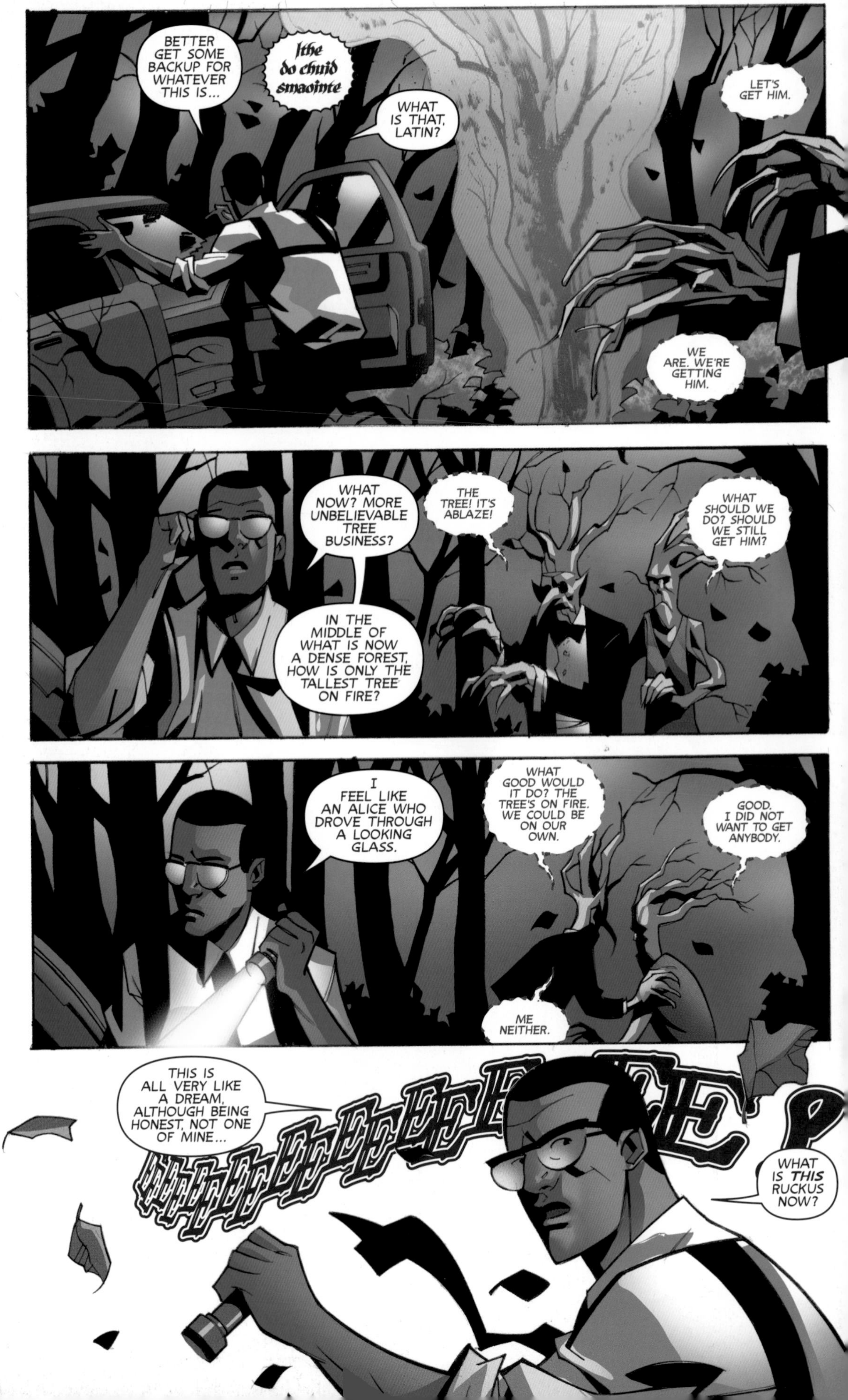
BETTER GET SOME BACKUP FOR WHATEVER THIS IS...
Ithe do chuid smaointe
WHAT IS THAT, LATIN?
LET'S GET HIM.
WE ARE. WE'RE GETTING HIM.
WHAT NOW? MORE UNBELIEVABLE TREE BUSINESS?
IN THE MIDDLE OF WHAT IS NOW A DENSE FOREST, HOW IS ONLY THE TALLEST TREE ON FIRE?
THE TREE! IT'S ABLAZE!
WHAT SHOULD WE DO? SHOULD WE STILL GET HIM?
I FEEL LIKE AN ALICE WHO DROVE THROUGH A LOOKING GLASS.
WHAT GOOD WOULD IT DO? THE TREE'S ON FIRE. WE COULD BE ON OUR OWN.
GOOD. I DID NOT WANT TO GET ANYBODY.
ME NEITHER.
THIS IS ALL VERY LIKE A DREAM, ALTHOUGH BEING HONEST, NOT ONE OF MINE...
WHAT IS **THIS** RUCKUS NOW?

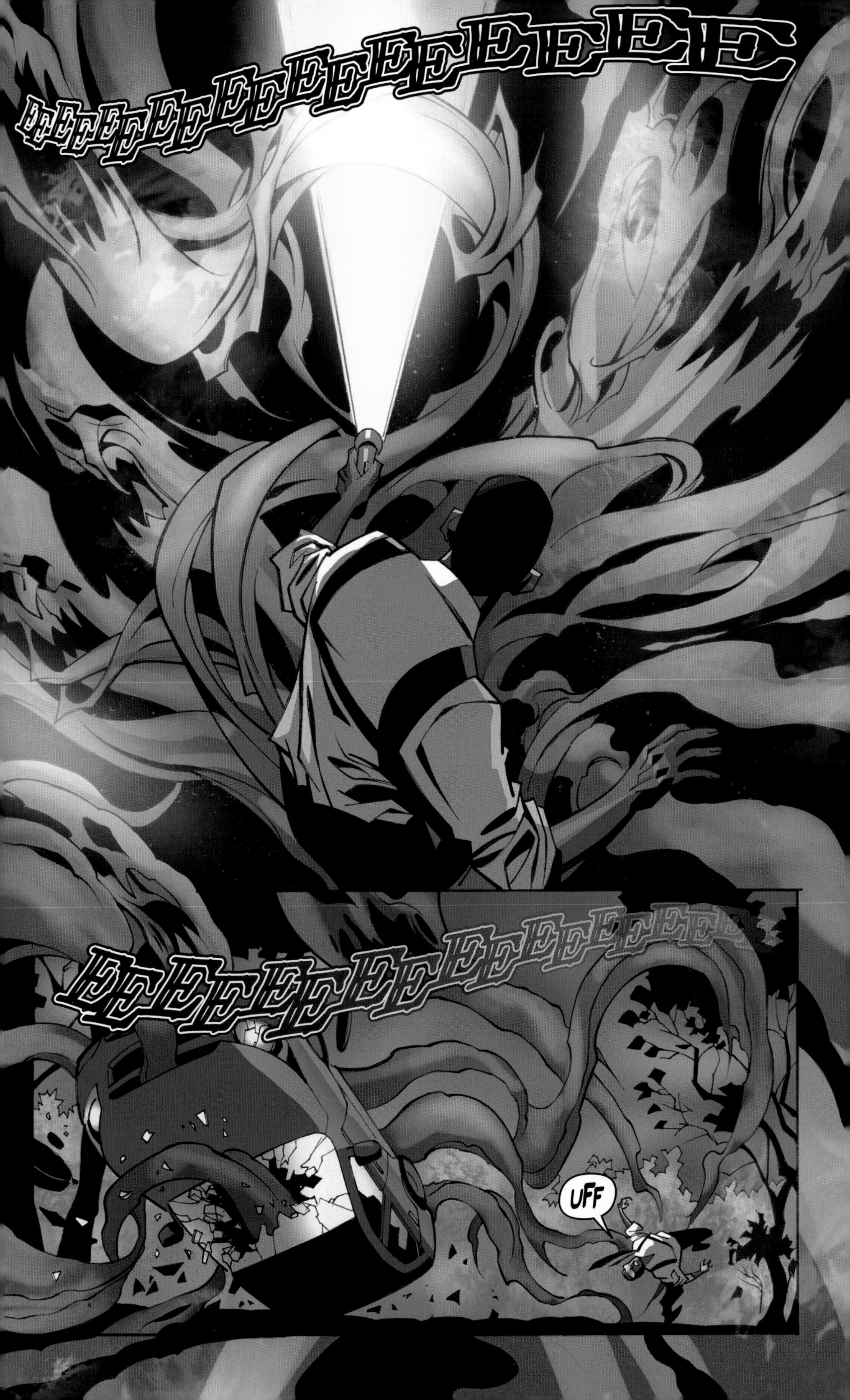

EEEEEEEEEEEEEEEE
EEEEEEEEEEEEEEE
UFF

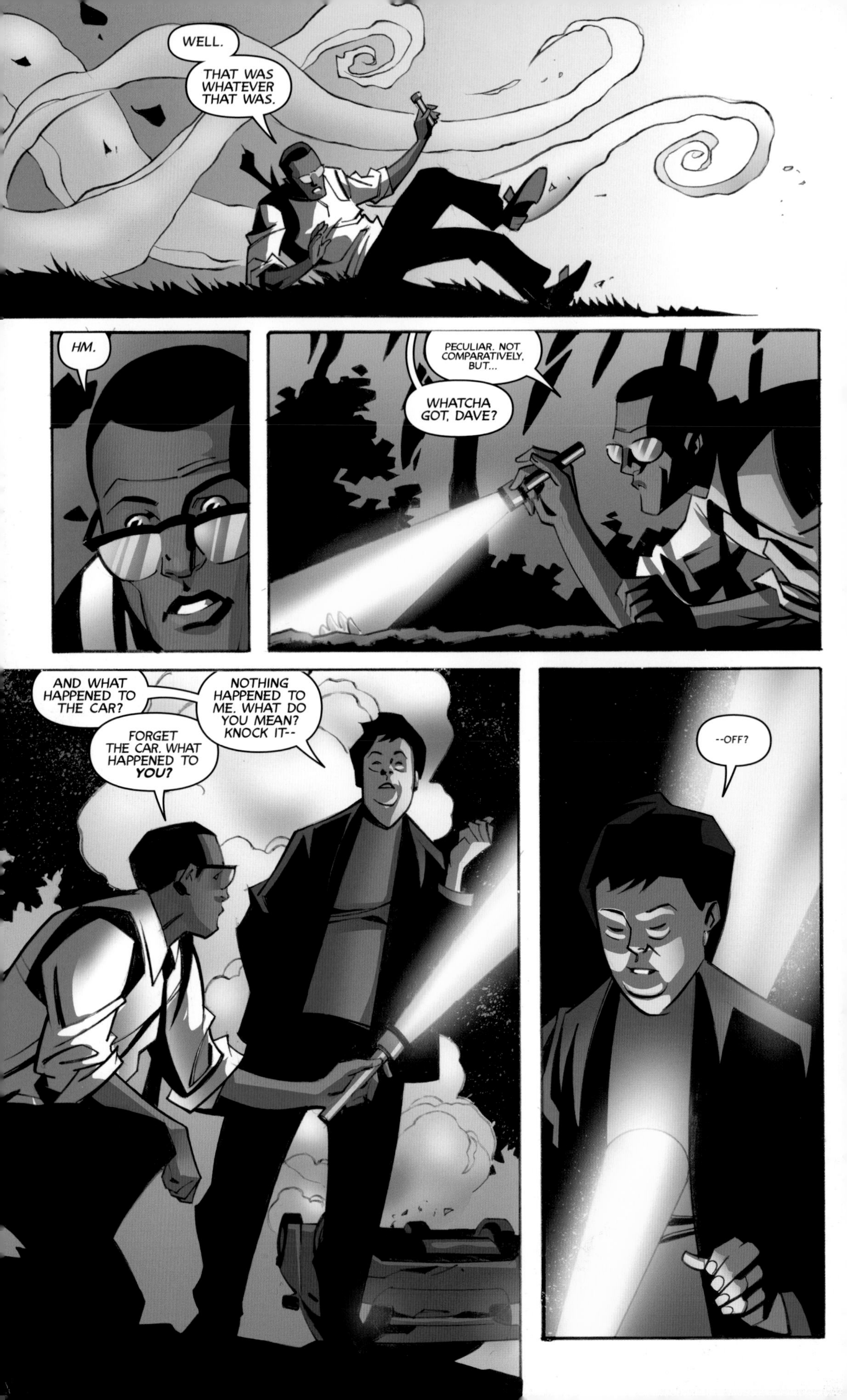
WELL.
THAT WAS WHATEVER THAT WAS.
HM.
PECULIAR. NOT COMPARATIVELY, BUT...
WHATCHA GOT, DAVE?
AND WHAT HAPPENED TO THE CAR?
FORGET THE CAR. WHAT HAPPENED TO *YOU?*
NOTHING HAPPENED TO ME. WHAT DO YOU MEAN? KNOCK IT--
--OFF?

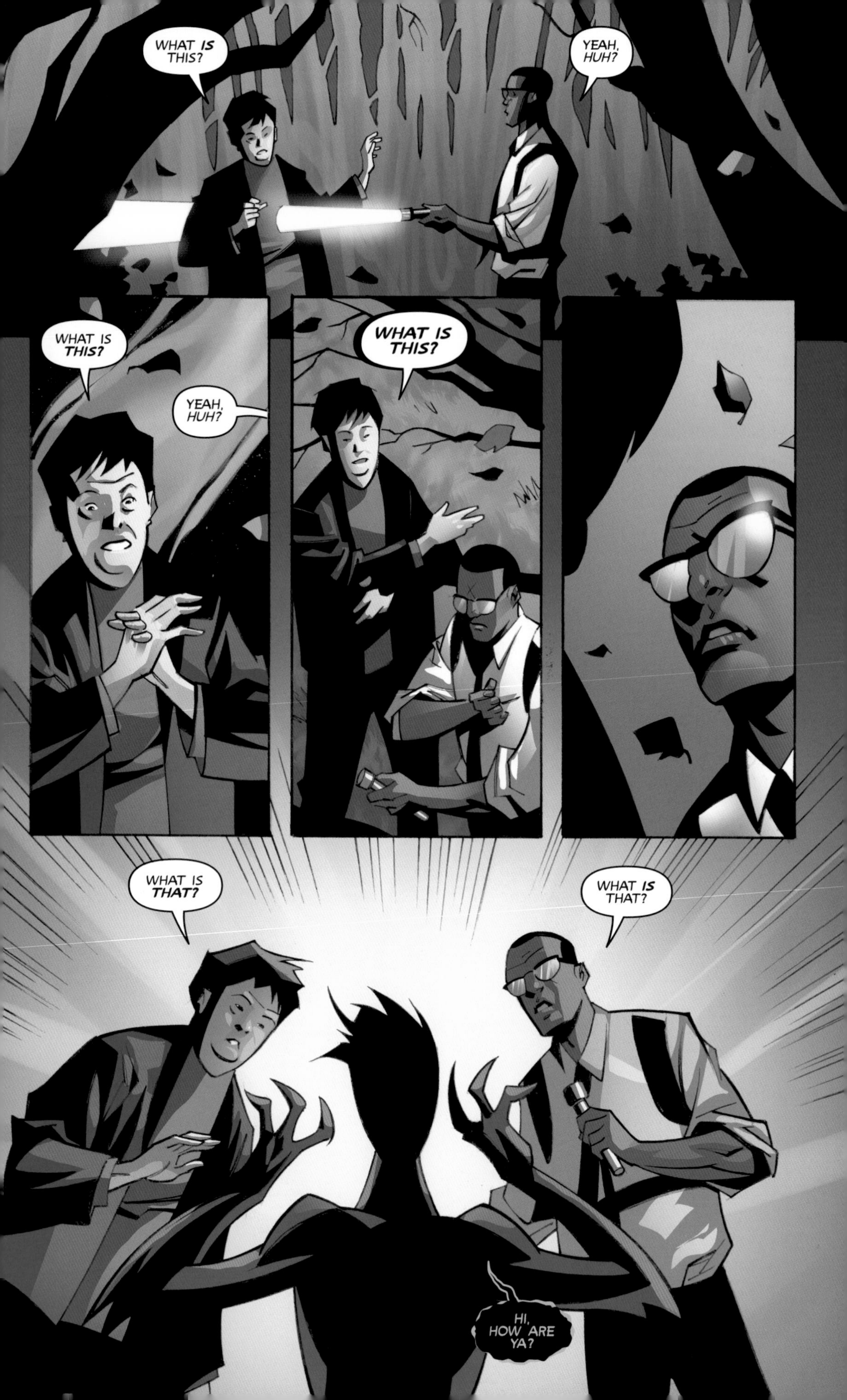
WHAT IS THIS?
YEAH, HUH?
WHAT IS THIS?
YEAH, HUH?
WHAT IS THIS?
WHAT IS THAT?
WHAT IS THAT?
HI, HOW ARE YA?

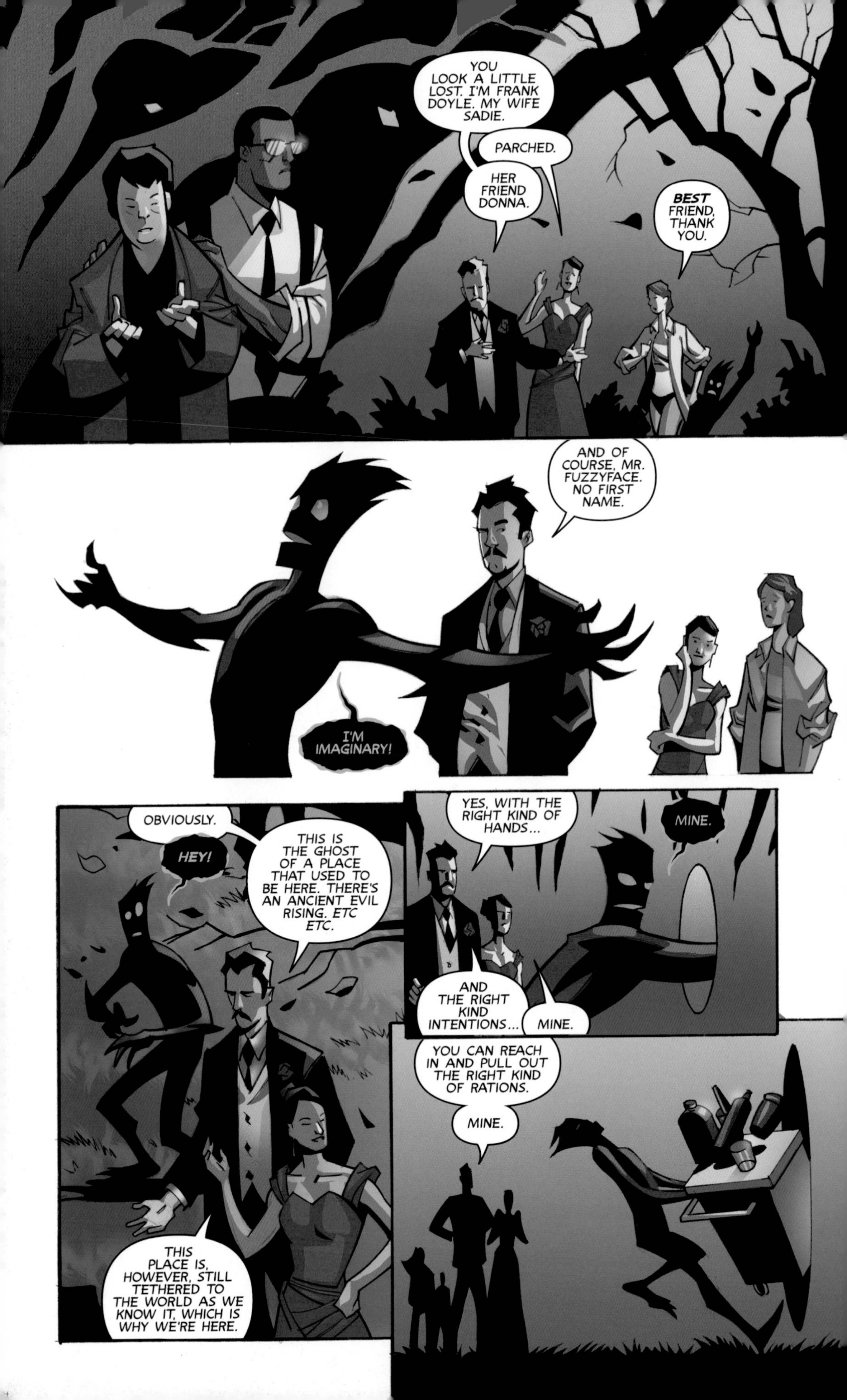

YOU LOOK A LITTLE LOST. I'M FRANK DOYLE. MY WIFE SADIE.
PARCHED.
HER FRIEND DONNA.
BEST FRIEND, THANK YOU.
AND OF COURSE, MR. FUZZYFACE. NO FIRST NAME.
I'M IMAGINARY!
OBVIOUSLY.
HEY!
THIS IS THE GHOST OF A PLACE THAT USED TO BE HERE. THERE'S AN ANCIENT EVIL RISING. ETC ETC.
THIS PLACE IS, HOWEVER, STILL TETHERED TO THE WORLD AS WE KNOW IT, WHICH IS WHY WE'RE HERE.
YES, WITH THE RIGHT KIND OF HANDS...
MINE.
AND THE RIGHT KIND INTENTIONS...
MINE.
YOU CAN REACH IN AND PULL OUT THE RIGHT KIND OF RATIONS.
MINE.

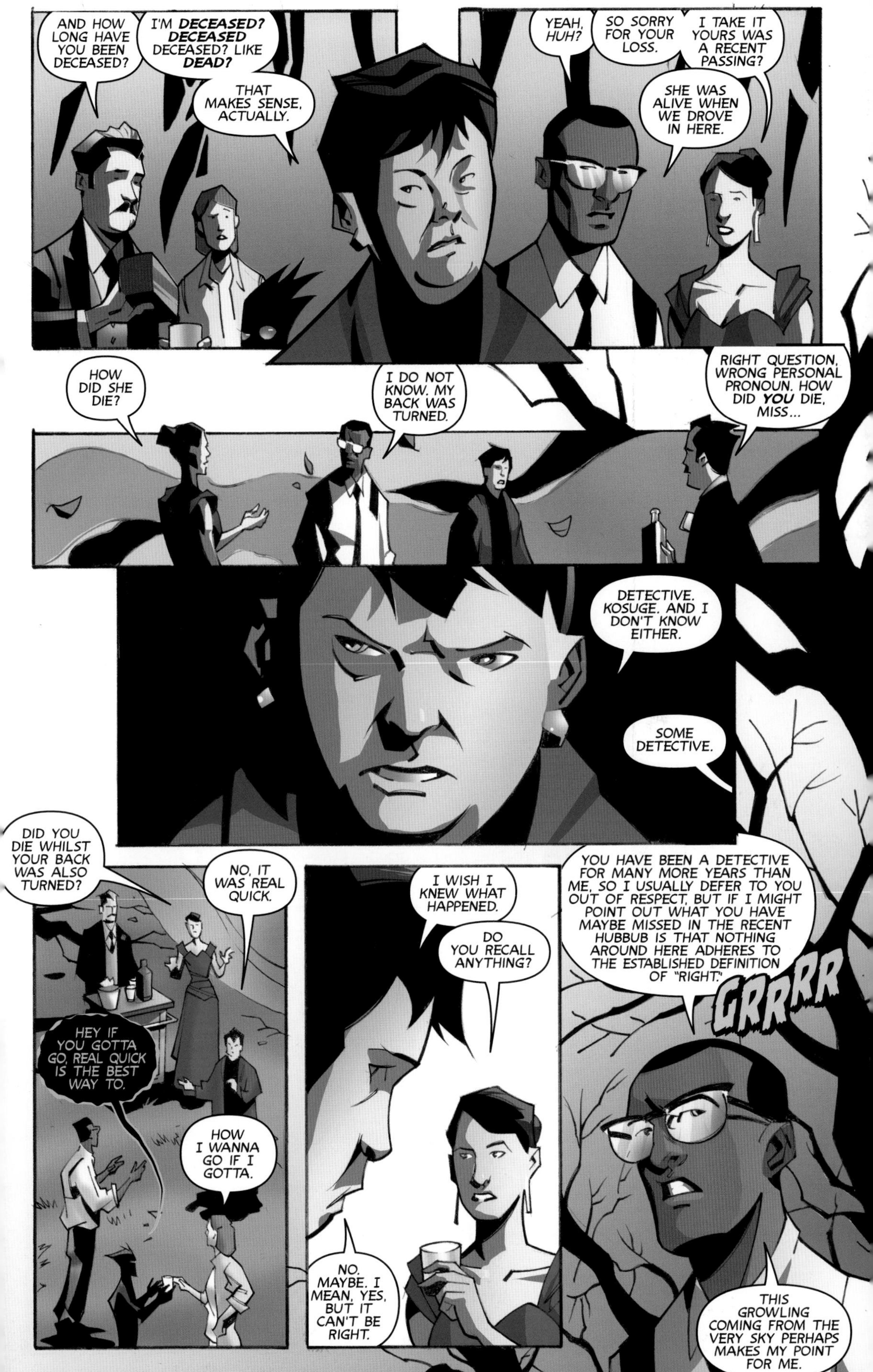
AND HOW LONG HAVE YOU BEEN DECEASED?
I'M **DECEASED? DECEASED** DECEASED? LIKE **DEAD?**
THAT MAKES SENSE, ACTUALLY.
YEAH, HUH?
SO SORRY FOR YOUR LOSS.
I TAKE IT YOURS WAS A RECENT PASSING?
SHE WAS ALIVE WHEN WE DROVE IN HERE.
HOW DID SHE DIE?
I DO NOT KNOW. MY BACK WAS TURNED.
RIGHT QUESTION, WRONG PERSONAL PRONOUN. HOW DID **YOU** DIE, MISS...
DETECTIVE. KOSUGE. AND I DON'T KNOW EITHER.
SOME DETECTIVE.
DID YOU DIE WHILST YOUR BACK WAS ALSO TURNED?
NO, IT WAS REAL QUICK.
HEY IF YOU GOTTA GO, REAL QUICK IS THE BEST WAY TO.
HOW I WANNA GO IF I GOTTA.
I WISH I KNEW WHAT HAPPENED.
DO YOU RECALL ANYTHING?
NO. MAYBE. I MEAN, YES, BUT IT CAN'T BE RIGHT.
YOU HAVE BEEN A DETECTIVE FOR MANY MORE YEARS THAN ME, SO I USUALLY DEFER TO YOU OUT OF RESPECT, BUT IF I MIGHT POINT OUT WHAT YOU HAVE MAYBE MISSED IN THE RECENT HUBBUB IS THAT NOTHING AROUND HERE ADHERES TO THE ESTABLISHED DEFINITION OF "RIGHT."
GRRRR
THIS GROWLING COMING FROM THE VERY SKY PERHAPS MAKES MY POINT FOR ME.

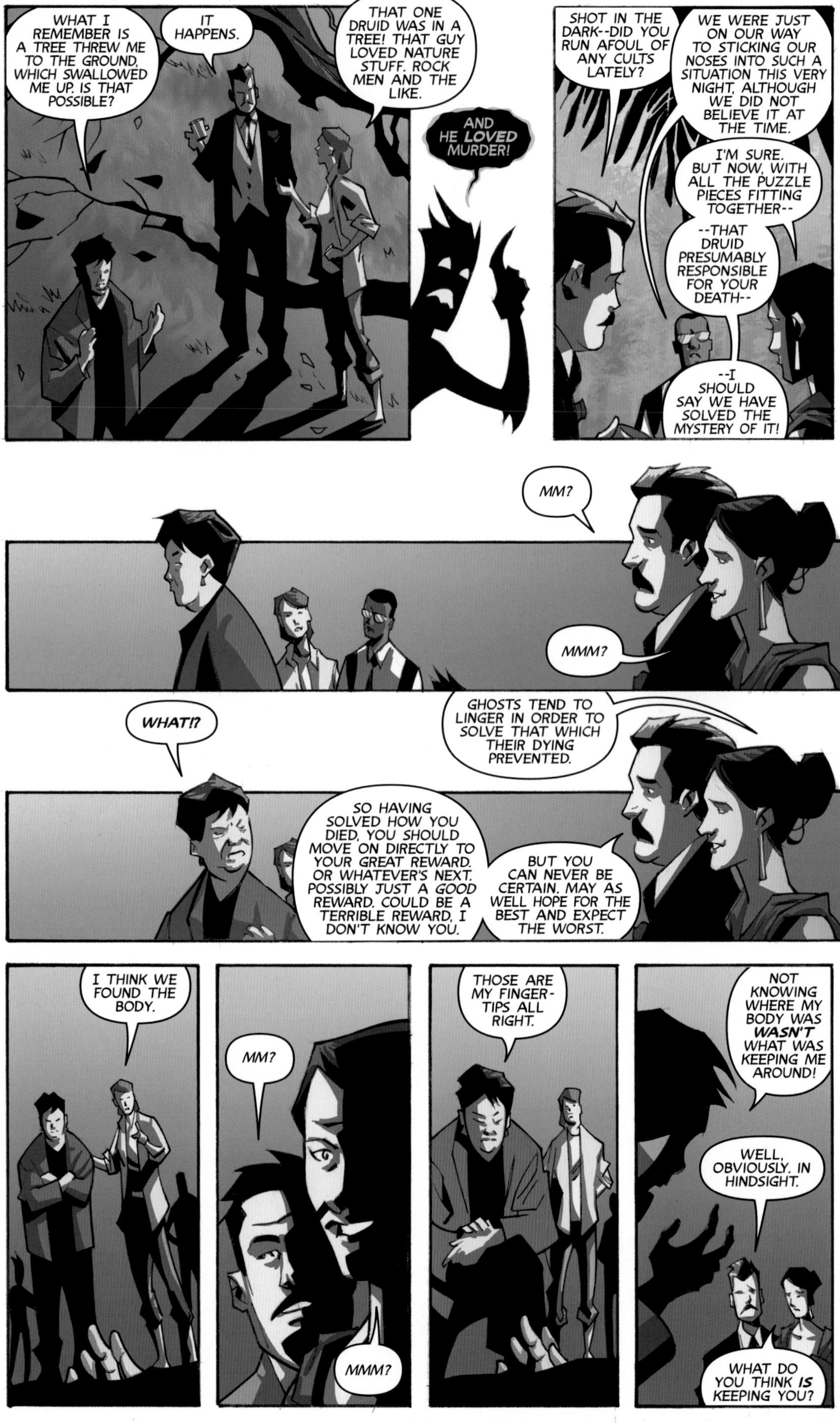
WHAT I REMEMBER IS A TREE THREW ME TO THE GROUND, WHICH SWALLOWED ME UP. IS THAT POSSIBLE?
IT HAPPENS.
THAT ONE DRUID WAS IN A TREE! THAT GUY LOVED NATURE STUFF. ROCK MEN AND THE LIKE.
AND HE *LOVED* MURDER!
SHOT IN THE DARK--DID YOU RUN AFOUL OF ANY CULTS LATELY?
WE WERE JUST ON OUR WAY TO STICKING OUR NOSES INTO SUCH A SITUATION THIS VERY NIGHT, ALTHOUGH WE DID NOT BELIEVE IT AT THE TIME.
I'M SURE. BUT NOW, WITH ALL THE PUZZLE PIECES FITTING TOGETHER--
--THAT DRUID PRESUMABLY RESPONSIBLE FOR YOUR DEATH--
--I SHOULD SAY WE HAVE SOLVED THE MYSTERY OF IT!
MM?
MMM?
WHAT!?
GHOSTS TEND TO LINGER IN ORDER TO SOLVE THAT WHICH THEIR DYING PREVENTED.
SO HAVING SOLVED HOW YOU DIED, YOU SHOULD MOVE ON DIRECTLY TO YOUR GREAT REWARD. OR WHATEVER'S NEXT. POSSIBLY JUST A *GOOD* REWARD. COULD BE A TERRIBLE REWARD, I DON'T KNOW YOU.
BUT YOU CAN NEVER BE CERTAIN. MAY AS WELL HOPE FOR THE BEST AND EXPECT THE WORST.
I THINK WE FOUND THE BODY.
MM?
MMM?
THOSE ARE MY FINGER-TIPS ALL RIGHT.
NOT KNOWING WHERE MY BODY WAS *WASN'T* WHAT WAS KEEPING ME AROUND!
WELL, OBVIOUSLY. IN HINDSIGHT.
WHAT DO YOU THINK *IS* KEEPING YOU?

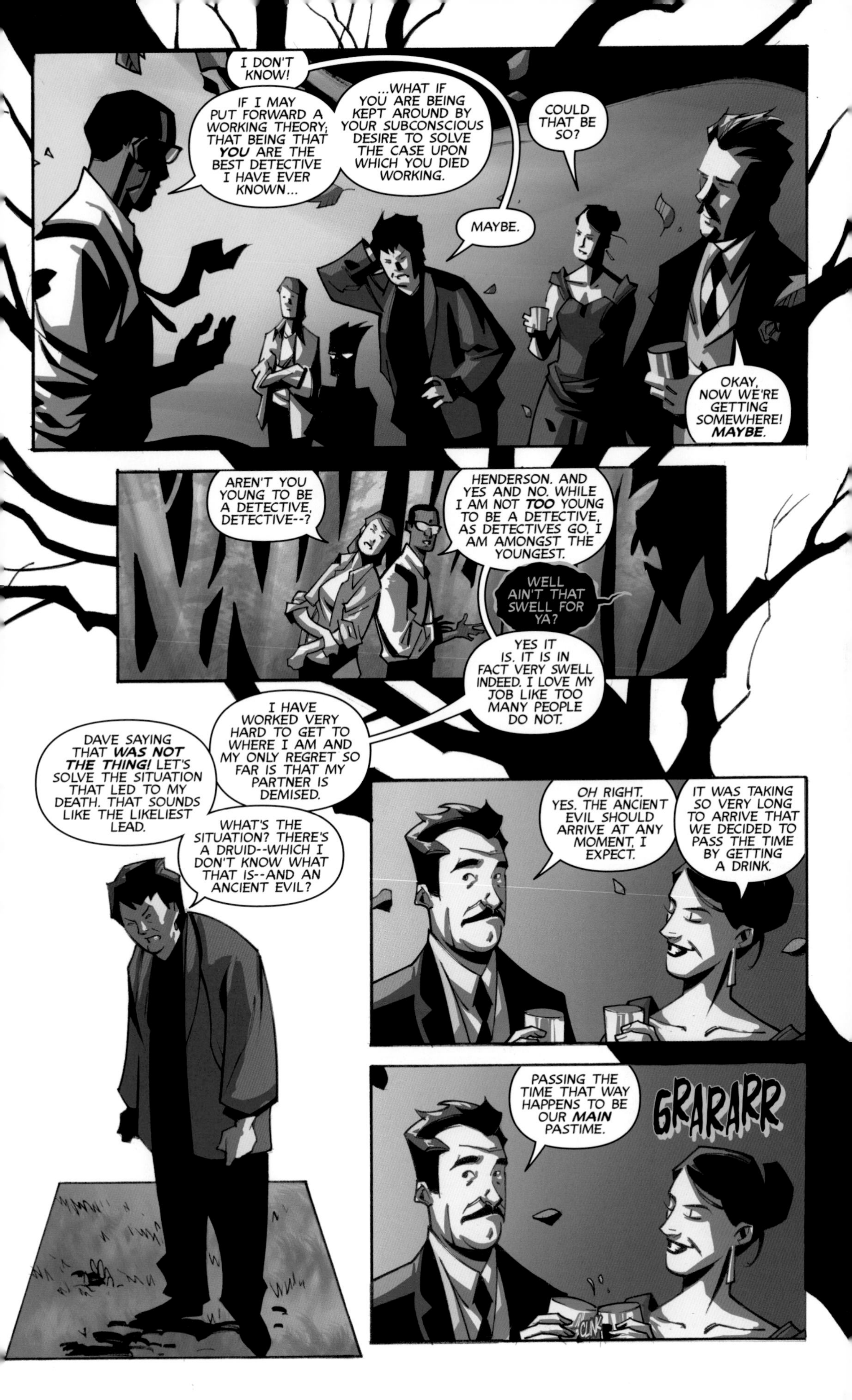

IF I MAY PUT FORWARD A WORKING THEORY; THAT BEING THAT ***YOU*** ARE THE BEST DETECTIVE I HAVE EVER KNOWN...
...WHAT IF YOU ARE BEING KEPT AROUND BY YOUR SUBCONSCIOUS DESIRE TO SOLVE THE CASE UPON WHICH YOU DIED WORKING.
I DON'T KNOW!
MAYBE.
COULD THAT BE SO?
OKAY, NOW WE'RE GETTING SOMEWHERE! ***MAYBE.***
AREN'T YOU YOUNG TO BE A DETECTIVE, DETECTIVE--?
HENDERSON. AND YES AND NO. WHILE I AM NOT ***TOO*** YOUNG TO BE A DETECTIVE, AS DETECTIVES GO, I AM AMONGST THE YOUNGEST.
WELL AIN'T THAT SWELL FOR YA?
YES IT IS. IT IS IN FACT VERY SWELL INDEED. I LOVE MY JOB LIKE TOO MANY PEOPLE DO NOT.
I HAVE WORKED VERY HARD TO GET TO WHERE I AM AND MY ONLY REGRET SO FAR IS THAT MY PARTNER IS DEMISED.
DAVE SAYING THAT ***WAS NOT THE THING!*** LET'S SOLVE THE SITUATION THAT LED TO MY DEATH. THAT SOUNDS LIKE THE LIKELIEST LEAD.
WHAT'S THE SITUATION? THERE'S A DRUID--WHICH I DON'T KNOW WHAT THAT IS--AND AN ANCIENT EVIL?
OH RIGHT. YES. THE ANCIENT EVIL SHOULD ARRIVE AT ANY MOMENT, I EXPECT.
IT WAS TAKING SO VERY LONG TO ARRIVE THAT WE DECIDED TO PASS THE TIME BY GETTING A DRINK.
PASSING THE TIME THAT WAY HAPPENS TO BE OUR ***MAIN*** PASTIME.
GRARARR
CLINK

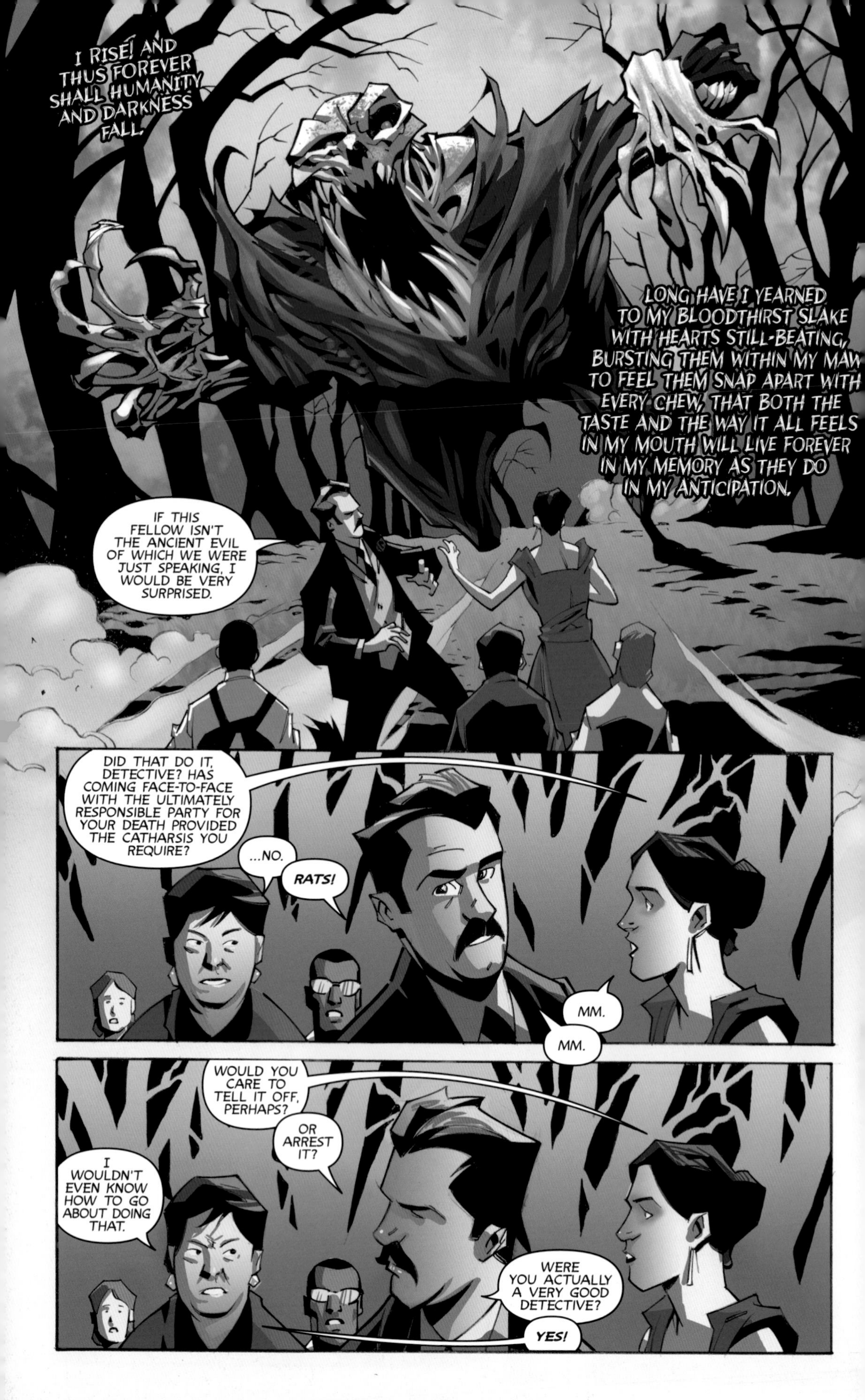
I RISE! AND THUS FOREVER SHALL HUMANITY AND DARKNESS FALL.
LONG HAVE I YEARNED TO MY BLOODTHIRST SLAKE WITH HEARTS STILL-BEATING, BURSTING THEM WITHIN MY MAW TO FEEL THEM SNAP APART WITH EVERY CHEW, THAT BOTH THE TASTE AND THE WAY IT ALL FEELS IN MY MOUTH WILL LIVE FOREVER IN MY MEMORY AS THEY DO IN MY ANTICIPATION.
IF THIS FELLOW ISN'T THE ANCIENT EVIL OF WHICH WE WERE JUST SPEAKING, I WOULD BE VERY SURPRISED.
DID THAT DO IT, DETECTIVE? HAS COMING FACE-TO-FACE WITH THE ULTIMATELY RESPONSIBLE PARTY FOR YOUR DEATH PROVIDED THE CATHARSIS YOU REQUIRE?
...NO.
RATS!
MM.
MM.
WOULD YOU CARE TO TELL IT OFF, PERHAPS?
OR ARREST IT?
I WOULDN'T EVEN KNOW HOW TO GO ABOUT DOING THAT.
WERE YOU ACTUALLY A VERY GOOD DETECTIVE?
YES!

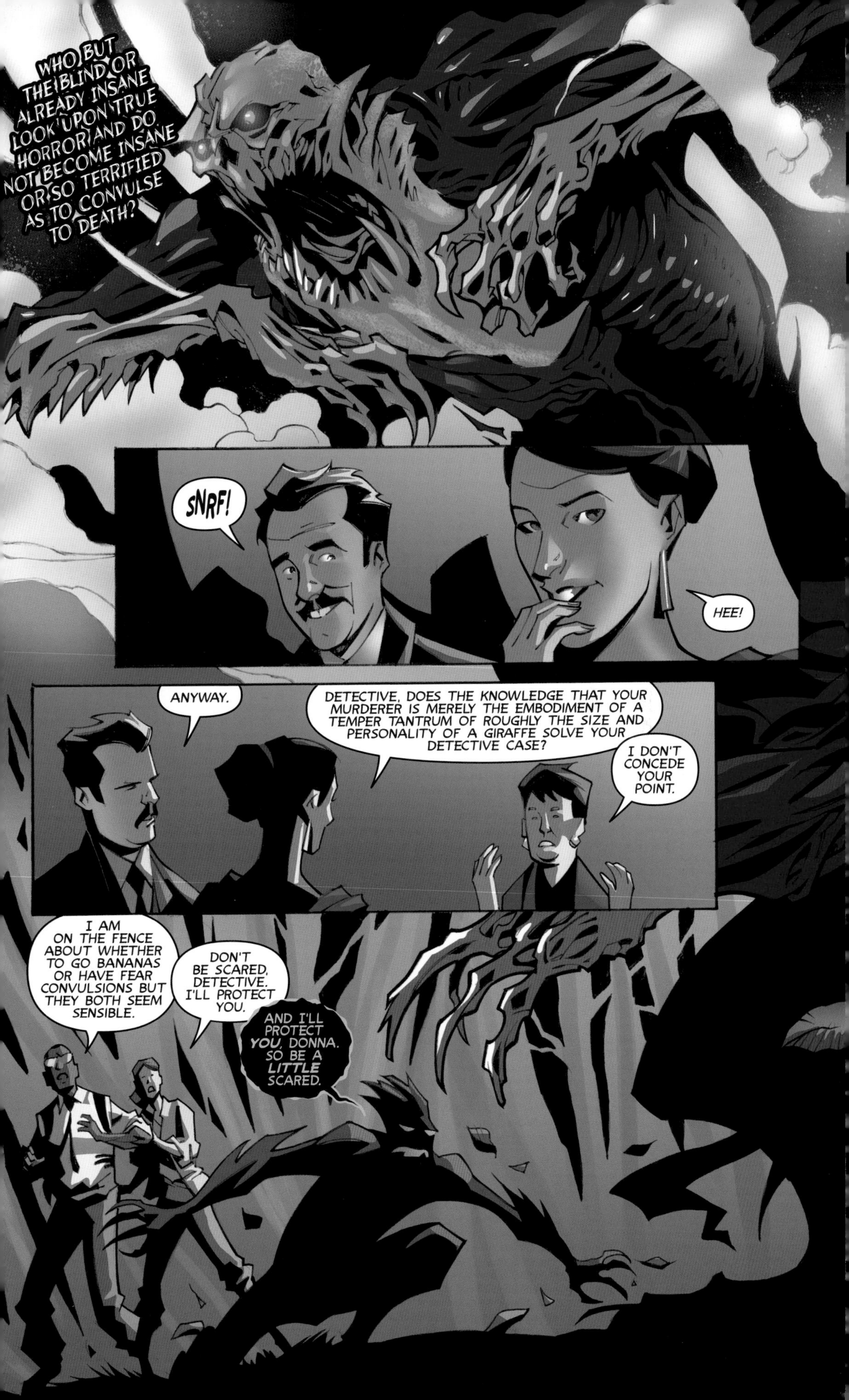
WHO BUT THE BLIND OR ALREADY INSANE LOOK UPON TRUE HORROR AND DO NOT BECOME INSANE OR SO TERRIFIED AS TO CONVULSE TO DEATH?
SNRF!
HEE!
ANYWAY.
DETECTIVE, DOES THE KNOWLEDGE THAT YOUR MURDERER IS MERELY THE EMBODIMENT OF A TEMPER TANTRUM OF ROUGHLY THE SIZE AND PERSONALITY OF A GIRAFFE SOLVE YOUR DETECTIVE CASE?
I DON'T CONCEDE YOUR POINT.
I AM ON THE FENCE ABOUT WHETHER TO GO BANANAS OR HAVE FEAR CONVULSIONS BUT THEY BOTH SEEM SENSIBLE.
DON'T BE SCARED, DETECTIVE. I'LL PROTECT YOU.
AND I'LL PROTECT YOU, DONNA. SO BE A LITTLE SCARED.

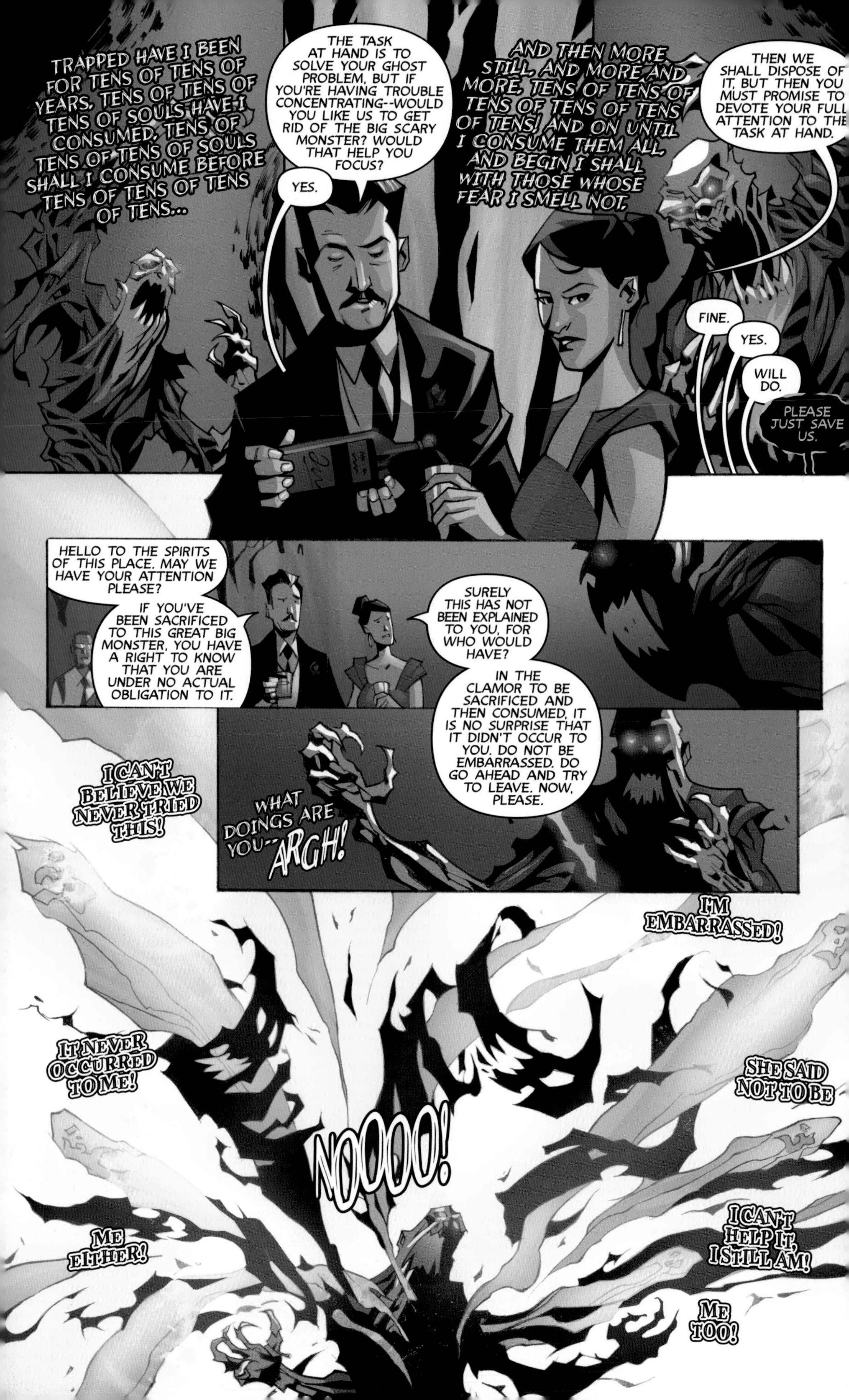
TRAPPED HAVE I BEEN FOR TENS OF TENS OF YEARS. TENS OF TENS OF TENS OF SOULS HAVE I CONSUMED. TENS OF TENS OF TENS OF SOULS SHALL I CONSUME BEFORE TENS OF TENS OF TENS OF TENS...
THE TASK AT HAND IS TO SOLVE YOUR GHOST PROBLEM, BUT IF YOU'RE HAVING TROUBLE CONCENTRATING--WOULD YOU LIKE US TO GET RID OF THE BIG SCARY MONSTER? WOULD THAT HELP YOU FOCUS?
YES.
AND THEN MORE STILL, AND MORE AND MORE. TENS OF TENS OF TENS OF TENS OF TENS OF TENS! AND ON UNTIL I CONSUME THEM ALL. AND BEGIN I SHALL WITH THOSE WHOSE FEAR I SMELL NOT.
THEN WE SHALL DISPOSE OF IT, BUT THEN YOU MUST PROMISE TO DEVOTE YOUR FULL ATTENTION TO THE TASK AT HAND.
FINE.
YES.
WILL DO.
PLEASE JUST SAVE US.
HELLO TO THE SPIRITS OF THIS PLACE. MAY WE HAVE YOUR ATTENTION PLEASE?
IF YOU'VE BEEN SACRIFICED TO THIS GREAT BIG MONSTER, YOU HAVE A RIGHT TO KNOW THAT YOU ARE UNDER NO ACTUAL OBLIGATION TO IT.
SURELY THIS HAS NOT BEEN EXPLAINED TO YOU, FOR WHO WOULD HAVE?
IN THE CLAMOR TO BE SACRIFICED AND THEN CONSUMED, IT IS NO SURPRISE THAT IT DIDN'T OCCUR TO YOU. DO NOT BE EMBARRASSED. DO GO AHEAD AND TRY TO LEAVE. NOW, PLEASE.
WHAT DOINGS ARE YOU--ARGH!
I CAN'T BELIEVE WE NEVER TRIED THIS!
I'M EMBARRASSED!
IT NEVER OCCURRED TO ME!
SHE SAID NOT TO BE
NOOOO!
ME EITHER!
I CAN'T HELP IT, I STILL AM!
ME TOO!

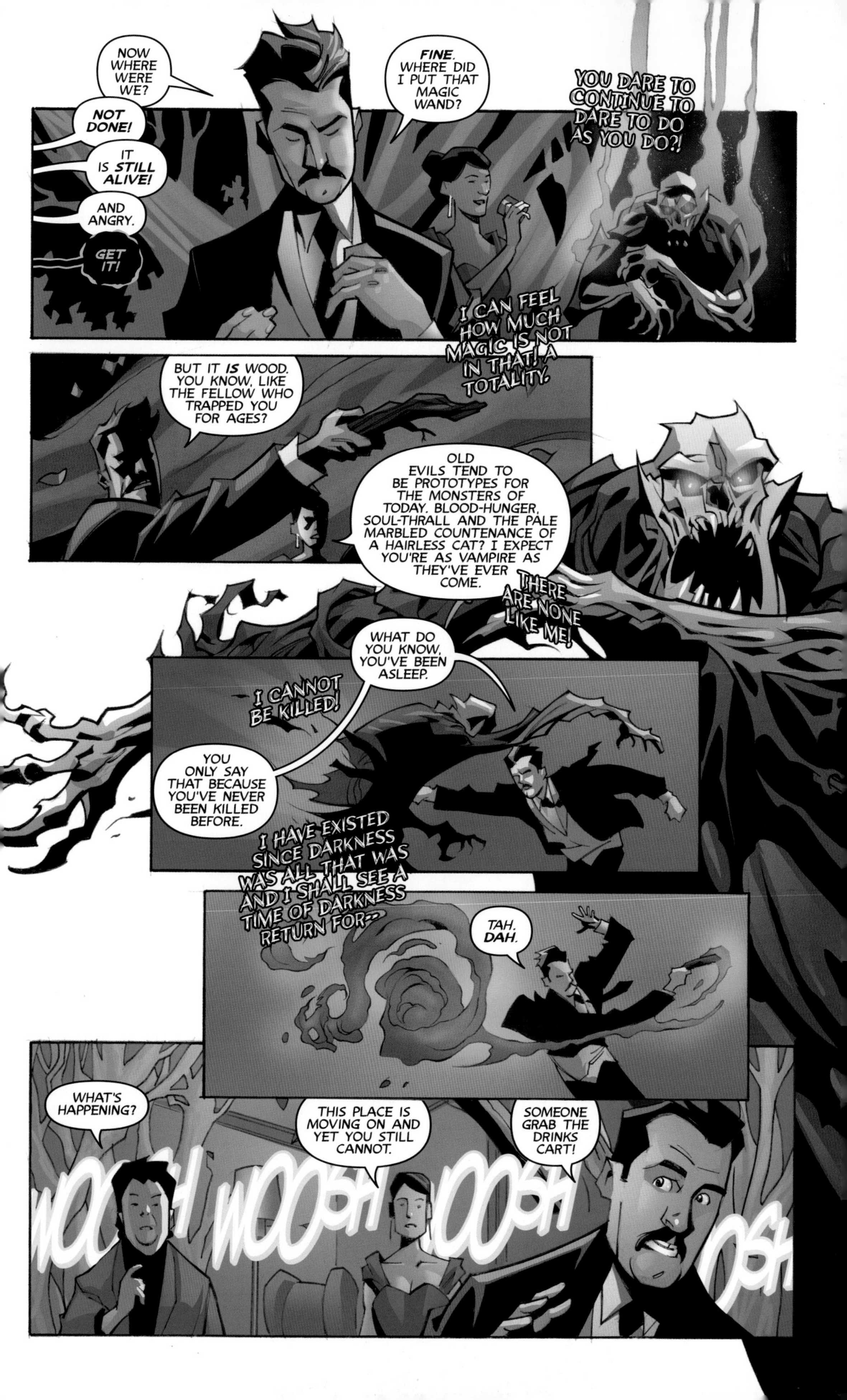
NOW WHERE WERE WE?
NOT DONE!
IT IS STILL ALIVE!
AND ANGRY.
GET IT!
FINE. WHERE DID I PUT THAT MAGIC WAND?
YOU DARE TO CONTINUE TO DARE TO DO AS YOU DO?!
I CAN FEEL HOW MUCH MAGIC IS NOT IN THAT! A TOTALITY.
BUT IT IS WOOD. YOU KNOW, LIKE THE FELLOW WHO TRAPPED YOU FOR AGES?
OLD EVILS TEND TO BE PROTOTYPES FOR THE MONSTERS OF TODAY. BLOOD-HUNGER, SOUL-THRALL AND THE PALE MARBLED COUNTENANCE OF A HAIRLESS CAT? I EXPECT YOU'RE AS VAMPIRE AS THEY'VE EVER COME.
THERE ARE NONE LIKE ME!
WHAT DO YOU KNOW, YOU'VE BEEN ASLEEP.
I CANNOT BE KILLED!
YOU ONLY SAY THAT BECAUSE YOU'VE NEVER BEEN KILLED BEFORE.
I HAVE EXISTED SINCE DARKNESS WAS ALL THAT WAS AND I SHALL SEE A TIME OF DARKNESS RETURN FOR--
TAH. DAH.
WHAT'S HAPPENING?
THIS PLACE IS MOVING ON AND YET YOU STILL CANNOT.
SOMEONE GRAB THE DRINKS CART!
WOOSH WOOSH WOOSH OOSH

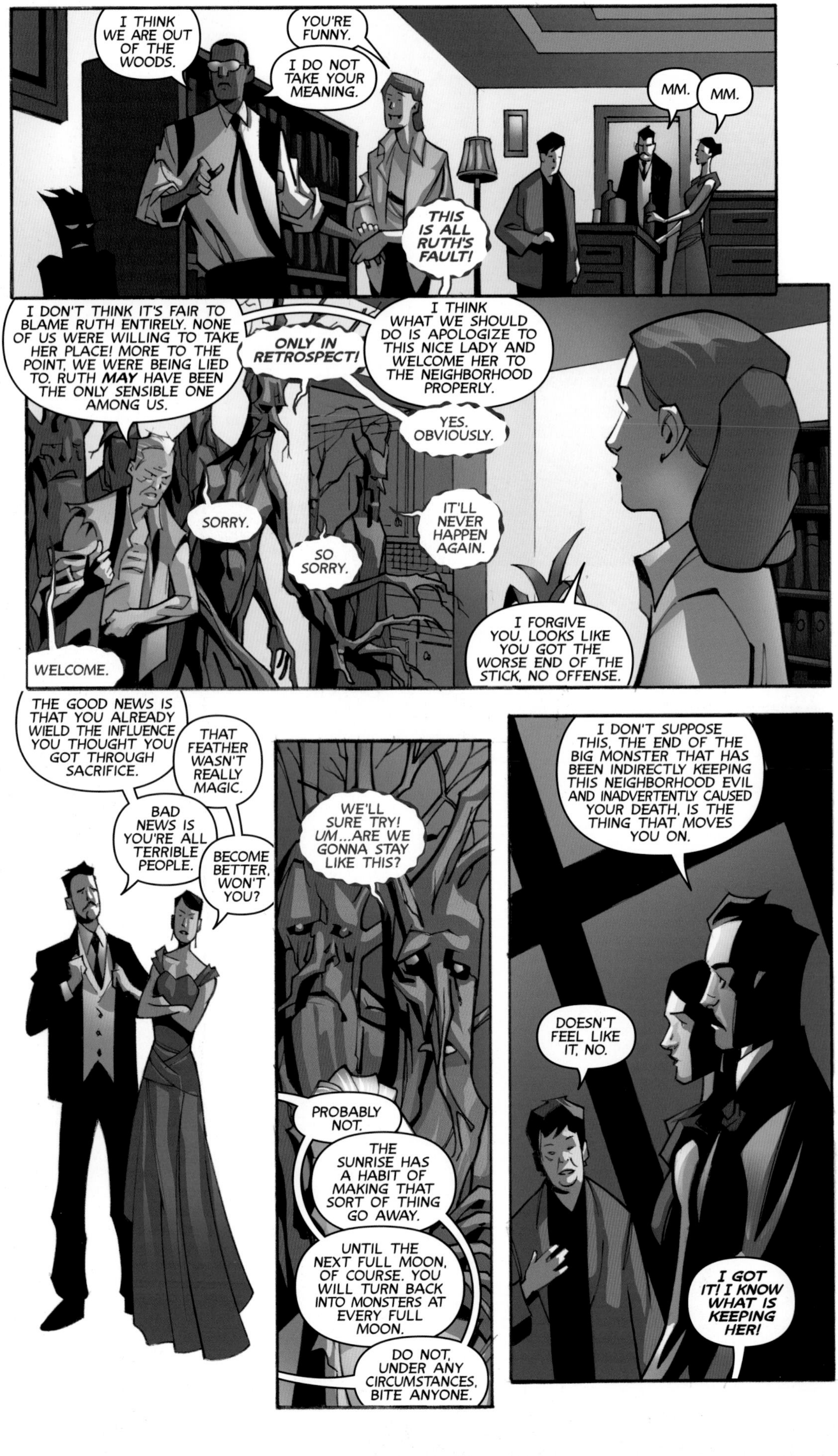
I THINK WE ARE OUT OF THE WOODS.
YOU'RE FUNNY.
I DO NOT TAKE YOUR MEANING.
MM.
MM.
THIS IS ALL RUTH'S FAULT!
I DON'T THINK IT'S FAIR TO BLAME RUTH ENTIRELY. NONE OF US WERE WILLING TO TAKE HER PLACE! MORE TO THE POINT, WE WERE BEING LIED TO. RUTH MAY HAVE BEEN THE ONLY SENSIBLE ONE AMONG US.
ONLY IN RETROSPECT!
I THINK WHAT WE SHOULD DO IS APOLOGIZE TO THIS NICE LADY AND WELCOME HER TO THE NEIGHBORHOOD PROPERLY.
YES. OBVIOUSLY.
SORRY.
SO SORRY.
IT'LL NEVER HAPPEN AGAIN.
WELCOME.
I FORGIVE YOU. LOOKS LIKE YOU GOT THE WORSE END OF THE STICK, NO OFFENSE.
THE GOOD NEWS IS THAT YOU ALREADY WIELD THE INFLUENCE YOU THOUGHT YOU GOT THROUGH SACRIFICE.
THAT FEATHER WASN'T REALLY MAGIC.
BAD NEWS IS YOU'RE ALL TERRIBLE PEOPLE.
BECOME BETTER, WON'T YOU?
WE'LL SURE TRY! UM...ARE WE GONNA STAY LIKE THIS?
PROBABLY NOT.
THE SUNRISE HAS A HABIT OF MAKING THAT SORT OF THING GO AWAY.
UNTIL THE NEXT FULL MOON, OF COURSE. YOU WILL TURN BACK INTO MONSTERS AT EVERY FULL MOON.
DO NOT, UNDER ANY CIRCUMSTANCES, BITE ANYONE.
I DON'T SUPPOSE THIS, THE END OF THE BIG MONSTER THAT HAS BEEN INDIRECTLY KEEPING THIS NEIGHBORHOOD EVIL AND INADVERTENTLY CAUSED YOUR DEATH, IS THE THING THAT MOVES YOU ON.
DOESN'T FEEL LIKE IT, NO.
I GOT IT! I KNOW WHAT IS KEEPING HER!

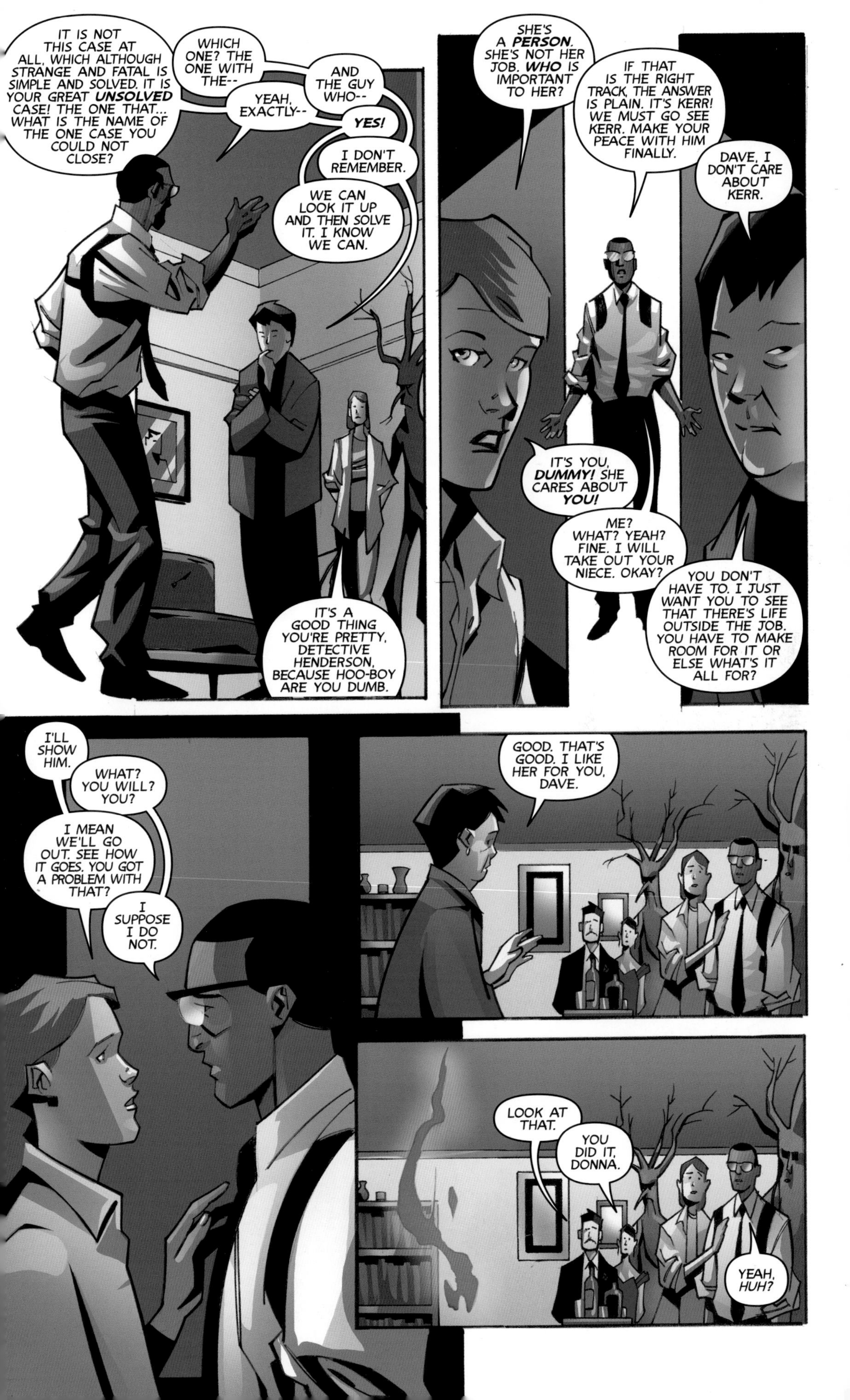
IT IS NOT THIS CASE AT ALL, WHICH ALTHOUGH STRANGE AND FATAL IS SIMPLE AND SOLVED. IT IS YOUR GREAT **UNSOLVED** CASE! THE ONE THAT... WHAT IS THE NAME OF THE ONE CASE YOU COULD NOT CLOSE?
WHICH ONE? THE ONE WITH THE--
AND THE GUY WHO--
YEAH, EXACTLY--
YES!
I DON'T REMEMBER.
WE CAN LOOK IT UP AND THEN SOLVE IT. I KNOW WE CAN.
IT'S A GOOD THING YOU'RE PRETTY, DETECTIVE HENDERSON, BECAUSE HOO-BOY ARE YOU DUMB.
SHE'S A **PERSON**. SHE'S NOT HER JOB. **WHO** IS IMPORTANT TO HER?
IF THAT IS THE RIGHT TRACK, THE ANSWER IS PLAIN. IT'S KERR! WE MUST GO SEE KERR. MAKE YOUR PEACE WITH HIM FINALLY.
DAVE, I DON'T CARE ABOUT KERR.
IT'S YOU, **DUMMY!** SHE CARES ABOUT **YOU!**
ME? WHAT? YEAH? FINE. I WILL TAKE OUT YOUR NIECE. OKAY?
YOU DON'T HAVE TO. I JUST WANT YOU TO SEE THAT THERE'S LIFE OUTSIDE THE JOB. YOU HAVE TO MAKE ROOM FOR IT OR ELSE WHAT'S IT ALL FOR?
I'LL SHOW HIM.
WHAT? YOU WILL? YOU?
I MEAN WE'LL GO OUT. SEE HOW IT GOES. YOU GOT A PROBLEM WITH THAT?
I SUPPOSE I DO NOT.
GOOD. THAT'S GOOD. I LIKE HER FOR YOU, DAVE.
LOOK AT THAT.
YOU DID IT, DONNA.
YEAH, HUH?

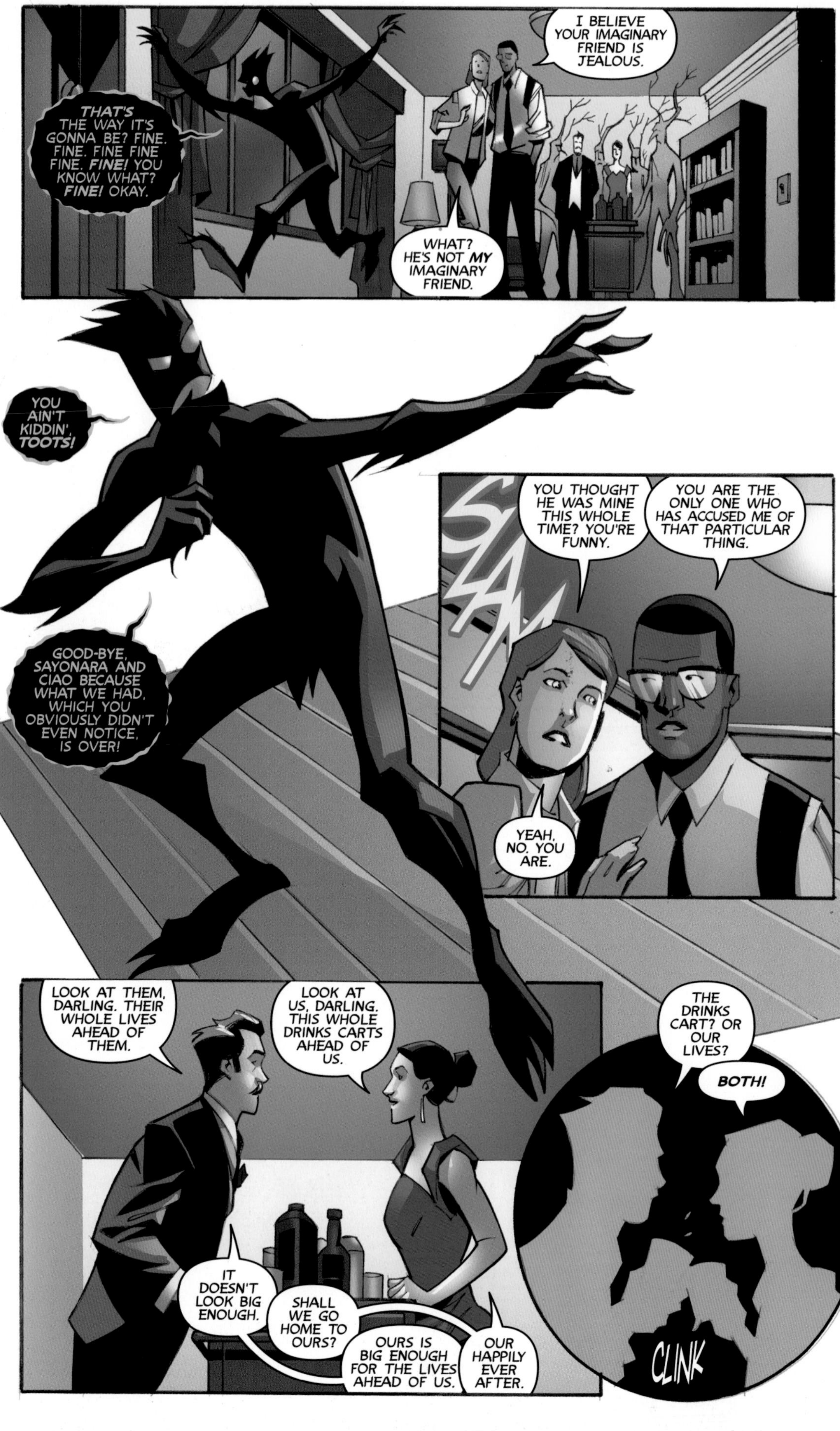
I BELIEVE YOUR IMAGINARY FRIEND IS JEALOUS.
THAT'S THE WAY IT'S GONNA BE? FINE. FINE. FINE FINE FINE. FINE! YOU KNOW WHAT? FINE! OKAY.
WHAT? HE'S NOT MY IMAGINARY FRIEND.
YOU AIN'T KIDDIN', TOOTS!
GOOD-BYE, SAYONARA AND CIAO BECAUSE WHAT WE HAD, WHICH YOU OBVIOUSLY DIDN'T EVEN NOTICE, IS OVER!
SLAM
YOU THOUGHT HE WAS MINE THIS WHOLE TIME? YOU'RE FUNNY.
YOU ARE THE ONLY ONE WHO HAS ACCUSED ME OF THAT PARTICULAR THING.
YEAH, NO. YOU ARE.
LOOK AT THEM, DARLING. THEIR WHOLE LIVES AHEAD OF THEM.
LOOK AT US, DARLING. THIS WHOLE DRINKS CARTS AHEAD OF US.
IT DOESN'T LOOK BIG ENOUGH.
SHALL WE GO HOME TO OURS?
OURS IS BIG ENOUGH FOR THE LIVES AHEAD OF US.
OUR HAPPILY EVER AFTER.
THE DRINKS CART? OR OUR LIVES?
BOTH!
CLINK

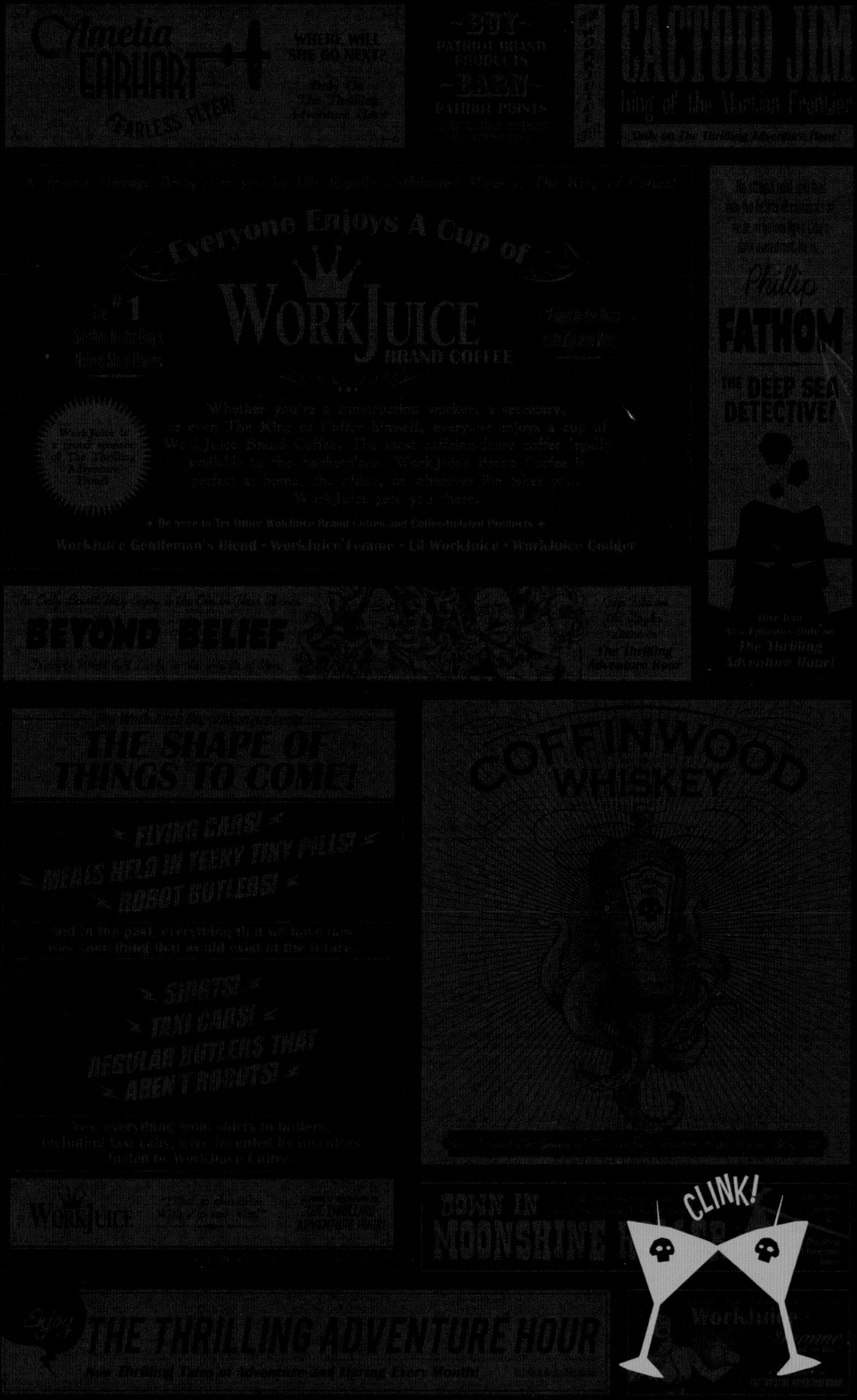

Amelia
EARHART
FEARLESS FLYER!
WHERE WILL SHE GO NEXT?
~BUY~
PATRIOT BRAND PRODUCTS
~EARN~
PATRIOT POINTS
CACTOID JIM
King of the Martian Frontier
Only on The Thrilling Adventure Hour
A Special Message Brought to you by His Regally Caffeinated Majesty, The King of Coffee!
Everyone Enjoys A Cup of
WORKJUICE
BRAND COFFEE
The #1 Solution for the Day's Natural Sleep-Downs
Whether you're a construction worker, a secretary, or even The King of Coffee himself, everyone enjoys a cup of WorkJuice Brand Coffee. The most caffeine-dense coffee legally available in the marketplace. WorkJuice Brand Coffee is perfect at home, the office, or wherever life takes you. WorkJuice gets you there.
Be Sure to Try Other WorkJuice Brand Coffee and Coffee-Related Products
WorkJuice Gentleman's Blend • WorkJuice Femme • Lil WorkJuice • WorkJuice Codger
Phillip
FATHOM
THE DEEP SEA DETECTIVE!
Dive Into New Episodes Only on The Thrilling Adventure Hour!
BEYOND BELIEF
THE SHAPE OF THINGS TO COME!
FLYING CARS!
MEALS HELD IN TEENY TINY PILLS!
ROBOT BUTLERS!
And in the past, everything that we have now was something that would exist in the future.
SHIRTS!
TAXI CARS!
REGULAR BUTLERS THAT AREN'T ROBOTS!
Yes, everything from shirts to butlers, including taxi cabs, were invented by inventors fueled by WorkJuice Coffee.
COFFINWOOD WHISKEY
WORKJUICE
DOWN IN MOONSHINE
CLINK!
Enjoy
THE THRILLING ADVENTURE HOUR
New Thrilling Tales of Adventure and Daring Every Month!
WorkJuice

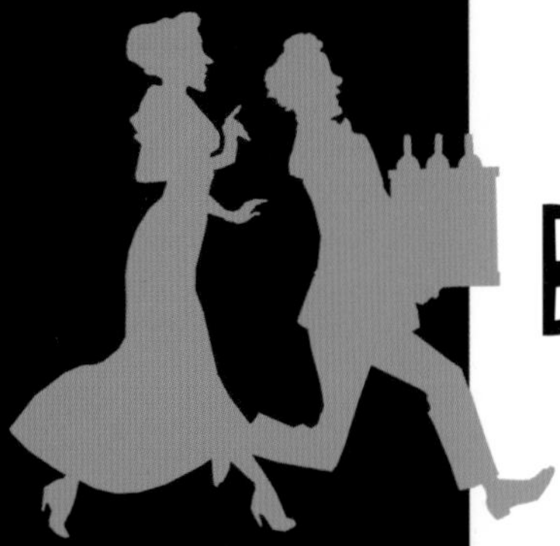

BEHIND-THE-SCENES

A LOOK AT THE ORIGINAL SCRIPT FOR ISSUE #0 WITH COMMENTARY BY WRITERS **BEN ACKER** AND **BEN BLACKER**.

PAGE ONE ---

Two columns of panels—Left side is Frank's (odd numbered panels). Right side is Sadie's. Behind columns, evoke the settings.[1] *Frank's in the catacombs of a museum. Sadie's in a bar called "PJ's Spirits."*[2]

Panel 1

In a room of British history, there are Heraldic flags on display, several of them in a line, all featuring Lion Rampants except one flag with a silhouette/empty space where the Lion should be—this is the monster attacking Frank.

The monster looks like a lion, sure, and Cookie Monster and the aliens in *Attack the Block*. Like readers won't know it's a monster version of Cookie Monster until they are told and then they'll be like "oh man! hilarious!"[3]

Frank's on his back fending off *ye olde C'thookie Monster*, tentacles issuing from its open maw that reach for Frank who holds the monster back with a hand on its throat and a knee in its belly. With his other hand, Frank reaches for something. But what? A sword. Is the answer. You can show some or all of it or not at all. Also please show Frank's bag—a satchel like on the poster for *The Exorcist*, turned on its side, opened and spilling out Frank's tools of the trade - most notably A JAR WITH SIGILS CARVED INTO IT.[4] Less important: a cross, a dog whistle, a gun and a flask.

CAP (FRANK): Despite everything looking terribly horrible, everything's right with the world.

Panel 2

Sadie sipping a martini, looking fabulous. Women want to be her and men do too.[5]

CAP (SADIE): Despite everything looking as it should, something is terribly horribly wrong.

Panel 3

Frank slices the monster's head off with a broadsword.

CAP (FRANK): When in doubt, chop off the head. Frank Doyle saves the day.[6]
SFX: SWISH!

Panel 4

Sadie SWIRLING a cocktail mixer.

SFX: SWIRL[7]
CAP (SADIE): This bar's bartender cannot make a decent martini. Sadie Parker saves the day.
SADIE: You can go ahead and burn that one.

[1] ***Blacker:*** *There was some discussion between us about how to write a Frank and Sadie origin story, as part of the fun of the Doyles is them together, bantering and being in love. Acker came up with what I think is a really brilliant execution—the side-by-side columns—so that, even while they're in their separate stories, they're read as a pair.*

Acker: *This idea to have the settings behind the columns of the panels was a straight rip-off of* Fables. *I don't think it made it in the issue.*

[2] ***Acker:*** *Sharp-eyed readers will see the name of the bar is one that implies ownership by a character established in the Beyond Belief-a-verse. Frank and Sadie's meeting was inevitable.*

[3] ***Acker:*** *Are you, dear reader, indeed like "oh man! Hilarious?" we hope so. Please let us know!*

[4] ***Blacker:*** *Frank's bag—the satchel used by the exorcist in* The Exorcist*—has been part of BB canon since the very beginning. We always loved the image of echoing the iconic Exorcist poster image with Frank standing outside of a house in which he's about to do some demon-busting work, only this exorcist isn't alone—his wife is by his side.*

[5] ***Acker:*** *I heard an interview with Brian K Vaughan where he described comics scripts, with their relative lack of codified form, at least as compared to, say, a screenplay, as a letter from the writer to the artist. I don't know if he invented that sentiment, but in terms of my frame of reference he did. That idea freed me up to have fun with comics scripts. To try to get the artist to get what I'm going for, as*

Panel 5

Frank, leaning on the suit of armor from which he took the sword and tossing the flag from which the monster came into the blaze on which he has set the monster.

CAP (FRANK): I need a drink.

Panel 6

Sadie is taking her drink with her to the party.

CAP (SADIE): I have everything I could possibly need.

PAGE TWO -

As before, left column—Frank, right column—Sadie. Behind column exteriors— Frank's in PJ's Spirits now. Sadie's in a brownstone. The captions on this page are word balloons (tailless? same speaker ones connected to each other?) floating around from the Frank panels to the Sadie panels.

Panel 1

Frank regards a martini. His doctor's bag on one side of him on the bar and the cocktail shaker is on the other side.

CAP (FRANK): PJ, this is better than your usual. And you're no usual slouch.
CAP (PJ): You just missed Bobo Brubaker and a dame far better than his usual, who, among other qualities, fixed that drink you're drinking. [8]
CAP (FRANK): What's a woman capable of doing *this* doing with Bobo Brubaker? [9]
CAP (PJ): Community service?

Panel 2

If this panel were a painting, it'd be Norman Rockwell's long lost "First Seance." An expansive upscale place with a smattering of young excited/scared Richie Riches with cocktails are in various stages of settling around a Ouija board. Bobo, a wolf among sheep, mans the Ouija and waves at Sadie to come over. Sadie judges him.

CAP (FRANK): Who's Bobo conning now, besides her?
CAP (PJ): He's staging scam seances for the rich and grieving. In, get this—the Willowbrook House.
CAP (FRANK): Why hold a phoney seance at an actually haunted house?
CAP (PJ): Verisimilitude?
CAP (FRANK): That's Bobo. Just dumb enough to be dangerous. [10]

Panel 3

Frank reaches panel-right for his bag.

CAP (FRANK): If there's a sensitive there...

Panel 4

Sadie reaches panel-left for the planchette.

CAP (FRANK): ...his hoax could take a turn for the real. [11]

Panel 5

Frank's gone from the bar. PJ drinking a beer.

CAP (PJ): Serves 'em right, you ask me.
CAP (FRANK): Him definitely.

opposed to worrying over specificity of layout.

[6] ***Acker:*** *In the history of the show, we'd never really written Frank in his monster-fighting days. We alluded to it in the finale episode, got a taste there, but we hadn't written that episode at the time we wrote this. It was a fun new place from which to write Frank.*

[7] ***Acker:*** *I hope I never get tired of verbs as sound effects. It is unique to comics and one of my favorite things in the world.*

[8] ***Acker:*** *Sharp-eyed readers who are also sharp-eared podcast listeners already knew this story had Bobo in it.*

[9] ***Acker:*** *Love at first sip!*

[10] ***Acker:*** *Frank's disdain for Bobo preceded his knowing Sadie.*

Blacker: *One of the hardest things about first issues or TV pilots is suggesting a life to your characters before the origin story you're presenting. We cleverly navigated this difficulty by writing these characters for over a decade before giving them a "pilot" story. Recommended!*

[11] ***Acker:*** *Look at young Frank knowing the rules and giving a care. Fun! Maybe we should do the Young Frank adventures someday.*

[12] **Blacker:** *I've never seen the movie The Beastmaster. I love the idea of hellhounds. And I like how they're paid off in this issue. Sorry if that offends you. I've never used a ouija board. Have you? Are you an artist? Will you make a Beyond Belief themed ouija board for me?*

[13] **Blacker:** *Harnesses=badassery. That's why horses are the baddest-assest animals.*

[14] **Acker:** *Oh he loooooooooves her!*

[15] **Blacker:** *These couple of pages had to do a lot of emotional heavy lifting. How do you show the reader that this is the beginning of a decade's worth of stories, a love story stronger than any supernatural force? I can compliment this, because my partner wrote it, and I think it does the job admirably. Staying in Frank's and Sadie's POVs gives a direct emotional impact.*

[16] **Acker:** *But really by Sadie. You got that, right? You did.*

Blacker: *. . . Not until this minute.*

[17] **Acker:** *He's so rugged.*

[18] **Acker:** *He's so not rugged.*

[19] **Acker:** *She's so rugged!*

[20] **Acker:** *Young Frank's first instinct is to scrap. Young Sadie's is to protect, save, defend. This is still who they are to some extent.*

[21] **Blacker:** *I think this is a variation of a joke we've used before, but it makes me laugh. And I'm surprised it was never used in a Marx Brothers routine or something.*

Panel 6
THE BEASTMASTER and HELLHOUNDS come out of the ouija board.[12] The Beastmaster is nothing like the dude from the movie Beastmaster. He is more like the library ghost in Ghostbusters. A scary floating head and torso with arms but no legs. He is dingy-colored and wears a crown. The Hellhounds are demonic wolfhounds with harnesses that make them look even more bad-assed. [13]

> CAP (FRANK): Not her. [14]

PAGE THREE -
Now they're both in the brownstone. Let it arc over these four panels and have a Frank and Sadie caption, his on the left, hers on the left, preceding the panels...

> CAP (FRANK): Once I met Sadie, everything that happened before felt like prelude. [15]
> CAP (SADIE): I always thought I had everything I could possibly need. Then I met Frank.

Panel 1
Frank and Sadie stock-still love-at-first-sighting each other as Beastmaster and Hellhounds terrorize and everyone human panicking and running.

Panel 2
Chaos continues around them. Frank shakes off the Disney moment. Sadie continues to stares at Frank intently.

Panel 3
Chaos still. Frank looks again. Sadie smiles.

Panel 4
Frank gets flipped, turned upside-down (by the monster). [16]

PAGE FOUR -
Panel 1
The Beastmaster holds Frank upside down.

> BEASTMASTER: YOU FEAR NEITHER ME NOR MY HELLHOUNDS! WHY?
> FRANK: It's not you, it's me. You're not my first monsters. You're not even my first monsters today. Let me just nip into my bag and we'll see who ought to fear whom and why.
> FRANK: Do put me right-ways up, though; we'd both hate for me to spill my belongings.

Panel 2
The Beastmaster knocks Frank's bag out of his hand. Bobo pulls at Sadie's hand. She still can't take her eyes off of Frank. Sadie's drink is behind her on the ouija board. It'd be good to see, but not crucial.

> FRANK: Guess that's "the easy way" off the table. Your remaining choices are "the hard way" and... no that's it. Your own fault. [17]
> BOBO: Come on! Let's split while it's distracted. Hello? Sadie? Earth to Sadie? It's me, Bobo. Bobo Brubaker. From right next to you. Hello? Sadie? [18]
> SADIE: You! Put that man down this instant! [19]

Panel 3

Angle on the faces of Frank (charmed) and the Beastmaster (all "who dares!")

Panel 4

The Beastmaster places Frank lightly down. He couldn't be more surprised about it. Frank is smug. The hellhounds snarl at Sadie, who is not having it. Bobo cowers, scared of the hellhounds. [20]

> HELLHOUNDS: Grrrrrrrrr...
> SADIE: Sit!

Panel 5

The hellhounds sit in an obedient row watching Sadie. Frank dusts himself off.
> FRANK: That's telling those ghosts. Thank you very much...
> SADIE: Sadie! Sadie Parker. And you are quite welcome, Mr...?
> FRANK: Doyle. Frank. Not in that order. [21]

PAGE FIVE -
Panel 1

Frank reaches into his coat. Sadie waves a hand through the Beastmaster. Bobo freaks out.

> SADIE: So ghosts are real and these are ghosts? Well!
> BOBO: Wait, wait, hang on. How'd you get them to - how'd you do that?
> SADIE: I haven't the foggiest idea. [22]

Panel 2

We're with Frank as he's crouching down drawing a sigil with chalk on the floor. Sadie's legs are in the panel - ooh la la. She's reaching for something and her shoe dangles off her foot. Bobo is bent over to ask Frank... [23]

> BOBO: How'd she do that?

Panel 3

Pull out some to see Sadie filling a martini glass. If we can see hers, it remains on the ouija board. Frank still crouched, drawing the most elaborate sigil, like a circle with criss-crossing fishhooks in it. Now that we have the full picture, we see how silly Bobo looks, butt out, all bent over like an exaggerated bow instead of crouching.

> FRANK: Could be any one of ten things...
> FRANK: Could be that she has a strong spiritual sensitivity. Could be she's what's known as a Ghost Yeller (if that were a thing). [24]

Panel 4

Frank comes up again and Sadie has a drink for him. She holds it out like a little girl presenting a flower, her belly pointed at him and one leg crossing behind the other.

> FRANK: Could be that she reminds him of someone important to him.

Panel 5

Frank takes the drink, but his eyes are on her. Can we see her reflection in his eyes? That'd be pretty dope.

> FRANK: Could be that anybody with half a brain in their head would do what Sadie Parker tells them to do. [25]

[22] **Blacker:** That Frank was acquainted with the supernatural from a young age but Sadie was new to it was not baked into the characters. When we started the show, they were fairly on equal footing. At some point, I think as we started to talk about origins for them, it emerged through conversation that their first experiences with the supernatural would help differentiate their approaches to it. Frank's first experiences were violent and scary, and thus (especially here, in his early life) he's more jaded and harder about dealing with nasties. Sadie's early experiences were so warm and comforting that she didn't even realize that she was dealing with the supernatural, and thus she's more open to engaging with ghosts and other creatures. Once we landed on that, it really informed how we wrote both characters going forward and, as in this origin story, backward.

[23] **Blacker:** Acker's stage directions are fun to read. We never got to do them in the radio show (obviously), so I'm glad they can be seen here! Worth the price of admission!

[24] **Blacker:** This is the kind of joke that one of us would make in a script that could turn into the basis for a full-blown story down the line. We use every part of the ghost buffalo.

[25] **Blacker:** This line pretty much sums up Frank's entire relationship with the woman who would become his wife. Left to his own devices, he'd hole up in his apartment (or, more likely, a bar) and not engage with the world. She draws him out and opens him to new experiences because she's open to new experiences. She's so irresistible to him that he very often is just following along.

[26] **Acker:** Oh look! Their first CLINK!

[27] **Blacker:** This isn't just a throw-away line. She really does like the way he thinks. As much as Sadie brings Frank into the world, he gives her a new way of looking at it. (They do that for each other). Young Sadie, in this issue, didn't realize that that was something she was missing.

[28] **Blacker:** Only now, years later, do I realize that this direction is sort of a cruel thing to ask of an artist or letterer. But man, does it look cool on the page!

[29] **Acker:** We rarely explain sigils in the podcast, because we hardly, if ever, used them there, but they keep showing up in Beyond Belief comics. Watch for more sigils and explanations of them in the next exciting adventure of Frank and Sadie Doyle!

[30] **Blacker:** One of the biggest challenges in adapting Beyond Belief (and any TAH property) to comics is that the podcast—by dint of being an audio medium and given our predelection for banter—is very dialogue-heavy. Comics can't bear the weight of too much dialogue. No one wants to read a sea of word balloons. But, Frank and Sadie wouldn't be Frank and Sadie unless they were bantering cleverly. So, I think the form caused us to sharpen their dialogue. Knowing we could only have so many balloons per panel, per page, but that we still needed to set a rhythm that "sounded" like the show (and The Thin Man and The Addams Family, Beyond Belief's biggest inspirations) led us to hone that dialogue. I think the result is something a bit more clever and layered with meaning than we usually did in the podcast.

[31] **Acker:** I think we had fun with plural personal pronouns with Sparks and Croach too. Maybe even in the zero issue. The only way to know for certain is to make sure you collect all both of them.

[32] **Acker:** Aw, Bobo, you dumb jealous goof!

Panel 6
They toast. Clink.

> SFX: CLINK! [26]
> SADIE: Oh, I like the way you think, Doyle Frank. [27]

PAGE SIX -
Panel 1
Frank sweeps arm from where the Beastmaster is to the sigil. Beastmaster blurs as he ends up in the sigil.

> FRANK: Okay, so... (magic language runestone letters) [28]
> FRANK: And... voila!

Panel 2
Sadie touches Frank's arm.

> SADIE: Now what is it you've done?
> FRANK: I've trapped him inside that sigil so he and his hellhounds can't cause any trouble while I figure out what to do with them. It'll hold him as long as it's in tact, so mind your step. [29]

Panel 3
On Bobo, rolling his eyes.

> SADIE: You do know your way around ghosts, don't you Mr. Doyle? [30]
> FRANK: I do, but if you don't call me Frank, you'll hurt my feelings.
> SADIE: I'd never hurt anyone's feelings, Frank. So there we are.

Panel 4
Sadie looks over her glass at Frank. Frank feigns modesty and shyness. So coy, this cat.

> FRANK: I must confess that being in a plural personal pronoun with you just now gave me quite a thrill.
> SADIE: You felt it too?
> FRANK: Seems as if we both did.
> SADIE: And there it is again! [31]

Panel 5
Bobo's toe, smudging the sigil.

> BOBO: Like, "oops." [32]

Panel 6
Beastmaster is excited.

> BEASTMASTER: Free!

PAGE SEVEN -
Panel 1
The Beastmaster lunges, tossing Bobo and Frank into the snarling circle of Hellhounds.

> BOBO: Not cool!

Panel 2
Sadie admonishes him.

    SADIE: You stop that at once and apologize!

Panel 3
The Beastmaster smiles a sinister smile.

    BEASTMASTER: ...No.

Panel 4
Sadie quizzical, motioning slightly OS.

    SADIE: Pardon me! Frank? It appears I'm not a "ghost yeller" after all.
    FRANK (OS): If that were a thing!

Panel 5
The Beastmaster reaches for her.

    BEASTMASTER: You'll never boss me again! [33]

PAGE EIGHT -
Panel 1
Hero shot of Frank holding the harnesses, having removed them from the hellhounds. The hellhounds are all around him, snarling at the Beastmaster now. Bobo is trying to get up. He's been chewed on some. [34]

    FRANK: Mind if I do, sport? [35]

Panel 2
Frank saunters over to the Ouija board.

    FRANK: Now correct me if I'm wrong, but I suspect the Ouija board was their gateway from the other side. [36]

Panel 3
Frank drops the harnesses into the Ouija board and they disappear into a vortex like flower petals down a well. Sadie looks over his shoulder at it.

    FRANK: Oh look, I'm right. [37]
    FRANK: That's why you could control them before, Sadie. You rested your glass on his gateway. Your possession of the drink extended to his gateway and to him and his hellhounds. But then you finished your drink.
    SADIE: That is rather my modus operandi, I'm afraid. [38]

Panel 4
The Beastmaster has a look on his face like he's been totally ripped off as Frank takes the crown off his head.

    FRANK: Don't be afraid. My *modus* is this.
    BEASTMASTER: No! That's mine!

[33] ***Acker:*** *I hope Blacker has something to say about this page, because I have nothing to say.*

Blacker: *...I really don't.*

Acker: *Does that mean it's perfect?*

Blacker: *I guess it does!*

[34] ***Blacker:*** *I love this stage direction because it asks the artist to differentiate between "chewed on some" and "chewed on a lot."*

[35] ***Acker:*** *I love a good "the hero explains it all" moment.*

[36] ***Blacker:*** *Classic ouija stuff.*

[37] ***Acker:*** *This is maybe the only time in Beyond Belief where Frank is ahead of Sadie.*

[38] ***Blacker:*** *Exposition is SO HARD, especially of made-up nonsense like this. We always try to deflate it or distract from it with a joke. I think Acker did that really well here with Sadie's line.*

[39] **Blacker:** *This is the kind of hand-waving exposition we'd do all the time in Beyond Belief stories where the "why" is never nearly as interesting as everything else. So, while "stop making astute observations" is something no one would ever say, it both closes the exposition book and (hopefully) gets a laugh.*

[40] **Blacker:** *Pants are the new harnesses.*

[41] **Acker:** *And really, she's ahead of him in the way that really counts.*

[42] **Blacker:** *This is a charming image, indicative of character, rendered charmingly. Sadie will hug a dog, even if it's a ghost dog.*

[43] **Acker:** *We knew the bones of this, Frank and Sadie's story—a meet cute in which Sadie's natural mediumistic intensity brought a fake séance to life and Frank came swinging in, but we didn't know the specifics. We didn't know the ghost's story. We figured out, though, that even though they fell in love from the moment they set eyes on each other, we wanted to end the story with their first proper date. The idea of this boozy picnic where they loosed puppy ghosts in a farm upstate was too adorable to shake and suggested hellhounds and the dogcatcher and everything we were missing.*

[44] **Blacker:** *I love that Frank sees empathy as a shortcoming. This line tells you all you need to know about their relationship and why it works. He'll always be dragged kicking and screaming into caring about anything but drinks and his wife, not in that order.*

[45] **Acker:** *I think this is the Frank and Sadie that the audience comes back for. "I love you" dressed in cleverness. It's also what we come back for. It's a pleasure to write. It always has been and always will be.*

[46] **Blacker:** *Bobo's passive acceptance of his rejection is so not-Bobo that I can only think he's biding his time until he can exact supernatural revenge upon the Doyles. Which he will, in several podcast episodes, including the first one we released...*

Panel 5

The Beastmaster becomes a shlubby DOGCATCHER whose uniform matches the color he was. His face is similarly colored as well. He's bald and he reaches for the crown, which has become his uniform's cap.

> FRANK: Dollars to donuts this expired dogcatcher was a fear-monger in life as in death. And the only ones he could scare were the dogs he caught.
> DOGCATCHER: Stop making astute observations about my shortcomings and give me back my hat! [39]

Panel 6

Frank stuffs the dogcatcher into the ouija board while Sadie fixes them more drinks.

> FRANK: Back you go. Followed by the Hellhounds, who I expect will wear the pants in your new afterlife. But what do I know? I'm only an expert. [40]
> FRANK: You ready to sic 'em boys? For the rest of forever?
> SADIE: Oh Frank, no! [41]

PAGE NINE -

Panel 1

Frank doesn't understand.

> FRANK: Your lips say "no," but the way this guy was a bully in life as well as death say "yes."

Panel 2

Sadie hugs a hellhound around its neck. [42]

> SADIE: If those dogs go back in there, that sad angry man will just get sadder and angrier, but now that he's been chastised, given a chance to think about what he's done, perhaps he'll come out of it improved, if he comes out of it again at all. And these dogs certainly deserve better. [43]

Panel 3

Frank picks up that jar with sigils on it.

> FRANK: Empathy, huh? I've heard of worse shortcomings. [44]
> FRANK: Luckily, "better" is something I can do.

Panel 4

She takes his hand.

> SADIE: Thank you.
> FRANK: You've taken my hand.
> SADIE: See if you get it back.
> FRANK: See if I want it back. [45]
> SADIE: Bobo, darling?

Panel 5

Bobo is all yeah yeah.

> SADIE (off): Consider yourself jilted.
> BOBO: Yeah yeah. [46]

PAGE TEN -

Blue sky countryside—Frank and Sadie have an all booze picnic as they let the ghost dogs—now puppies—out to frolic forever.

Frank reclines and Sadie rests against him, the both of them looking in the direction of the dogs and boy, they're smiley in love. Smiling to themselves, not even for each other's benefit or anything.

Also they are clinking martini glasses together, even in their weird configuration. Frank's holding his glass out and Sadie clinks hers to his. The pimentos in the olives in the martinis in the glasses make the teensiest heart. Only the keenest-eyed people or the ones who read the backmatter will notice it. [47]

And the last caption where THE END would go at the bottom right, reads...

CAP: CLINK!

[47] ***Acker:*** *Some of the stuff will always only be for you, the completists. We hope you live happily ever after.*

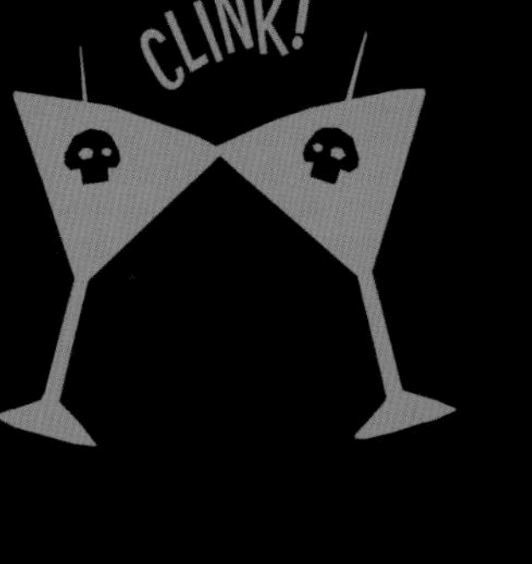
CLINK!

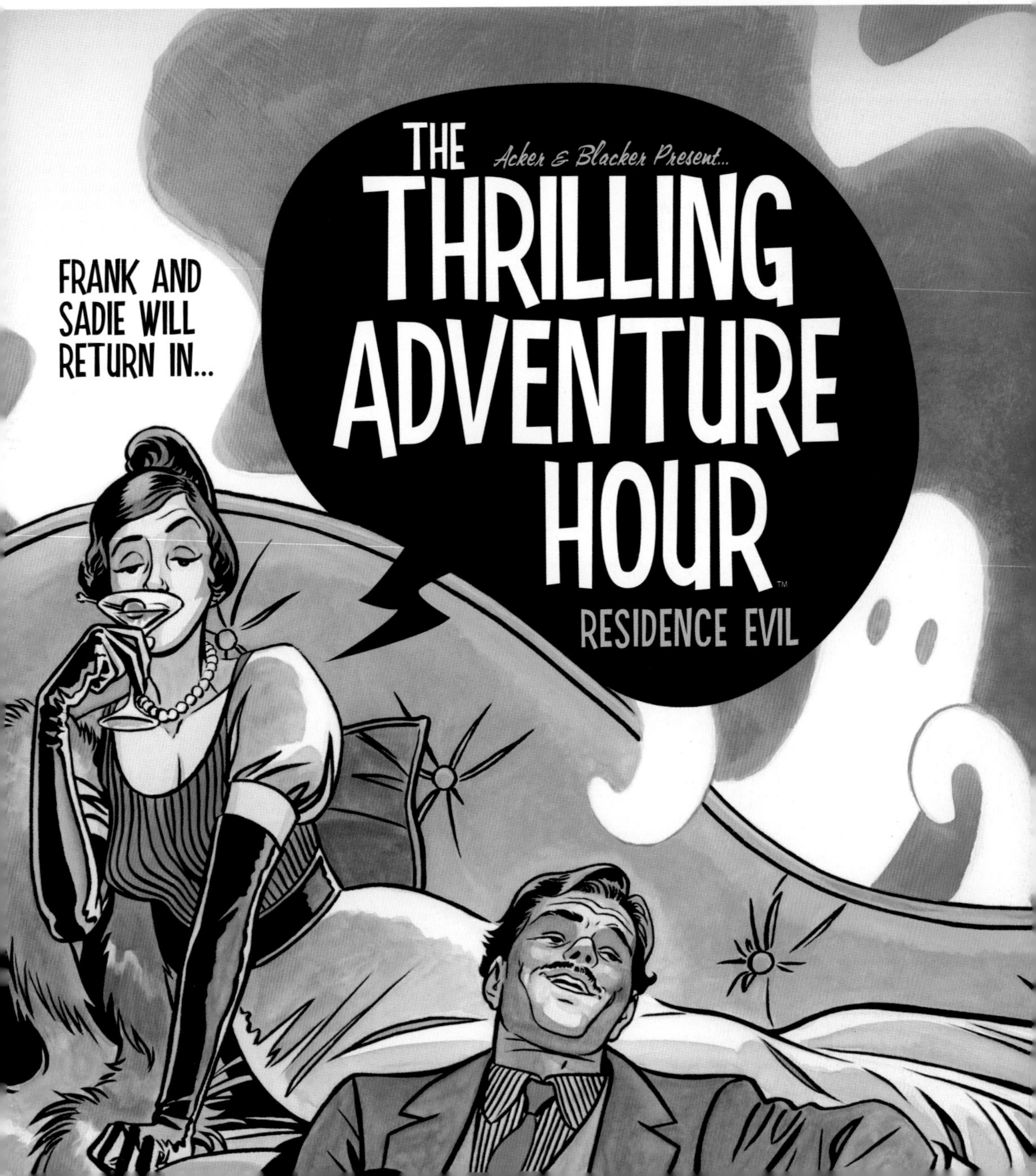
THE
Acker & Blacker Present...
THRILLING ADVENTURE HOUR
™
RESIDENCE EVIL
FRANK AND SADIE WILL RETURN IN...

DISCOVER
VISIONARY CREATORS

THE WOODS
JAMES TYNION IV • MICHAEL DIALYNAS
VOL. 1
THE ARROW

"The Spire is fantastic! My kind of genre free-for-all."
—BRIAN K. VAUGHAN (Saga)
THE SPIRE
SIMON SPURRIER
JEFF STOKELY
ANDRÉ MAY

MARK WAID • PETER KRAUSE
IRREDEEMABLE
AFTERWORD BY GRANT MORRISON

J.G. JONES
MARK WAID
STRANGE FRUIT
Foreword by
ELVIS MITCHELL

MICHAEL ALAN NELSON
DAN MORA
GABRIEL CASSATA
HEXED
THE HARLOT & THE THIEF VOLUME ONE

ABNETT & CULBARD
WILD'S END
FIRST LIGHT
"IT'S REALLY GREAT!"
JEFF LEMIRE

BOOM! STUDIOS

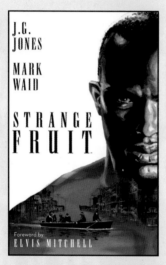

AVAILABLE AT YOUR LOCAL COMICS SHOP AND BOOKSTORE
WWW.BOOM-STUDIOS.COM

James Tynion IV

The Woods
Volume 1
ISBN: 978-1-60886-454-6 | $9.99 US
Volume 2
ISBN: 978-1-60886-495-9 | $14.99 US
Volume 3
ISBN: 978-1-60886-773-8 | $14.99 US

The Backstagers
Volume 1
ISBN: 978-1-60886-993-0 | $14.99 US

Simon Spurrier

Six-Gun Gorilla
ISBN: 978-1-60886-390-7 | $19.99 US

The Spire
ISBN: 978-1-60886-913-8 | $29.99 US

Weavers
ISBN: 978-1-60886-963-3 | $19.99 US

Mark Waid

Irredeemable
Volume 1
ISBN: 978-1-93450-690-5 | $16.99 US
Volume 2
ISBN: 978-1-60886-000-5 | $16.99 US

Incorruptible
Volume 1
ISBN: 978-1-60886-015-9 | $16.99 US
Volume 2
ISBN: 978-1-60886-028-9 | $16.99 US

Strange Fruit
ISBN: 978-1-60886-872-8 | $24.99 US

Michael Alan Nelson

Hexed The Harlot & The Thief
Volume 1
ISBN: 978-1-60886-718-9 | $14.99 US
Volume 2
ISBN: 978-1-60886-816-2 | $14.99 US

Day Men
Volume 1
ISBN: 978-1-60886-393-8 | $9.99 US
Volume 2
ISBN: 978-1-60886-852-0 | $9.99 US

Dan Abnett

Wild's End
Volume 1: First Light
ISBN: 978-1-60886-735-6 | $19.99 US
Volume 2: The Enemy Within
ISBN: 978-1-60886-877-3 | $19.99 US

Hypernaturals
Volume 1
ISBN: 978-1-60886-298-6 | $16.99 US
Volume 2
ISBN: 978-1-60886-319-8 | $19.99 US